The Impasse of European Communism

Also of Interest

Communism and Political Systems in Western Europe, edited by David E. Albright

The Euro-American System: Economic and Political Relations Between North America and Western Europe, edited by Ernst-Otto Czempiel and Dankwart A. Rustow

The Foreign Policies of the French Left, edited by Simon Serfty

Ideology and Politics: The Socialist Party of France, George A. Codding, Jr., and William Safran

Social Structure in Italy: Crisis of a System, Sabino Acquaviva and Mario Santuccio

The Spanish Political System: Franco's Legacy, E. Ramón Arango

Marxism in the Contemporary West, edited by Charles F. Elliott and Carl A. Linden

† *The Unfinished Revolution: Marxism and Communism in the Modern World,* revised edition, Adam B. Ulam

† *History of the International: World Socialism 1943–1968,* Julius Braunthal

Innovation in Communist Systems, edited by Andrew Gyorgy and James A. Kuhlman

† *Fascism in the Contemporary World: Ideology, Evolution, Resurgence,* Anthony James Joes

Worker Participation and the Crisis of Liberal Democracy, Sherri DeWitt

The Socialist Industrial State: Toward a Political Sociology of State Socialism, David Lane

† *Theories of Comparative Politics: The Search for a Paradigm,* Ronald H. Chilcote

† *The Letters of Rosa Luxemburg,* edited and translated by Stephen Eric Bronner

† Available in hardcover and paperback.

About the Book and Author

The Impasse of European Communism
Carl Boggs

The major Communist parties in Western Europe claim a commitment to a "democratic road to socialism." Often this is a genuine evolution of traditional Marxist/Leninist ideology based on the assumption that political and economic power can be obtained through gradual change rather than revolution and through the utilization of democratic processes. How well is this strategy working? Not very well, concludes the author of this book.

Carl Boggs bases his analysis on a theoretical assessment of the historical and strategic development of Eurocommunism — of those parties and movements (notably in France, Italy, and Spain) that seek a transition to socialism based on the democratization of existing political and economic structures (the so-called parliamentary road to socialism). After examining the logic and premises of this conception, he moves to a critique of the major Eurocommunist theoreticians — e.g., Togliatti, Berlinguer, Ingrao, Napolitano, Carrillo, Marchais, Elleinstein, Poulantzas, and Claudin. He concludes that their ideas fail to resolve the historic Marxist conflict between democratization and rationalization (understood here in terms of the drive toward statism, bureaucratization, and further refinement of the social division of labor under capitalism). In fact, says Dr. Boggs, Eurocommunism will probably represent a sort of historical resolution of legitimation and production crises within Mediterranean capitalism that extends rather than overturns hierarchical social and authority relations, the capitalist state, and the social division of labor. Such a resolution might broadly parallel the function of social democracy in Northern Europe in a previous phase of capitalist development.

Carl Boggs is a visiting professor in the Political Science Department at the University of Southern California. He has also taught at the University of California, Los Angeles, at Washington University, St. Louis, Missouri, and at the University of California, Irvine. Dr. Boggs has conducted field research in Italy and is the author of *Gramsci's Marxism*.

The Impasse of
European Communism

Carl Boggs

Westview Press / Boulder, Colorado

Copyright © 1982 by Westview Press, Inc.

Published in 1982 in the United States of America by
  Westview Press, Inc.
  5500 Central Avenue
  Boulder, Colorado 80301
  Frederick A. Praeger, President and Publisher

Library of Congress Cataloging in Publication Data
Boggs, Carl.
  The impasse of European communism.
  Includes bibliographical references and index.
  1. Communism—Europe. I. Title.
HX238.5.B63   335.43'094   81-22005
ISBN 0-89158-784-5   AACR2
ISBN 0-86531-285-0 (pbk.)

Printed and bound in the United States of America

Contents

Preface

To speak of the "impasse" of European Communism in the highly explosive and unpredictable political milieu of the 1980s is to raise questions that go far beyond the analysis of any specific party or regional grouping of parties. Thus, while I have concentrated on the postwar development of the Mediterranean Communist parties, most of the general conclusions presented in the following pages will probably apply to the experience of any advanced capitalist country where mass-based "Marxist" parties or movements are pursuing structural reformist strategies. In a broader sense, the arguments developed in this book can be understood as part of an effort to illuminate what has become a fundamental crisis within Marxist theory itself.

When "Eurocommunism" became a lively media and academic theme in the mid-1970s, the Italian Communist Party (PCI) seemed to be on the verge of entering national government. The political, economic, and even military implications of such a historic event were generally seen as momentous. The PCI could not build upon its stunning electoral victories in the 1975 regional balloting, however, and hence suffered at least a temporary setback in its political march forward. The media response was to proclaim the "death of Eurocommunism"; overnight the parties that had seemed so close to making history were reduced to collective corpses. In one important respect such proclamations were not only premature but were also grossly insensitive to the very deep economic and social processes that gave rise to that nervous anticipation in the first place. For even if the Italian and French Communist parties were now further removed from national power, the plethora of issues, debates, and circumstances that surrounded the Eurocommunist phenomenon in the 1970s are still very much alive and will no doubt remain so for the indefinite future. Indeed, class conflict in the Mediterranean has intensified; working-class and popular movements still confront the same strategic choices; the ruling classes are still desperately trying to recover their fragile hegemony; and the Communist parties have scarcely vanished from the political terrain. One could go further: The atmosphere of urgent debate generated by Eurocommunism was connected to an entire tradition of Marxist theoretical and strategic discourse that has its origins in the classic turn-of-the-century exchanges involving Eduard Bernstein, Karl Kautsky, Lenin, and Rosa Luxemburg.

But there is yet another sense in which Eurocommunism could be described as "dead"—or more appropriately, stillborn. The very theory and strategy that underlie the Eurocommunist "third road" (or "democratic Road to Socialism") have been riddled with serious contradictions from the outset. For reasons I shall elaborate in the text, this approach supplies no adequate grounding for socialist transformation in the advanced countries.

The dramatic gains of Eurocommunism in the mid-1970s were commonly interpreted, by Marxists and non-Marxists alike, as a historically necessary response to the fading appeals of both social democracy and Leninism in Western Europe. The fact that the Italian, French, and Spanish Communist parties managed to create a mass presence through primarily electoral methods while retaining their Marxist identities seemed to validate this notion. Moreover, by distancing themselves from the Soviet bureaucratic-centralist model in the popular consciousness, they could present a more convincing image of themselves as democratic and respectable parties suitable for major governing roles in their political systems. But this political viability was purchased at a very high price; success in moving out of the Leninist (or Stalinist) straightjacket paved the way not to the much-celebrated "third road" but to a replay of earlier social-democratic illusions. The great electoral advances of parties like the PCI therefore merely conceal a deeper set of dilemmas, which logically flow from a theory that I have referred to as "structural reformism." Although this theory contains various innovative features, in the end it owes more to the evolutionist model of Eduard Bernstein (and to its later adaptation by Palmiro Togliatti) than to the counter-hegemonic strategy of Antonio Gramsci that it often claims as its heritage.

The repeated failure of the Western European Communist parties to sustain any anticapitalist mobilization—to go beyond the limits of parliamentarism—does not stem from a tactical or momentary deviation on the part of shrewd leaders. Nor is it a matter of "revisionist" leaders betraying the masses. What is at issue, and what needs to be analyzed, is a lengthy historical *process* that has led to a fundamental reorientation of political commitment in all areas of party activity. I view this as a tendency toward social democratization, which would (if successful) serve to reconsolidate a stagnating capitalist system on new structural and ideological foundations. The theme of social democratization furnishes the organizing principle of this study.

I have included abundant references to the French and Spanish Communist parties, but the Italian party (and the Italian context in general) is the case study underlying my central arguments. There is no denying the differences between these parties at the level of leadership, organization, social composition, and tactics. Even within the parties, moreover, a variety of policy and tactical preferences can readily be identified. But when it comes to distinctly strategic considerations, such differences are clearly subordinate to the common outlook and organizational patterns associated with structural reformism. Despite a variety of national traditions, the overall patterns of evolution that I set out to clarify reflect more or less uniform tendencies. In this respect the PCI might best be understood as the most "advanced" embodiment of both structural reformist strategy and the larger trend toward social democratization, as it is the Italian situation that displays the outlines of these phenomena in sharpest relief. Whether or not other parties are destined to follow the PCI's trajectory is still an open question. To pose the issue of social democratization, after all, is to suggest long-term historical tendencies rather than any rigidly predictable outcome.

The dilemmas of Eurocommunism, as I have indicated, also both reflect and contribute to the deeper crises of Marxism. For in great measure the inability of Communist parties to significantly advance revolutionary struggle reveals an underlying theoretical weakness. Not only is the actual vision of socialist transformation a narrow one, but the rationalizing programs of the parties inevitably give birth to new bureaucratic and statist obstacles. Hence the goal of democratic renewal, which is the cornerstone of the PCI model, remains trapped within pluralist categories. In the absence of any real theory of socialist democracy it is hard to comprehend how such an objective could ever achieve institutional expression. The problem ultimately derives from a certain deficiency of political thinking within Marxist theory. Like Leninism and social democracy before it, Eurocommunism has never really conceptualized the kind of political forms, institutions, and processes that might be compatible with a democratic socialism rooted in a network of workers' control and community self-management.

The conservatism of structural reformist parties on a wide range of political, social, and cultural issues can no longer be explained away by historical contingency; nor can it be justified as a set of tactical maneuvers to meet changing pressures. The overall patterns have been in place far too long. To some extent this eclipse of democratization represents the eclipse of the emancipatory side of Marxism—at least of its major political expressions in the twentieth century. Eurocommunism boasts of having outgrown Stalinism, the Soviet model, and the "dictatorship of the proletariat." Yet the inability of Eurocommunism even to depart from the old bureaucratic conceptions suggests that such a predicament goes to the very core of Marxism. The issue here concerns not some rapid or utopian leap to the sphere of direct democracy, but rather the capacity of Marxist parties and movements to produce a viable critique of bureaucracy and the authoritarian state, to lay the basis of a politics consistent with a genuinely transformative strategy.

The viewpoint most compatible with such a critique and strategy—that of the radical left—is the one that shapes the main outlines of this book. Building upon the traditions of council Communism, Western Marxism, the new left, and feminism, the radical strategy embraces a vision of democratization quite at odds with that of structural reformism (or Leninism). Radicalism looks not toward the reconstruction of the bourgeois state but toward creation of a generalized system of dual power and popular self-management leading to a qualitatively new state. It does not seek to extend statist forms of economic planning and rationalized administration; instead it envisages a socialization of production grounded in workers' control and local democracy. And it invests its political energies not merely in the parliamentary realm of legislative reforms but in a broader process of social struggle and cultural revolution. If the radical alternative too has historically fallen short, its predicament has differed qualitatively from that of Eurocommunism: Its political presence in various European countries (Germany, Hungary, Spain, France) was generally short-lived, and where it did grow into a durable movement (as in Italy during the 1970s) it often became the victim of its own fragmentation and spontaneism. But the continued impasse of the older strategies (including their updated versions) might well signal a rebirth and maturing of the radical left on a scale unprecedented in the advanced capitalist countries—especially if the global crisis of capitalism intensifies. Whatever the past failures of radicalism, the point I wish to emphasize is that the following critique of Eurocommunism rests upon separate premises—and therefore follows quite separate lines—from those based upon conventional Leninist, Trotskyist, Maoist, or (in a very different vein) liberal assumptions.

This book is the outgrowth of a project begun in 1977 and later published as an anthology that I coedited with David Plotke, entitled *The Politics of Eurocommunism* (Boston: South End Press, 1980). The extensive gathering and analysis of materials needed to assemble that volume contributed greatly to the present study. In addition, the concluding essay I wrote for that anthology—"The Democratic Road: New Departures and Old Problems"— laid much of the groundwork for this book. An earlier version of that article ("Eurocommunism, the State, and the Crisis of Legitimation") appeared in the *Berkeley Journal of Sociology* (Vol. 23, [1978-1979], pp. 35–82), and I wish to express my thanks to the journal editors for their encouragement and helpful suggestions in response to the original manuscript. The epilogue is a rewritten and substantially lengthened version of the article "Gramsci and Eurocommunism," which was initially published in *Radical America* (May-June 1980). I would like to thank members of the *Radical America* collective who sent me their insightful comments and criticisms on the first draft of that manuscript. For valuable editorial and substantive advice at various stages in the preparation of this volume I wish to thank Doug Appel, Michael Albert, Dan Cohen, Arlene Dallalfar, Allen Hunter, Andrew Feenberg, John Friedmann, John Kautsky, Clarence Lo, David Plotke, Jose Rodriguez-Ibáñez, Clare Spark, and Paul Thomas. For contributing immensely in various ways to the end result—even where she may have disagreed with a number of my conclusions—I wish to thank Michele Prichard. And, lastly, for constant encouragement and friendly prodding throughout my work on this project I wish to thank Lynne Rienner of Westview Press.

Carl Boggs

1

Introduction: Marxism, Democracy, and Eurocommunism

The emergence of strong Eurocommunist parties in Italy, France, Spain, and elsewhere in the advanced capitalist world during the mid-1970s was seen by many political activists and observers, Marxist and non-Marxist alike, as a dramatic break with the past — the beginning of a new, expansive phase in European socialist development. After the debacle of Stalinism, the declining appeal of the Soviet model, the paralysis of social democracy, and the failures of the new left, the long-established and once stagnant Communist parties seemed to be in the midst of unprecedented political revitalization, even to the point in some instances of becoming real contestants for national power. With their mass support expanding and their organizational strength intact, and with the capitalist economy in an intensifying global crisis, these parties appeared ready to escape their legacy of impotent opposition with its obsolete theories, strategies, and practices. Democratic socialism was at last a concrete alternative to continued futile sectarian activity.

This was the sentiment that moved Pete Hamill to write that "a new generation of Communists is taking its place on the world stage. They are from the Mediterranean, and they are championing the communism that Karl Marx had in mind from the beginning: a communism that is just and liberating, by definition democratic." Hamill suggested that "they are not interested in being members of dry little sects eternally debating the catechism of Karl Marx. . . . So they are developing a communism that is democratic before it is anything else, a communism that is interested in results, that is empirical and moral, that is alert to and shaped by local conditions."[1]

The Historical Break

Much of this book is devoted to analyzing the premises and validity of such a widely encountered optimism, filtered primarily through the struggles and "results" of the Italian Communist party (PCI) over roughly the past two decades. As we shall see, party statements, intentions, promises, and even theories are one thing; the judgment of political history is something else entirely. What must be noted at the outset, however, is what the Hamill statement unambiguously reflects: that Eurocommunism, whatever its serious weaknesses and contradictions, has raised anew—emphatically and in concrete terms—the problem of the relationship between socialism and democracy. More specifically, it has opened new areas of discussion on the relationship between Marxist parties and *parliamentary* democracy in the advanced countries.[2] It is this relationship, more than the general and often abstractly defined question of *revolutionary* democracy, that has posed such a dilemma within the socialist tradition. Yet strangely enough, this dilemma has rarely been the object of Marxist theoretical reflection since the issue first presented itself in European politics at the turn of the century.[3] The resulting vacuum in the distinctively political side of Marxist theory and practice has encouraged, more or less by default, the triumph of antidemocratic, statist currents that run from traditional social democracy and Leninism through Stalinism and the bureaucratic centralism of contemporary Soviet-style regimes. Therefore Eurocommunism, whatever its theoretical flaws or its ultimate political future, has through its very historical reality forced Marxists to confront questions that have been deferred for much too long. What is the actual character of the bourgeois state, and what is its (potential) role in the transition to socialism? What has been the long-term impact of Socialist and Communist involvement in parliamentary structures upon the ideological and organizational development of these parties? What revolutionary strategy is likely to succeed in overthrowing the various modes of bourgeois domination and in laying the basis of a truly egalitarian society? What institutional forms of socialist democracy might be expected to shape this process?[4]

There is no simple way to explain why Marxism, which is after all a highly politicized system of thought, has failed to address these crucial themes in more than a partial or tangential fashion. Rather there are several possible reasons for this lapse, some historical and contingent, others rooted in the very logic of Marxist theory.

In the first place, Marxism has evolved within an essentially productivist framework—that is, its methodology stresses the primacy of issues related to accumulation, production, class forces, and capitalist economic development over those related to the state, organizational forms, and political strategy. The famous base-superstructure dichotomy represents the crudest expression of this bias, but even where strict interpretations are abandoned in favor of some notion of reciprocity the role of economics in "the last instance" generally seems to confine the sphere of politics to epiphenomenal status. Insofar as the political is denied any real degree of autonomy, it necessarily lacks its own historical dialectic; it can be understood only as shaped or "determined" by some deeper underlying force.[5]

Second, there is a powerful current within Marxism (and Leninism) that insists that "democracy," however it is defined, will emerge more or less organically and dialectically as the working class begins to assert its hegemony through a long process of social transformation. Here the proletarian conquest and consolidation of state power is automatically equated with a trend toward democratization. As the specificity of revolutionary change cannot be anticipated in advance, efforts to outline the organizational forms of socialist democracy would make little sense; they would be utopian, ahistorical. Thus democratic participation as such poses no real problems, because what really matters is the balance of class forces, and, ultimately, the capacity of an emergent Marxist party to establish a new power apparatus and new social priorities. Nonclass forms of domination (e.g., bureaucracy) are dismissed as a bourgeois mystification or a syndicalist distraction.

Third, movements, parties, and regimes within the socialist tradition have often, many times for good reason, succumbed to an instrumentalism generated by an urgent sense of tactical immediacy. For example, in the case of the Bolshevik Revolution, postrevolutionary pressures, such as civil war, economic crisis, and international isolation, helped to solidify a bureaucratic centralism that became a permanent feature of the Soviet regime. In the case of European social democracy, transitional struggles and demands such as state planning and nationalization took on the status of ultimate socialist goals.[6] In both instances, the vision of a new kind of society embracing a qualitatively different set of social and authority relations was effectively destroyed.

Fourth, the overwhelming Marxist commitment to scientific and technological progress has sometimes justified, both ideologically and materially, the resort to rationalized (and therefore centralized) modes of state and economic administration no less repressive than the bourgeois hierarchical structures it replaced. The logical reverse of this, especially where Marxist movements have come to power, is to downplay noninstitutionalized social and cultural forces and thereby forestall attempts to create local forms of workers' control and self-management grounded in the transformation of everyday life.

Fifth, the fact that all major Communist revolutions have occurred in largely preindustrial societies, where antiimperialist struggles necessarily defined political strategy, meant that until recently few Marxists paid much attention to the conditions and imperatives of socialist transformation in the advanced capitalist countries, where the tradition of bourgeois democracy is of course strongest. Ironically, this is a turnabout from Marx's own concerns, which revolved around developmental patterns in the industrialized countries (Britain, France, Germany). Although it is true that much of Western Marxism since the 1920s has sought to rehabilitate these themes—through contributions in the areas of class consciousness, ideological hegemony, culture and media, and so on—it has done so by virtually ignoring issues of state power and political strategy. Necessarily distanced from those movements that had come under the spell of Stalinism, this tradition (with the notable exception of Gramsci) represented in its own terms a certain flight from politics.[7]

Sixth, most of the politically influential Marxist theorists of the twentieth century—e.g., George Plekhanov, Lenin, Trotsky, Rosa Luxemburg, Antonio Gramsci, and Mao—had little or no experience with parliamentary democracy, and where they did (as in Germany and Italy) its institutional development was very weak. Moreover, the era of mass Communist parties in the advanced countries did not really begin until after World War II, by which time the character of the bourgeois state had undergone profound transformations.

Finally, the conventional notion of the "dictatorship of the proletariat" has immobilized Marxist thinking about the state, democracy, and political strategy to the extent that a simplistic, outmoded formula became a substitute for real theoretical discussion and analysis. Within the Communist tradition—even in Western Europe—the terms "dictatorship" and "democracy" were always viewed as synonymous, as the former rested upon an imputed working-class majority. As could be expected, such verbal obfuscation blocked any real structural analysis of the Soviet party-state. And the Trotskyist tradition, which did produce a critique of Stalinism, never grasped the systemic features of bureaucratic centralism because Trotskyism too accepted these authoritarian principles of social organization.

The failure of the most successful Marxist currents to elaborate a coherent approach to either bourgeois or socialist democracy is all the more striking given the strong commitment of both Marx and Engels to democratization. In contrast to the liberals, they saw it as something far more than a strictly political process. The themes of proletarian self-emancipation and full democratic collectivity are at least implicit in much of their work; and one can find periodic critiques of Blanquism and Jacobinism as well as references to the "withering away of the state"—a utopian schema premised on the eventual abolition of the social division of labor. Still, in actuality neither Marx nor Engels confronted the issue of democracy as such in either theoretical or strategic terms, despite their many penetrating analyses of European political struggles (most notably of the Paris Commune). Such analyses, commentary, and periodic insightful passages, like Marx's often-quoted statement from *The Civil War in France*—"the working class cannot simply lay hold of the ready-made state machinery, and wield it for its own purposes"—or the optimistic thought Engels frequently expressed in his later years that peaceful, legal methods of struggle might supplant insurrectionary tactics once workers achieved suffrage, do not constitute a theory or strategy.[8]

Of course it would be unrealistic to expect a full-blown theory of the capitalist state or of democratic self-management from socialists whose formative concepts were developed more than a century ago. The point is not so much that their work was unfinished (especially as it applied to the state), but rather that their major contributions preceded the era of parliamentary democracy and mass socialist parties. Engels lived long enough to witness the origins of the German Social Democratic party (SPD) as a mass-based electoral party, but the SPD was only in its infancy when he died in 1895, thus ruling out the possibility of reflective historical judgment and analysis. It can be safely argued that neither Marx nor Engels had any real experience with bourgeois political forms and that, moreover, there is little in their writings that anticipates the great transformations that have occurred in the modern bourgeois state. This left the terrain wide open for subsequent movements and theorists to articulate political strategies more or less *de novo* in the fluid and divisive period between 1895 and the mid-1920s, as they struggled to come to grips with the legacy of classical Marxism.

Four Marxist Strategies

Out of the debates, struggles, and schisms of this period evolved four identifiable Marxist tendencies: the "orthodox" or "centrist" (the Karl Kautsky–August Bebel prewar influence within the SPD, Austro-Marxism), the reformist-evolutionist (Bernstein, Filippo Turati, much of the European trade-union leadership), the vanguardist-insurrectionary (Lenin, Amadeo Bordiga, the early Comintern), and the radical left (Luxemburg, the council tendency). Each represented an often coherent, sometimes chaotic groping for political solutions during a time of social turbulence, war, and the emergence of new issues posed by imperialism and the Bolshevik Revolution. And each operated, often implicitly, from a distinct set of premises concerning the transition to socialism: the nature of the state, the overall assessment of capitalist development and imperialism, the problem of democracy, the source of class consciousness, and so forth. Naturally, attitudes toward parliamentary democracy varied greatly, even if these attitudes did not always produce concrete strategies and tactics.

Kautsky was the original theorist of what today is called the parliamentary road to socialism. Whatever the nuances of his approach to the problem of crisis or the changes in his perspective after 1914, he never wavered from his commitment to parliament as the center of political activity. The economic and social complexity of advanced countries like Britain and Germany, along with new opportunities provided by the growth of suffrage, mass working-class parties, trade unions, and legislatures, made insurrection outdated. Kautsky assumed that with the gradual expansion of proletarian organizations necessarily generated by capitalism, and with the corresponding diffusion of socialist political and ideological strength, the state as it was constituted by the bourgeoisie could be used for anticapitalist ends.[9] Granted that the German state was still a class state, one that had historically been controlled and manipulated by the ruling strata for their own ends, this relationship could be turned around once the process of democratization succeeded in provoking a crisis of legitimacy leading, ultimately, to direct frontal struggles and a break with the capitalist system. Leaving aside the controversy over the mythical "51 percent," the advantages of a parliamentary strategy were for Kautsky quite clear. It would introduce the workers to norms of democratic participation, help build toward a new consensus that would stimulate favorable conditions for class struggle, and minimize the need for violence, while presumably at all stages curbing the authoritarian power of the military and state bureaucracy.[10]

Although Kautsky's concept of the transition required a fundamental overturning of the capitalist economy, it did not anticipate the kind of "automatic" collapse or catastrophic rupture that is commonly read into his theory. True, the Erfurt Programme of 1891 (written jointly by Kautsky and Bernstein) did endorse the breakdown scenario—without, however, drawing out the strategic consequences of such a scenario. But this perspective is not really advanced in any of Kautsky's major writings. The theory he most consistently adhered to from beginning to end was that of a series of economic crises building toward class confrontation and a break with the outmoded structure of capitalist production.[11] In other words, the economy was seen as the locus of sharpening contradictions produced by objective historical forces while the political system (i.e., bourgeois democracy) was viewed as a stable, more or less durable form that would persist through all stages of socialist transformation.[12] But here Kautsky remained forever vague about how and through what mechanisms the break was expected to occur.

When Kautsky argued for a merging of socialism and democracy, it was always parliamentary democracy that he had in mind; one does not encounter a discussion of socialist democracy anywhere in his work, or even an extensive critique of the bourgeois state.[13] He was implacably hostile to all types of nonparliamentary activity (e.g., "direct legislation," the mass strike), the more so after 1914 when his famous debates with Lenin came into the open. He regarded antiinstitutional struggles as a residue of preindustrial politics, appropriate only to the adventurism and irrationality of romantic sectors of the peasantry and the petty bourgeoisie. As for the administration of the state and economy in general, the requirements of planning and coordination in a complex society would leave no alternative to a centralized bureaucratic apparatus, even under socialism.[14]

In contrast with Kautsky's "orthodoxy," Bernstein's political evolutionism actually corresponded more directly to the immediate practical interests of the SPD's trade-union and parliamentary leadership and, moreover, better reflected the party's actual strategic development. Bernstein shared Kautsky's commitment to parliamentarism and to the idea that socialism, if it is to be democratic, must inherit and expand rather than overturn the liberal tradition.[15] But he came to diverge sharply from the conventional Marxist assumption, which was closely identified with the late Engels, Kautsky, and Bebel, that capitalism generated within it unresolvable contradictions that would propel it toward crisis and polarized class conflict, leading eventually to a rupture in the old social relations of production. Bernstein viewed capitalism in the advanced countries as stable and adaptable enough to contain imminent crises; an expanded public sphere, the vitality of electoral politics, a flourishing trade-union movement, and increased levels of prosperity all indicated the possibility of a reconstituted capitalism that, as it became progressively democratized, could evolve toward socialism. Although he posed his theory as a critique of the breakdown scenario, it was really something else — a complete rejection of the notion that capitalism cannot survive its own internal crises, that the transition to socialism requires a qualitative break.[16]

If both Kautsky and Bernstein shared hostility to insurrectionary politics, the latter went much further in his conceptualization of a unilinear, relatively harmonious, and crisis-free transition to socialism. For Bernstein, the ultimate goal would be realized not through the intervention of historical laws but simply through the new opportunities that a developing capitalism presented. In this sense, the bourgeois state was understood as much more than a simple organ of class domination; its gradually expanding democratic forms actually favored the progress of the working class and its allies toward emancipatory objectives. The greater the parliamentary strength of socialists, the better their capacity to achieve genuine reforms that would whittle away at capitalist domination and create a new balance of political forces.[17] In the context of the SPD, Bernstein thought that accumulated reform successes could bring the party to power within the German state and provide the umbrella for a restructuring of the economy (including the proliferation of cooperatives). Kautsky, on the other hand, had no such illusions and insisted that reforms were worth winning only insofar as they strengthened the working-class movement.

To an even greater degree than Kautsky, Bernstein believed in the efficacy and permanence of bourgeois political institutions, not simply as transitional forms but as structures that would help define (and set limits to) the new society. Talk of socialist democracy was regarded by Bernstein and the SPD right as romantic gibberish; references to the "withering away of the state" were seen as hopelessly utopian. Like Kautsky, he accepted as inevitable the reproduction of the centralized state apparatus with its various hierarchies and professional bureaucrats, and he saw in voting the main expression of political involvement. Given their agreement on these basic premises, it is hardly surprising to find the earlier differences between Kautsky and Bernstein disappearing (and collapsing into the Bernsteinian evolutionary schema) in the 1920s, with the impact of the Russian Revolution and rise of a more democratized Weimar Republic.[18]

The prerevolutionary Russian context that provided the backdrop of Leninist theory and Bolshevik practice, on the other hand, lacked even the bourgeois democratic trappings of the Wilhelminian state. Most oppositional political activity was denied legitimacy under tsarism, forcing the left parties to conduct their struggles underground in an atmosphere of repression and quasi-military combat. Clearly, Lenin's theory and strategy drew more or less exclusively from this experience. He was familiar with European parliamentary systems and even commented at length on how Marxists should approach the relatively open terrain of elections, legislatures, and trade unions (as in *Left-Wing Communism*), but his concern was mainly tactical rather than theoretical. Hence it is fair to say that Lenin's theory of the state—and the political strategy it inspired—was essentially a theory of the authoritarian *tsarist* state even though Lenin employed the term "bourgeois state" quite loosely in his writings.

Understandably, Lenin defined the state that his party had to confront as a repressive apparatus built for the defense and reproduction of ruling-class interests. Insofar as "the state is the product of the irreconcilability of class antagonisms" and constitutes "an organ for the oppression of one class by another,"[19] it stands as an alienated structure above civil society, detached from mass struggles and from the interests of the vast majority of people. The core element of the state, bourgeois or otherwise, is the central bureaucracy—the main locus of class rule even where parliamentary forms exist. Although Lenin thought that with capitalist development the bourgeoisie would allow, and possibly even thrive on, limited democratization, he anticipated that the bureaucratic side would reassert itself and close off this space in response to the impact of economic crisis, imperialism, and war. He viewed bourgeois democracy therefore as both illusory and fragile: illusory in that during stable times it would be manipulated by the ruling class to instill in the masses a false sense of participation, fragile in that it was not likely to survive the advanced stages of imperialism. In Russia, the frail beginnings of democratization (the dumas, constituent assemblies, and so on) were cut short when the traditional regime tried desperately to maintain its hegemony in the midst of crisis and popular upheaval.

Lenin bitterly attacked the thesis (supported in Russia by the Mensheviks) that the existing state forms, no matter how "democratic" they appeared, could be internally restructured and taken over for socialist purposes. Efforts to route the class struggle primarily *through* such a state would inevitably run up against the bureaucratic Leviathan, which would reduce any "democratic" strategy to a sad illusion. Hence the only viable solution was one of frontal assault channeled through mass mobilization outside the institutions of state power and directed toward their eventual dismantling. The only rationale for participating in those institutions was tactical, to prepare for their destruction. In their place would be erected new proletarian forms of power, the nucleus of a new state (the dictatorship of the proletariat) that would lay the basis for the transition to socialism. Although these forms would initially require a degree of centralization and hierarchy, their content would be far more democratic then any preceding system because they represented the historical interests of the vast majority (the working class).

At this point, Lenin's thinking moved in two directions. There is the Lenin who argued for direct democracy in *State and Revolution,* who called for "dual power" and "all power to the Soviets" during the revolutionary events of 1917, and who in his final months expressed great anxiety over the party-state bureaucracy that was already getting out of control. And there is Lenin the architect of the vanguard party, the believer in firm political discipline, and the worshipper of capitalist forms of technology and administration.[20] In the course of history the second Lenin readily prevailed over the first: the dictates of the revolution itself, the Civil War, and international isolation favored centralization of power, while "democracy" (both within the Bolshevik party and in Russian society) came to be viewed as a "petty-bourgeois illusion." Embryonic structures of self-management (notably the soviets and factory committees) were destroyed or disappeared within a few short years after the October Revolution; and by 1921, the struggle for internal party democracy had been resolved on the side of the centralists. The dictatorship of the proletariat thus already contained the seeds of bureaucratic centralism that were later to find such fertile soil under Stalin.[21]

The key to understanding Lenin's centralist impulses lies in his theory of the vanguard party, which was a continuous element in his approach after 1903 and most closely corresponded to Bolshevik practice. Against this, the visionary antistatism of his *State and Revolution* could produce no real antistatist strategy, no real concept of socialist democracy grounded in new forms of public authority; his uneasiness with the authoritarian excesses of the young Soviet regime could generate no critique of bureaucracy;[22] and his commitment to workers' control of industry did not preclude his introduction of "one-man management" and the general incorporation of bourgeois methods of organization.[23] All of this made sense within the context of a political strategy designed to overthrow an autocratic tsarist state and consolidate Bolshevik power under harsh conditions.

The fourth tendency to evolve out of the classical Marxist debates was represented by the German-Dutch radical left, which originated as a critique of the statist instrumentalism that shaped both social democracy and Leninism. In the aftermath of the 1905 revolution in Russia, prominent figures like Rosa Luxemburg, Anton Pannekoek, Hermann Görter, and Henriette Roland-Holst mobilized a small nucleus of radicals who were prepared to challenge the narrow parliamentarism of the Second International, especially the sort practiced by the SPD. In rejecting the strategic alternatives presented by Kautsky and Bernstein, they looked to spheres of combat that would supersede conventional party and trade-union maneuvers: the mass strike, popular insurrection, factory committees, and workers' councils. Their concept of democracy, inspired by a rediscovery of Marx's theme of proletarian self-emancipation, consisted of new revolutionary forms and processes that would extend beyond the limits of the bourgeois state as well as of (later) the Leninist system of "proletarian democracy" in Russia.

For Luxemburg, the democratic pronouncements of SPD and Bolshevik leaders were both devoid of content. Democratization for her meant more than programmatic statements, efforts to "broaden" liberal institutions, or promises of political equality to be introduced by benevolent, tutelary leaders at some later stage. She viewed it as the expression of a deeper process of social transformation rooted in mass self-activity. Within the SPD, Luxemburg fought against elitism, bureaucracy, and authoritarian manipulation that was often justified by appeals to a "scientific" Marxism; against this she countered with the more or less unmediated subjectivity of the proletariat, which she fully expected to culminate in a revolutionary democracy characterized by the "self-administration" of the masses. In contrast with most of the SPD hierarchy, she appeared to be always on the lookout for new opportunities, new avenues of struggle, new forms of popular initiative. She found her inspiration in the dramatic mass strike based upon the 1905 Russian model.[24]

The entire foundation of Luxemburg's strategic orientation, as for the radical left in general, was the imminent crisis of capitalism, which ruled out any real internal transformation of the bourgeois state. With the advancing crisis, growing popular upheavals would force the bourgeoisie into an authoritarian posture to defend its threatened class interests; under such circumstances, electoral victories would turn out to be hollow, and social reforms — even where possible — would only help to stabilize a faltering capitalist system. The parliamentary road was a myth, as it never challenged the real centers of bourgeois power nor did it look to the masses themselves as the real protagonists of democratic socialism.[25] Luxemburg insisted, in opposition to Bernstein, that no concept of transition was possible without a theory of crisis based upon the necessary contradictions of capitalist development. And she emphasized, in opposition to both Bernstein and Kautsky, that democratization involves proletarian control of production as well as of the state. Her conclusion: The leading SPD strategists had become hopelessly trapped within a bourgeois conception of democracy.

As for Lenin, she shared only his views that capitalism was in the throes of global crisis, that parliamentary systems were in this situation little more than adornments of bourgeois power, and that therefore the established state apparatus would have to be overthrown, destroyed, and replaced by a revolutionary state. (Here of course Luxemburg had in mind the prewar German state.) But they differed fundamentally over the essence of the new state, as well as over the political methods for achieving it. Luxemburg's viewpoint was that the vanguard party necessarily violated democracy in the name of organizational "effectiveness," that in the end it reabsorbed the masses into a new system of bureaucratic authority. She believed that Lenin's authoritarian means would subvert his proclaimed emancipatory ends. The problem with vanguardist strategy lies in its obsession with leadership, which emerges as a substitute for mass activity and social struggle; true, the mobilization of popular support is necessary for the revolutionary conquest of power, but the active, decisive component remains the party.[26] Lenin sidestepped this dilemma in two ways—through a definitional technique (dictatorship of the proletariat equals democracy) and by deferring the issue to a future stage (when the withering away of the state would presumably accompany the development of full Communism).

Luxemburg was the first important Marxist theorist to pose the question of socialist democracy. Yet, unlike Kautsky, Bernstein, and Lenin, she never actually developed in her work an integrated political strategy that could produce concrete tendencies within the mass struggles of the time. In her rejection of the twin extremes of parliamentarism and vanguardism she found refuge in the "masses" as she struggled to counter the powerful antidemocratic currents at work within Marxism. But her vision of the mass strike—and her call for a "dialectic" between leaders and followers—furnished no tangible solution to the problem of building a sustained democratic socialist movement. Her tremendous faith in the mass strike resembled more than anything else a Sorelian myth that enabled her to avoid the intricate questions of consciousness and organization. It also allowed her to ignore the question of democracy in its concreteness, as part of the struggle to create alternative non-bureaucratic forms of economic and political control.

The task of elaborating the constituent elements of a democratic socialist strategy was left to Pannekoek and the council communists, whose main premises (imminent crisis, proletarian self-management, direct mass action, and so on) were identical to Luxemburg's. Not content with the diffuse spontaneism of the mass strike scenario, they looked to the *organizational* development of local forms of democracy (soviets, factory committees, workers' councils) that appeared in the 1905 revolution in Russia and later grew into sizable political movements not only in Russia but in Italy, Germany, the Netherlands, and elsewhere. They saw in the council form the embryo of a revolutionary system of power more collective and transformative than anything envisioned by either social democracy or Leninism.

Pannekoek's analysis of the SPD situated the party within the early phases of capitalist expansion; once having developed an institutional-ized presence within the political system (facilitated by the eclipse of the anti-Socialist laws), the party soon adopted the very logic of the bourgeois revolution. The SPD thus came to embody not the subversion of bourgeois society but its rationalization, to the extent that it stabilized the existing state apparatus by reinforcing the methods of formal democracy, initiating limited social reforms, and integrating large sectors of the working class into the system. Thus, "In Germany, the develop-ment of the party form was subject to the particular conditions of the bourgeois revolution and served, through its Marxist imagery, to achieve for the emergent proletariat a secure place within capitalism."[27] The growth of imperialism, which fostered a militant nationalism within large strata of the proletariat, further encouraged this tendency. By 1908 — at about the time Luxemburg, Robert Michels, and Gustav Lan-dauer were refining their own critiques of German Social Democracy — Pannekoek had concluded that the historical task of the SPD was to "reorganize capitalism on a new foundation," on the assump-tion that the working class could through its parliamentary and trade-union strength eventually dominate the state machinery. The reality, however, would be a new system of domination (state capitalism) erected behind the "facade of socialism."[28]

Because of this line of thinking, Pannekoek found himself engaged in a head-on theoretical clash with Kautsky in 1912; writing in *Neue Zeit*, Kautsky chastised the radical left for its seeming anarchistic indulgence of undisciplined mob politics and its lack of organizational focus — a generalization that was perhaps valid for certain radical elements. Panne-koek responded that Kautsky's single-minded parliamentarism, along with his equation of socialism with nationalization and state planning, led him into a theoretical and strategic impasse: preservation of bourgeois political structures at all costs. For Pannekoek, it was more than a question of Kautsky's failure of imagination: "It is simply that our perspectives correspond to different stages in the development of organization, Kautsky's to the organization in its first flowering, ours to a more mature level of development" in which a variety of forms of ac-tion (insurrectionary as well as legal) could be integrated into a total revolutionary process, all leading to the dissolution of the capitalist state.[29] Kautsky was so preoccupied with organizational growth and sur-vival that virtually his entire theory and tactics served to shield the bureaucratic apparatus from the risks of social revolution.[30] The fatal defect of parliamentarism was that (despite the disclaimers of its sup-porters) it saw electoral activity "not as a means of increasing proletarian power, but as the battle itself for this power," which led sooner or later to an institutionalized political division of labor within the movement. Observed Pannekoek, "If one holds that political conflict should occur exclusively within parliament, then the parliamentarians are the only people called upon to wage it. It is not the working masses who are involved, but their representatives who fight on their behalf. The masses only figure at the ballot boxes. . . . The party deputies thus take up a vanguard position; they become a special class, the 'guides.'"[31]

The foundations of a new order, therefore, would have to be built outside the large-scale Marxist parties and trade unions, for the leadership of such organizations was too committed to preserving its bureaucratic status within a stable, administered system of social relations ever to be the repository of democratic impulses. The best "strategy" was ultimately what the workers could fashion themselves by means of their own activity; all other "solutions" that delivered mass initiatives over to "representatives" of one sort or another were illusory, for in Pannekoek's words, "The real forces of revolution lie elsewhere than in the tactics of parties and the politics of governments."[32] The institutional alternative to a party-centered socialism would be a federative system of local councils. In the highly charged atmosphere of postwar Europe, with capitalism in crisis and social democracy in shambles, the council radicals thought that the tremendous upsurge of proletarian militancy would generate, organically and spontaneously, a flowering of revolutionary organs at the point of production—a dream that was to be at best only partially and briefly fulfilled. Pannekoek was convinced that the emergent "soviet system" would in time uproot and abolish the state bureaucracy, transferring the management of production and society into the hands of the masses and laying the basis of a fully socialized state. This process was expected to mature through internal proletarian struggles, as a by-product of capitalist evolution, rooted in the "natural groupings of workers in the process of production, the real basis of society."[33] Here Pannekoek shared Luxemburg's critique of the Bolshevik Revolution, but he carried the analysis even further. He concluded that in Russia "Marxism" (or Leninism) became the modernizing ideology of a radical intelligentsia bent on mobilizing a small proletariat behind essentially state capitalist objectives. The predictable result was a new system of production directed by a state bureaucracy and rationalized by means of a centralized planning apparatus, with the workers forming an exploited class.[34]

From the standpoint of democratic vision, the council communists opened up new theoretical and strategic terrain within the Marxist tradition. Yet their framework too was riddled with ambiguities and contradictions. A theory of self-conscious proletarian struggle, it lapsed at times into a rigid economic determinism; an effective critique of statism, it failed to develop an alternative conception of the state upon which a viable political strategy could be constructed; a compelling theory of democratic transformation, it expressed an extreme productivism that gave rise to a narrow workerism—with its faith in a heroic unitary proletariat—that precluded any conception of *generalized* self-management or of social revolution outside the workplace. As for the council movement itself, insofar as its strength depended upon extreme crisis its trajectory was bound to be unstable and ephemeral. Unable to understand this limitation, Pannekoek could never come to grips with the incapacity of the postwar council insurgency—including the one he experienced closely in Germany—to survive as a democratizing force.[35] Ironically, the productivism and localist impotence of the council tendency arose from the same mechanical separation of politics and economics that was the theoretical flaw of social democracy, with the order of emphasis reversed.[36]

Democracy or Statism?

The fate of European Marxist parties and movements in the twentieth century has been decisively influenced by these early struggles and debates, which seem to reappear in each new setting. It is noteworthy that every major current placed great emphasis on democracy as an integral part of socialist transformation, consistent with Marx's original vision, but none actually developed a comprehensive theory of *socialist* democracy. Each was therefore partial, having failed even to put forward those objectives necessary for democratization: generalized self-management, reconstitution of social life, overturning of the bourgeois division of labor. And not coincidentally, each downplayed or ignored the issue of popular consciousness—that is, the sphere of active, subjective intervention in everyday life vital to the unfolding of self-emancipating human personalities and social relations. For Kautsky and Bernstein, the problem was a theory confined to the very assumptions of bourgeois politics and to the failure to extend even their limited conception of democratization into the sphere of civil society. The radical left was able to overcome this problem in its emphasis on direct, non-bureaucratic forms of struggle but ended up without a *political* strategy that could give shape to such forms; it either dismissed the role of organizational mediations altogether (Luxemburg), or it lapsed into a strict production-centered schema that turned the whole of bourgeois society into an immense factory (the council communists). Finally, Lenin's Jacobin preoccupation with the primacy of politics simply deferred the question of democracy through its instrumentalist drive toward state power in circumstances that demanded statist methods of mobilization and control.

What all of these currents shared, however deep their differences, was a mechanistic conception of the state that detached politics from the economy, indeed from the totality of civil society.[37] What the theories lacked was a vision (and strategy) pointing toward a unified transformation of each sphere of bourgeois society. Of course such theories were the product of an earlier (competitive) phase of capitalism, when the state was much less developed and less organically merged with the broader system; political institutions were not yet involved on any large scale in accumulation or legitimation functions. Under such conditions, a relatively feeble and isolated state apparatus appeared more vulnerable, either to a simple process of internal democratization or to direct overthrow from outside. The anticipation of massive crisis and upheaval, shared by all in this period except Bernstein (who abandoned any revolutionary pretensions), reinforced this rather cavalier attitude toward the state. Like Marx in the 1840s, these currents embraced a triumphalism that looked to the imminent dissolution of capitalism and a rapid march toward socialism. This helps to account for the exceptionally vague discussion of the transition during this period (again, with the qualified exception of Bernstein). It also explains the simplistic dichotomies that characterized the strategic debates of the times: parliamentarism versus insurrection, reform versus revolution, internal democratization versus vanguard seizure of power.

The failure of the European radical left to break out of its insularity and generate a sustained movement beyond the postwar crisis meant that the Marxist legacy would be appropriated by social democracy and Leninism (or its Stalinized version) until at least the 1960s. In both cases, the theory eventually became the legitimating world view of political elites and cadres, industrial managers and planners, parliamentarians and trade-union bureaucrats – all of whom, whatever their motivations, would use their power to maintain their privileged status over the "masses" they claimed to represent. The result was that, although social democracy and Leninism pursued completely different roads to power, both strategies led to the same antidemocratic politics: extension of bureaucracy in both the state and workplace, political division of labor within the movement, suppression of the social revolution. By the late 1920s, and emphatically by the 1930s, the idea of socialism had become inseparably connected with the reality of authoritarian politics.

Social democracy presented itself as following the "democratic road," but its efforts to internally transform the capitalist state either collapsed in the midst of crisis (Germany) or brought "working-class" parties into power (or a share of power) where they set out to administer a rationalized state capitalism (Sweden). Nowhere did social democracy seriously attack the exploitative features of bourgeois society—the class system, hierarchy, the market economy. The expansion of parliamentary democracy only masked the essence of a social order characterized by generalized domination and by a widening gulf between state and civil society. In the course of Soviet development, Leninism embodied the institutionalization of a "proletarian" democracy in the single-party state. It too manufactured a popular democratic mythology—the vanguard party as bearer of the historical will of the masses—in order to conceal the actuality of bureaucratic centralism. In both instances, the democratic socialist ideal amounted to little more than a mystifying facade: either distorted by the imperatives of capitalist production or thrown up against the power of an authoritarian state. Political and cultural space for local organizational forms, for workers' self-management, and for popular initiative narrowed where it did not vanish altogether.

From this standpoint, "successful" Marxist strategies contained three defining elements—a statist politics, a commitment to rationalization of production, and the hegemonic role of technocratic intellectuals—each of which was incompatible with any sustained democratization. Statism concentrated power within a governmental apparatus that became the primary locus of accumulation and legitimation functions and that reproduced its own interests and identity apart from the spheres of popular control. Paradoxically, just as the working class was being integrated into the various state, party, and interest-group structures for the first time, the very opening for expanded democratic participation collapsed. Rationalization involved the drive to eliminate the residues of traditionalism—the institutional and ideological barriers to economic productivity and growth—that required an administered and centralized system of planning, technological development, and labor discipline. In this sense Marxism itself emerged as an ideological expression of the bourgeois division of labor, reproducing and legitimating old forms of domination (e.g., class, bureaucratic, patriarchal) in new settings.[38] The vehicle of this dialectic was a rationalizing elite stratum that mobilized its intellectual capital (knowledge, communication skills, technical expertise, and so on) to create a new power bloc through an alliance with the proletariat. Ideologically committed to advancing the class struggle, this stratum in time (especially where it came to power) constituted itself as a dominant technocratic force over the masses.[39]

For European social democracy, the main direction was toward a restructuring of capitalism within a multiparty framework, allowing for the freer development of "social capital." In Soviet-type bureaucratic regimes, the single-party state utilized its controlling presence to carry out a range of "modernizing" goals dependent upon central planning and rapid industrialization. In both cases, the outcome was similar: the ascendance of a rationalizing political force that, beneath its dedication to "socialism," would carry out (in extended and progressive form) the historic tasks of the bourgeois revolution where the bourgeoisie itself was too weak or otherwise incapable of organizing the economy and winning the support of the working class.

The Rise of Eurocommunism

In the context of those twin failures, and following several decades of Stalinist organizational and theoretical constraint within the international Communist movement, the first stirrings of Eurocommunism in the 1970s signaled to many the long-awaited appearance of a fundamentally new strategy—a "third road"—that could effectively merge the goals of socialism and democracy.[40] The illusions of the past, whether those of social democracy or of Leninism, would be transcended.

Whatever their various historical and political differences, the Eurocommunist parties have one major defining characteristic in common—commitment to a democratic transition to socialism that is engineered through the political institutions of advanced capitalism. For its architects in the Italian, Spanish, and French parties, the democratic road assumes that the historic Marxist goals of expanded production and social equality can (and must) be realized through a progressively democratized bourgeois state.[41] This means a long-term strategic emphasis on electoral politics, extension of parliamentary forms, and preservation of civil liberties; the actual conquest of state power is seen as evolving gradually out of an increasingly favorable balance of forces. Parallels with some of the dominant motifs in classical social democracy will appear quite obvious. But Eurocommunism presents itself as a tendency *sui generis,* as clearly distinct from this tradition. In contrast to Kautsky, it rejects a scenario of sudden or qualitative rupture; in contrast to Bernstein it sustains a theory of social contradictions and class struggle that has always been the core of Marxism. And of course it has departed significantly from its own Leninist origins, having long ago (at least in practice) abandoned the idea of an insurrectionary frontal assault on the bourgeois state apparatus.[42] In contrast, the third way establishes claim to a strategy of socialist transformation that is more coherent and more solidly grounded in the conditions of late capitalism—a strategy that anticipates a prolonged systemic contestation for hegemony, in which the "democratization of the state" occurs organically and as peacefully as possible, with no dramatic collapse or upheaval, in a period of relative institutional stability.

Even this reconstituted theory of the democratic road, however, goes back to the immediate post–World War II years when a few innovative Communist parties (notably the Yugoslav and Italian) were beginning to reassess the Stalinist legacy. Although the phenomenon of Eurocommunism is in many respects novel, its guiding concepts actually go back to this period. The theory of "structural reforms" of the Italian Communist party (PCI), for instance, can be traced back to the years 1944–1947, when Palmiro Togliatti first outlined a *via italiana* that was motivated by strategic protection of republican institutions. Only crudely sketched at first as a response to fascism and later denied full expression by the cold war, this model was followed rather faithfully in practice and, in the period after 1956, was refined by Togliatti and his successors, who in the early 1970s introduced the "historic compromise"—the idea of a governing alliance with the Christian Democrats. The Spanish Communist party (PCE), while struggling as an underground party to survive Franco's authoritarian rule, endorsed the democratic road as early as the late 1960s, even in the absence of electoral possibilities before mid-1977. Santiago Carrillo's increasingly bold critique of the Soviet system, the publication of his *Eurocommunism and the State* in 1977, and the PCE's jettisoning of "Leninism" in favor of a "revolutionary, democratic, and Marxist" party at its Ninth Congress in April 1978 all marked the culmination of a long process of ideological transformation. The decision by the French Communist party (PCF) to abandon the "dictatorship of the proletariat" concept at its twenty-second Congress in February 1976 was, likewise, really a theoretical codification of the party's ongoing political involvement since World War II.

In each case, continued adherence to Leninist theory and the Soviet mystique served more as a fiction to reinforce party identity than as a strategic guide to action. The appearance of "Eurocommunism" in the mid-1970s thus signified above all a final and irrevocable shift of this identity from a Soviet-defined international movement to a national or regional one where indigenous local factors play the overwhelming role. Only to a lesser extent did it reflect the sudden emergence of new democratizing impulses within the parties, although such impulses cannot be discounted.

What is new, however, is the following: the exacerbation of the global and European crisis of capitalism, which is especially acute in the Mediterranean countries owing to their subordinate position in the international division of labor; the electoral successes of the PCI, legalization of the PCE, and the PCF's entry into a left alliance with the Socialists (since disbanded), conferring on these parties an image of respectability and in the case of the PCI bringing national governmental power closer; and the more self-conscious theoretical and political assertion of the democratic road strategy, thus widening and solidifying the breach with the Communist Party of the Soviet Union (CPSU).

Fascinating as these developments are, a familiar question presents itself: Given the general premises of the Eurocommunist parties and the conditions they face, how far in political reality can they hope to advance along the path of democratic socialist transformation—assuming that is what the parties envision? Here Eurocommunism, like other Marxist movements before it, confronts an old dilemma: how to achieve instrumental (efficiency and power-oriented) goals without undermining revolutionary (democratic and egalitarian) ones. This poses in turn the theme of rationalization, which is the reverse side of the dialectic of democratization and which will shape much of the following analysis. If we reflect upon the totality of Eurocommunist strategies, programs, and intentions, it is clear that alongside the commitment to democratization is the long-range project of rationalization—the augmenting of economic productivity and institutional cohesiveness by means of stripping away precapitalist residues (e.g., traditional social relations, outmoded techniques, parasitism, clientele networks), expanding the role of science and technology, building new planning mechanisms, expanding and professionalizing the public sector, and stabilizing the political system. To some degree, this project has always been central to Marxism, especially where movements have come to power (usually in preindustrial countries) and set in motion a modernizing process of "socialist construction," exemplified by the pattern of Soviet development already mentioned. This secularizing, rationalizing side of Marxism has usually coexisted in some fashion with its democratizing, emancipatory side. The difficulty is that in the historical formation of Marxist party-states, rationalization has often prevailed in a way that generates profoundly antidemocratic consequences: bureaucratic centralism, routinized and alienated labor, mass depoliticization.

But if such movements have yielded to certain imperatives of rationalization, then surely the Eurocommunist parties, situated in relatively developed countries with (Spain excepted) institutionalized bourgeois democratic traditions, could hope to escape its authoritarian logic. Clearly, the strategic potential for a democratic transition to socialism is greater in Western Europe today than it was, for example, in Russia at the time of the Bolshevik Revolution. Yet, from the standpoint of dilemmas associated with the politics of industrialization, most of the old obstacles and limitations remain in new forms. In the first place, Mediterranean capitalism is today characterized by growing production and legitimation crises that open up new terrain for rationalization within a bourgeois framework. Second, where the Eurocommunist parties are able to win at least a share of power — and the PCI has long been doing so in local Italian politics — one outcome might be the gradual displacement of traditional capitalist domination rooted in private property with a bureaucratic system of rule linked to a more encompassing state apparatus. Third, bureaucratic obstacles to the democratic road are in fact strengthened by the presence within Eurocommunism of the very strategic tendencies that shackled traditional social democracy, notably the attempt to chart a path primarily through the existing state and the absence of a fully developed theory of socialist democracy that spells out new forms of popular control.

Of course the historical circumstances are too different to permit the drawing of simple parallels between earlier forms of social democracy and contemporary Eurocommunism, whatever their theoretical similarities. Moreover, the Eurocommunists (especially in Italy and Spain) do stress such objectives as "decentralization," "democracy at the base," and even *"autogestion";* they are obviously aware of the pitfalls associated with a narrow parliamentary and trade-unionist strategy; and they are more sensitive to the role of popular movements (around issues related to women, youth, the environment, the neighborhoods) even if they remain fundamentally ambivalent about such movements.[43] Still, to the extent that this new version of the democratic road lacks a revolutionary conception of the state, the strategy could be rendered inert when confronted with the process of rationalization, paving the way to a bureaucratic-statist outcome behind a pluralist facade.

Expressed in these terms, the conflict between democratization and rationalization involves several roadblocks that Marxist parties have rarely managed to avoid. Socialist transformation in the advanced countries will surely be unpredictable, open-ended, conflictual, at times even chaotic. It follows that a major predicament for such parties — especially those restricting their activity largely to the dominant political-institutional sphere — is that of trying to expand the democratic and liberating potential of the existing structures within a framework that in many ways protects hierarchical and exploitative social relations. For Eurocommunism, therefore, the strategic march toward state power inevitably runs across the problems of legitimacy and bureaucratic domination. At this point several crucial questions need to be posed. How can the diffusion of technocratic rationality be compatible with a broadening of democratic participation? How can state planning and social investment (even with a dose of decentralization) be increased without risking further bureaucratization? How can the participatory side of government be further democratized while curtailing and streamlining its administrative side?[44] Finally, to what extent can the rather stable institutional order that is required for the Eurocommunist concept of transition be maintained in the midst of accelerating social, economic, and political crisis?

We are not yet in a position to offer final answers to such questions. The difficult struggle to create innovative and successful theories of revolutionary change in the advanced capitalist countries is really just beginning. The growing impasse of Eurocommunism in the early 1980s does suggest, however, that the logic of its strategy is beset with enough contradictions and pitfalls to call into question the basis of the exuberant optimism noted at the outset. My central purpose is to explore this logic by assessing Eurocommunist political strategies and economic programs of the postwar period and by analyzing their relationship to actual historical processes and events. Of course the ultimate question is whether the modern variant of the democratic road can sustain its promises of real socialist transformation (assuming it ever gains power) or is destined to become a recycled version of conventional social democracy.

systems. After the failure of European Resistance movements to generate a revolutionary transformation in any developed country, the long-cherished hopes of insurrection were abandoned (although they were routinely mentioned in official party statements). Not only in France and Italy, but in many other European countries—Greece, Denmark, Austria, Norway, Belgium, Luxembourg, Finland, and Iceland—Communist parties entered national governments after the war, moving into opposition only when the cold war made continued collaboration with bourgeois parties impossible. Many of these parties maintained an extensive presence in local governments, and some returned to a share of national power (as in Finland) once East-West tensions were softened in the 1960s. Even in opposition, however, the Communist parties abided strictly by the norms and practices of bourgeois democracy; not only did they consistently shy away from activities involving class confrontation or mass mobilization, their entire political outlook shifted toward advocacy of extreme moderation.[2]

During the immediate postwar years, some Communist parties were trapped in a dual politics of duplicity, suspended between Leninist ideological identity and everyday parliamentarism. In the PCI, this strategic ambivalence was concretely resolved by 1953 in favor of Togliatti's concept of structural reforms, which the party later openly championed in the wake of the 1956 events: the initial stirrings of de-Stalinization in the USSR (including tentative approval of "different" or "national" paths to socialism); the Hungarian uprising; and the first appearance of polycentrism in the world Communist movement, which Togliatti outlined at the Eighth PCI Congress in 1956. In the PCF under Maurice Thorez, dual politics continued well into the 1960s, its contradictions mystified and repressed by a residual Jacobin ideology, a heavy-handed organizational centralism, and a sense of embattled political isolation (explained by the party's failure to build its popular support beyond the early postwar peak). Although it had engaged in frontist and electoral politics since the mid-1930s, only after 1964 did the PCF begin to present a strategic self-conception in tune with this history and critical of the Leninist insurrectionary model. Even so, it took the leadership a decade to abandon the pretense that Leninism and the democratic road were somehow compatible.[3]

Once the PCI and PCF moved to reassess their identities openly and systematically, once their indigenous political entanglements began to take precedence over Soviet "internationalism," their adoption of structural reformism became more uncompromising and irreversible. The strategy of democratization, however limited, was less a matter of choice than a requirement of political success, or even survival; it was, above all, geared to a phase of capitalist development in which the monopolistic rule of a single party seemed no longer defensible or plausible. This process advanced more rapidly in the PCI than in other Communist parties, largely because of its very size (which offered more promising chances of electoral success) and the guiding strategic influence of Togliatti. It was accelerated by the internal triumph of the PCI's right wing in the late 1960s, culminating in the expulsion of the leftist Il Manifesto group in 1969. The arguments of the right — that the conditions of "neocapitalism" allowed for and required a reformist insertion of the party into the bourgeois state — coincided with the PCI's expanded role in Italian society.[4] Other parties were not so immediately confronted with these kinds of pressures, opportunities, and choices.

Events of the late 1960s and early 1970s added to the momentum favoring the democratic road. These included (1) the decline of Gaullism as a hegemonic force in France and the immobility of the center-left coalition in Italy; (2) the Soviet invasion of Czechoslovakia, which the PCI and PCF vigorously protested and which further illuminated the issues of pluralism and national autonomy; (3) the challenge of the new left and feminism (dating from the May 1968 events in France and the "hot autumn" of 1969 in Italy), which dramatized the authoritarian character of the Communist parties and ultimately softened their resistance to new ideological currents; (4) the leftist defeats in Chile and Portugal, which revealed the need for broad popular alliances extending beyond the traditional proletariat; (5) a mellowing of the postwar Socialist antagonism toward the Communists, clearing the way for greater unified leftist action, including the formation of new coalitions and alliances; and (6) the consistent election gains of the PCI, which for the first time won more than one-third of the vote in the 1975 (regional) and 1976 (national) elections, carrying it to the threshold of national power.[5]

Beneath this were four significant long-term factors: the visible erosion of bourgeois and Catholic dominance in Italy and France, détente between the United States and the Soviet Union, the Sino-Soviet split and the rise of pluralism within the world Communist movement, and, perhaps most crucial, the stable institutionalized involvement of the two parties in parliamentary politics. These developments contributed to the legitimation of the parties domestically (reflected in the decline of anti-Communism) and to their innovative flexibility vis-à-vis the USSR and the Marxist tradition in general.

The PCE's transformation, on the other hand, occurred later but more abruptly. After nearly four decades of clandestine activity under the Francoist dictatorship, the PCE leadership was anxious to shed its "outlaw" status and switch to legal means of struggle. Underground politics took its toll, not only physically but ideologically: The PCE grew more and more insulated and detached from social reality during the harsh and repressive generation following the Civil War. Especially before 1956, the PCE's Leninism meant a rigid attachment to Bolshevik strategy and passive subservience to the CPSU line and Soviet foreign policy. Throughout this period its centralized apparatus remained intact.

The first signs of change appeared in the mid-1960s with the Franco regime's slippage and the PCE's growing presence in the new workers' commissions (*comisiones obreras*), which in areas like Catalonia had established bargaining relationships with management. Then, in 1968, Carrillo stepped forward as a vocal critic of the Soviet intervention in Czechoslovakia, seizing upon this moment to attack Soviet bureaucratic centralism and, by extension, the concept of the dictatorship of the pro-letariat, which he now argued was outmoded and incompatible with revolutionary goals. From this standpoint, and with the expectation that the decaying Franco dictatorship would soon crumble and give way to bourgeois democracy, the PCE embraced the democratic road. It was not until 1977, however — after Franco's death, the legalization of the PCE, and the holding of Spain's first national elections since 1936 — that the party could implement the strategy in practice.

What distinguishes the situation of the PCE from that of the PCI and PCF, of course, is that bourgeois democratic institutions had not yet fully appeared in Spain. Throughout the 1970s, the requirements of anti-fascist struggle still weighed heavily on the Spanish left. This reality has permeated every aspect of the PCE's program and strategy; it is reflected in Carrillo's books, interviews, and statements.[6] It also defines the two-stage conception of the transition advanced by Carrillo: First destroy the remnants of fascism and secure liberal democracy, then begin the process of socialist transformation. In Carrillo's words, "The great thing today is to smash the forced integration constituted by fascism. In order to do this, what is needed is a coalition government which will restore liberties. Tomorrow the advance to socialism will be posed."[7] This is not to deny that the PCI and PCF have also been preoccupied with fascism and the threat of reaction, but merely to indicate that Spain today is at a dif-ferent level of political development from either Italy or France. Hence the PCE in 1980 seeks to play an integral role in a pluralist transforma-tion of Spanish society while staking out its own claim to legal opposition.

With the strategic outlook of the three parties changing drastically, new theoretical formulations (e.g., on the state, concept of the party, class forces, nature of the transition) were bound to follow. Interestingly enough, it was the theoretical codification of already established organizational practices—a step coinciding with the *political* birth of Eurocommunism—that provoked so much controversy and triggered the initial Soviet response.[8] The Eurocommunist position was strongly affirmed and defended (notably by Carrillo and Berlinguer) at the June 1976 meeting of twenty-seven Communist parties in East Berlin; although criticisms of the Soviet model were muted, CPSU leaders were forced to yield on every major issue.[9] In this case, as in others, the conflict focused on Lenin—or at least what passed for Leninism within the Communist tradition.

The Departure from Past Myths

What the Eurocommunist parties ultimately had to confront, and reject, was the traditionally sacred notion of the dictatorship of the proletariat. For, as we have seen, although Leninism as a concrete strategy never really took hold in the advanced capitalist societies, its lingering mystique and symbolic imagery did have political consequences for an entire range of party activities. It is therefore significant that, although the official break did not occur until the 1975–1978 period, the implications for such a departure were already present in Togliatti's postwar writings on the *via italiana*, which he tried to square with ideological convention by employing the innovative term "democratic dictatorship of the proletariat."[10] Togliatti's concept of "progressive democracy," sketched in 1944–1946, necessarily required for its actualization a nonvanguardist party—a mass, nonsectarian organization that represented the working class and allied strata within the framework of pluralist competition. At this time the PCI set for itself the basic goal of consolidating bourgeois democracy in the continuing struggle against fascism; the transition to socialism would be delayed until domestic and international power relations were more favorable (a phase, however, that was never seriously discussed in the party literature). Immediate political efforts were largely tactical, directed toward broadening space within the existing institutional spheres. The impetus for this departure came not only from the Resistance, which transformed the Communist party from a small sect into a diversified mass party, but from the frontist policy of interclass alliances laid down at the Seventh Comintern Congress in 1935.[11]

In Togliatti's view, the PCI was but one part of the state and society alongside other parties and forces; thus, no single party had an exclusive moral claim to rule and no Marxism possessed absolute scientific authority. A democratic transition would require the PCI's continuous institutional presence in a "secular, non-ideological, and pluralistic" state. Togliatti noted, accurately, that the dictatorship of the proletariat was always a vague concept in classical Marxism and that its only historical embodiment (in the Soviet Union) was not something that the vast majority of Italians, with the memories of Mussolini's authoritarian state still fresh, wanted to duplicate. Yet, despite the obvious contradictions between the *via italiana* and Bolshevik strategy, Togliatti, owing to his long and deep attachment to the USSR, could never break with the party's official Leninism.

At the same time, Togliatti was the first leader within international Communism to argue that Stalinism was a systemic deformation not reducible to the personal machinations of a single leader; implicit here was a more general critique of the Soviet model and of Leninism, even if Togliatti himself stopped short of such a critique during his lifetime. More explicit were a number of related issues that the theory of the dictatorship of the proletariat had obscured: the vast economic and political differences between Russia in 1917 and postwar Western Europe; the role of parliamentary institutions in the transition; the nature of popular alliances and the task of maximizing participation at the base; the question of internal party democracy; and so forth. Ferment over these issues within the PCI began to spread in the late 1950s[12] until at the Tenth Congress in 1962 Leninism (in its Soviet-defined form) finally came under open attack. Togliatti now conceded that Lenin no longer provided a final guide to action for Marxist parties in the developed countries.[13] The unmistakable thrust of Togliatti's writings and statements in the years before his death in 1964 was clearly "Eurocommunist" — a *via terza* (third way) that embraced the national autonomy of parties, a nonbureaucratic and pluralistic socialism, and the goal of internal democratization of the bourgeois state.[14]

To fill the void created by the departure from Leninism, the PCI turned to Antonio Gramsci, one of the party's founders and a theorist whose influence was just becoming visible within Western European Marxism. Gramsci's notion of a gradual transformation of civil society as the prelude to the conquest of state power soon constituted the rationale for the *via italiana*.[15] Filtered through Togliatti, the PCI's "Gramscian Marxism" allowed the party to occupy a new (parliamentary) strategic terrain while retaining its nominal Leninism.[16] Despite strong pressure from the most militant electoralist faction (led by Giorgio Amendola), however, the leadership under Luigi Longo somehow clung to its "Leninism" throughout the 1960s. These pretensions were abandoned only in the aftermath of the Thirteenth Congress in 1972, when Berlinguer introduced the historic compromise tactics.

Fueled by electoral successes and the decline of Christian Democratic strength, the PCI could realistically focus its sights on national power. Under such conditions, the authoritarian heritage of Leninism would constitute a severe handicap by enabling opponents to raise the bogey of Soviet dictatorship. The PCI's strategic approach to the state now differed more explicitly and fundamentally from Lenin's; bourgeois political institutions were viewed as integral to all phases of socialist transformation, while longstanding commitments to nationalization of industries and centralized economic planning were sharply revised. Yet even the most profound changes were presented as an expression of continuity from Leninism through the "new course" to the *compromesso* policy of the 1970s.[17]

In this sense, the PCI has yet to fully surmount its dualistic legacy of the early postwar years—the surface persistence of Leninism as a source of organizational identity alongside the electoralism and trade unionism of its everyday practice. As late as 1979 Berlinguer could say, "It is not our intention to fuel petty polemics or partisan controversies over 'Leninism.' At the same time, we have no intention of disowning or minimizing our party's historical ties with the October Revolution and Lenin's work."[18] In any case, the theoretical innovations that grew out of the Thirteenth Congress hastened the PCI's liberation from past myths, legitimating in unambiguous terms its strategic adaptation to representative democracy and prefiguring the rise of Eurocommunism.[19]

Both the PCE and PCF, on the other hand, experienced a later and much briefer process of internal debate over Leninism, but once the process was under way (in the early 1970s), party leaders resolutely swept aside orthodox symbols in their eagerness to demonstrate their Eurocommunist credentials. They wasted little time in jettisoning the dictatorship of the proletariat, which, as in the case of the PCI, imposed a tremendous ideological burden upon those organizations engaged in electoral activity or committed to the revitalization of bourgeois democracy. Carrillo argued that Leninist strategy had lost its rationale in the advanced capitalist systems (presumably including Spain): Not only armed insurrection, but the vanguard party (and the single-party state) were increasingly obsolete owing to the diversification of social forces and the complexity of political structures. By 1976, he rejected bureaucratic centralism of the Soviet type in principle, referring to the USSR as occupying a position "somewhere between capitalism and socialism." The formal rights and liberties produced by the bourgeois revolution, far from simply reflecting capitalist needs, as many Leninists had assumed, must be deepened and carried forward under socialist development. Hence Carrillo could "easily imagine a socialist regime governed jointly or even alternatively by Communists, Socialists, and Christians who are in favor of socialism: a socialist state with a plurality of parties."[20]

As Spanish fascism was still very much alive in the 1970s, Carrillo's preoccupation with liberal forms makes sense as part of a transitional program that, once carried out, would finally enable the PCE and other radical forces to pose the question of socialism. The irony here is obvious. Although Spain lacked any representative tradition, the positions staked out by the PCE at the Ninth Congress in 1978 expressed the deepest commitment to pluralist democracy of any Communist party in history.[21]

The PCF has been neither so critical of the CPSU nor so devoted to pluralist forms as the PCE. At the Twenty-Second Congress in 1976, Marchais concluded that the terms "dictatorship" and "proletariat" were negative symbols that isolated French Communism — the former conjuring images of Hitler, Mussolini, and Franco (and presumably Stalin), the latter suggesting a restricted working-class rather than a "mass" base. In the new phase of struggle, characterized by the crisis of monopoly capital, radicalization of the middle strata, and "peaceful coexistence," socialism could be advanced without civil war or an overturning of bourgeois state power — assuming, of course, that the PCF could mobilize a broad antimonopoly social bloc.[22] At the same time, the PCF leadership has been less willing to question its avowed vanguardism, as manifest in the idea that the party alone is the judge of Marxist theory and strategy, that it must exercise control over the mass organizations, and that it is the sole representative of the working class. It has been equally reluctant to part with democratic centralism. In this area, to a greater degree than in either the PCI or the PCE, the residues of Leninism survive in the PCF.[23]

In the debates over these departures from orthodoxy within international Communism, the CPSU presented itself as the guardian of Leninism. The Soviets have accepted in principle the concept of differing roads to socialism since 1956, but they still look to general patterns of historical change (above all the "leading role" of the revolutionary party) that cannot be violated without sacrificing basic Marxist objectives. CPSU theorists in fact do not reject the strategic use of parliamentary institutions in advanced capitalism, or even the possibility of a peaceful transition; the problem with Eurocommunism, in their view, is the "opportunistic" extremes to which the parties have gone in practice. Thus the abandonment of Leninism is viewed not merely as a theoretical deformation, but as a further step toward the parties' subordination to the bourgeois state apparatus and the market economy. In Soviet terms, the Eurocommunists have forgotten that the endemic crises of monopoly capitalism inevitably point toward rupture and transcendence of the old structures, even where parliamentary forms are utilized to prepare the way.[24] This Soviet renunciation of pluralist socialism is really the heart of the matter, as the Eurocommunist model constitutes a direct challenge to bureaucratic centralism and to the facile equation of democracy with the dictatorship of the proletariat not only in the USSR but also in Eastern Europe.[25] The CPSU leaders have every reason, therefore, to defend "Leninism" against the incursions of Carrillo, Berlinguer, and Marchais.

The stripping away of Leninist strategic imagery, even where old organizational principles linger, is thus the hallmark of Eurocommunism. It would be easy to analyze the transformation as merely symbolic, as the delayed theoretical recognition of routinized political practices. But that would be only half true; the break with Leninism has also cleared away obstacles to change within the parties, permitting them to glimpse a more comprehensive democratic theory of transition. Contradictions naturally remain, but the foundations of a contemporary structural reformism are more solidly established.

A Mediterranean Structural Reformism

Within the international Communist tradition, the presence of more than a dozen parties adhering to a reconstituted democratic road strategy gives rise to tremendous diversity—in levels of political development, organizational strength, social composition, international ties, and even in degrees of attachment to ideological orthodoxy. And of course each party, no matter how integrated into a global movement or loyal to the Soviet Union, is shaped by a unique national history and culture. The party leaderships, moreover, are factionally divided into "left," "right," and "center" tendencies despite sometimes tortured efforts to convey a public image of unity. Still, a common strategy does run through all the differences and idiosyncracies, one that can be defined as "structural reformist" or, in the looser parlance of the 1970s, "Eurocommunist." Although the parties are very much in a state of flux and transition and must confront historical conditions that are even more destabilizing, I believe their strategic orientation is more or less fixed and (barring a massive disruption of the political system) will constitute their guidepost to the future. In the case of the Mediterranean Communist parties, this commonality is enhanced by certain shared geographical and cultural bonds, as well as by a shared history that has facilitated political linkages.

The components of a non-Leninist transition developed within the evolving Eurocommunist movements can thus be elaborated as follows:

1. Utilization of the forms and practices of bourgeois democracy—elections, parliament, local government, interest groups—as the fundamental means of achieving a power transfer. Whereas Lenin emphasized the tactical importance of this sphere, arguing that it could help realize limited objectives, the Eurocommunists view it as the locus of a long-range strategy for dismantling bourgeois power and moving toward socialism. Insofar as the objective conditions exist within capitalism for democratization of the state apparatus, no forcible destruction of bourgeois democratic institutions is necessary; on the contrary, these institutions are to be vigorously defended throughout all phases of socialist transformation. The postwar Italian, French, and Spanish parties have all followed this prescription as far as possible, committing the vast bulk of their resources to electoral politics and avoiding direct encounter with the state at all costs (e.g., Italy in 1945 and France in 1968). Eurocommunism therefore represents an extension of earlier patterns, an institutional refinement of Togliatti's "new course" most of all in its celebration of pluralist forms. In Togliatti's words:

> We are democrats because we move in the framework of the Constitution, within democratic traditions and legality, and we expect from everyone all due respect for this legality and the application of all constitutional norms. . . . We have conquered the terrain of democracy in order to advance beyond it, toward socialism. It would therefore be absurd to negate it. On the contrary, we defend it. In fact, the urgency of socialist renewal . . . allows us to see in the norms of democratic and constitutional life not an obstacle, but a positive force for the construction of socialism.[26]

2. The theory of structural reforms—the concept of a gradual democratization of representative institutions that infuses old forms with new content, as the working class and other popular strata achieve a steadily more powerful voice, sense of citizenship, and political strength—as the dynamic underpinning of the transition. Each electoral advance and institutional gain permits the capture of new positions within the state, creating new space in which the left is better able to subvert bourgeois hegemony and assert its control over the main sectors of the economy and society. The PCI and, to a lesser extent, the PCE advertise this strategy as a modern Gramscian "war of position" capable of generating an authentic mass party and new levels of collective participation. Only through such a "modification of structures"—one that brings the working class to power and supersedes the narrow (formal) definition of freedoms typical of the liberal stage—can democracy be fully "completed."[27] For the PCF, this approach is more strictly conceptualized as a "transition from a state of the monopolies to the state of the working people" in which "advanced democracy is a step toward socialism."[28]

3. The preservation of constitutional rights and liberties, including those of political opposition, through the transitional period and into socialism itself. The Eurocommunist parties view pluralist forms and traditions as more compatible with egalitarian social development than is Soviet-style bureaucratic centralism, whatever the economic arguments on behalf of the latter. The indissoluble connection between democracy and socialism means, according to PCI theorist Luciano Gruppi, that "the struggle for human liberty, for parliamentary democracy, does not constitute a tactical moment, but is an essential part of the struggle for socialism as an ultimate goal."[29] Gruppi added that not only does parliament ideally play an active, decisive role in the transition, it is the "political system most appropriate to socialism."[30] Eurocommunist theorists conceive of the state as an arena of contestation, where diverse social forces struggle for expression, rather than as an instrument for the imposition of one set of political or religious ideologies. A wide variety of traditions and viewpoints (excluding fascism) is regarded as legitimate in principle; political solutions to the crisis of capitalism necessarily demand contributions from many sources—Marxist and non-Marxist, public and private, secular and religious.[31] To guarantee this kind of pluralism, the political system requires constitutional and structural provisions for open dissent and free alternations between parties. It is true that all currents within the Second International also accepted pluralist democratic norms, but their strategic understanding of postcapitalist politics remained hazy, bound as they were to such incompatible concepts as the withering away of the state and the dictatorship of the proletariat.

4. As a corollary to the acceptance of ideological and cultural diversity, a jettisoning of the vanguard theory of political and social organization—although except in some of Carrillo's statements this cornerstone of Leninism has not yet been completely overturned. Carrillo's position, adopted at the Ninth PCE Congress, is that genuine pluralism compels the party to abandon its "scientific" claim to be sole bearer of working-class interests; he saw the PCE as part of an unfolding "new political formation" in which other parties and mass organizations play equal roles, in which the party and state are not identical.[32] Carrillo's model also abolishes the Leninist "transmission belt" concept of party control over popular movements, such as the workers' commissions, trade unions, and neighborhood organizations. The PCI too has long endorsed ideological and religious pluralism (necessary for survival in a largely Catholic setting) and more recently accepted the principle of trade-union autonomy. According to Pietro Ingrao, the party is still a "leading" force insofar as it must shape state institutions, and yet it cannot become

totally submerged in the state.[33] In fact, the PCI retains significant vestiges of vanguardism, as reflected in the tenacity of its "scientific" Marxism and in its persistent drive to control mass organizations.[34] The PCF, meanwhile, has departed very little from its entrenched vanguardism and centralism, but how long this rigidity can be reconciled with its general strategic reformulations remains problematic.[35]

5. An alliance politics that attaches new significance to the expanding "middle strata" (civil servants, professionals, technicians, and so on) broadens the definition of "social bloc" to include all social forces (potentially) opposed to the monopolies, reaches out to Catholicism, and encourages electoral or governing coalitions with nonsocialist parties. Superficially resembling the Popular Front, Eurocommunist strategy differs from frontism to the degree that it is primarily anticapitalist rather than antifascist and ostensibly strives for mobilization toward socialism instead of being preoccupied with immediate defensive maneuvers. The PCI's skillful use of alliance strategy has been vital to its development of a large, heterogeneous popular base and an extensive administrative power network throughout Italy. The strategy is rooted in what the PCI sees as a convergence of urban social forces growing out of the conditions of advanced capitalism—industrial workers squeezed by the economic crisis, the middle strata radicalized by loss of job control and social issues, the petty bourgeoisie suffocated by the growing power of monopolies.[36] The PCF and PCE share the PCI's goal of a broadening social bloc tied to progressive electoral successes, and both are committed to mobilizing the new middle strata. But they are more skeptical of party coalitions than is the PCI, in part because they lack the PCI's strength and hence risk being dominated by larger Socialist parties.

6. Commitment to a process of institutional "renewal" at all levels of state activity. The starting point is professionalization of the civil service, including the elimination of huge patronage networks, nepotism, and corruption along with the simplification of the system of governmental ministries and agencies.[37] The goal is to make the public sector more accountable to the general population, first, by undermining monopoly and "parasitic" influences through strengthened parliamentary control; second, by democratizing the police, the military, and the court systems; and third, by decentralizing state power, which means turning over more decision-making authority to local and regional governments and (in the case of the PCE) encouraging the growth of popular democratic structures such as neighborhood councils. The PCE and PCI have both established a material basis for this strategy, the PCE in the workers' commissions, mass organizations, and (more ambivalently) the separatist movements, the PCI in municipal and provincial governments. In cities

like Bologna, where Communist administration goes back as far as 1945, the PCI has sought to develop "new norms of public life," which means alternative approaches to urban management and planning that maximize local participation (for example, through neighborhood councils that in limited form have appeared in some areas), and abolish *clientelismo*.[38] Party strategy here involves gradual development of a "democratically planned economy" with a mixture of state and small-scale private enterprises.[39] The PCF agrees with much of this in theory, but has a weaker local base from which to pursue it and thus its centralism tends to prevail by default.

7. The beginnings of an internal party democratization, typified by slow and cautious moves away from hierarchical, disciplined, cell-based structures toward broader participatory organizations that allow a freer exchange of ideas and influences. If none of the Eurocommunist parties has fully disavowed the concept of democratic centralism (although the PCE did entertain this notion at its Ninth Congress), each finds it more and more difficult to resolve the contradictions of pursuing a non-Leninist strategy while retaining a Leninist structure. First, the impact of the new left and mass movements since the late 1960s has forced the parties to confront new issues and adapt to a more participatory style. Second, in recent years internal debates have taken place over the many issues posed by Eurocommunism—for example, in the PCF and PCE over the break with Leninism, in the PCF following the dissolution of the Common Program and the left's electoral setback in March 1978, in the PCI around whether to pursue the historic compromise. As the party leaders can no longer prevent those struggles from moving into the open and perhaps taking a mass character, the Leninist fiction of internal secrecy, and with it a variety of other centralist norms, is rapidly becoming obsolete.

8. The assertion of political and strategic independence from the CPSU and the Soviet model, which has lost most of its appeal to the Western European left since the 1960s. New areas of autonomy were encouraged by de-Stalinization within the USSR and, later, by the diversity made possible in great measure by the Sino-Soviet conflict. The difficulties that Western Communist leaders encountered in trying to reconcile their domestic priorities and needs with the bureaucratic centralism of "actually existing socialism" in the USSR and Eastern Europe fed the drive toward a distinctly indigenous, non-Soviet-oriented model. For most of the parties, the 1968 Soviet overthrow of a Czech regime that had made serious inroads into Stalinist hegemony was the last straw. The PCI had since 1956 affirmed the right of parties to autonomy within international Communism—a direction already implicit in the *via italiana*

strategy. More recently, Berlinguer has clearly indicated that autonomy for the PCI means not only the freedom to carve out a "national" or regional strategy (an issue resolved earlier) but the pursuit of an independent global Communist presence outside the two major power blocs.[40] Carrillo's defense of these positions, both in *Eurocommunism and the State* and in party statements since the early 1970s, were even more forceful. He rejected the legitimacy of the "directing center," long associated with Soviet domination; the PCE had no interest in returning to outmoded conceptions of "proletarian internationalism," nor did it have any identification with the Soviet model of revolutionary transformation.[41]

The PCF leadership has been more sanguine and ambivalent in its attitude toward the CPSU. The French Communists have endorsed the principle of "national roads," but they have often yielded to Soviet foreign policy interests (for example, in their open support of the Soviet invasion of Afghanistan). At the same time, they have generally sided with the PCI and PCE on major issues. At the East Berlin conference all three parties affirmed what have become the defining features of Eurocommunism: strategic independence, no special status for the USSR, abandonment of the Soviet position on proletarian internationalism. Only Berlinguer and Carrillo, however, declared that they would refuse to participate in another Soviet-sponsored conference.[42]

9. The geographical proximity and cultural similarity of the Mediterranean parties have encouraged formation of a common regional or European-based perspective not only on matters of political strategy but on questions of international politics. Contacts among Western European Communist parties became more regular and intimate in the late 1960s, following the events in Czechoslovakia, to the extent that by 1973 regular conferences were being held. A loose alliance among the PCI, PCE, and PCF quickly emerged, leading to a joint Italian-Spanish declaration of July 1975, an Italian-French statement of November 1975, and the common declaration of all three in Madrid in March 1977. At the same time, the parties moderated their initial hostility to the North Atlantic Treaty Organization (NATO) and the European Economic Community (EEC) (as well as to the parties of the Socialist International) as a prelude to their increasing acceptance of European integration.[43] The PCI sent the first Communist delegation to the European parliament in 1969; since then the PCI and other parties have announced their support of European federal institutions, and some chose to work for a strengthening of the parliament through the introduction of popular elections, which first took place in April 1979. Having now established a strong minority representation within this body, the PCI

and PCF anticipate the formation of a broad left coalition incorporating the German Social Democrats, the French Socialists, and the British Labour Party. The PCE, for its part, supports Spanish entry into the EEC—which it sees as a crucial step toward legitimizing its "European" status—that would give the PCE representation alongside the PCI and PCF. The strategic basis of Eurocommunist regionalism is a more global version of the theory of structural reforms: Enter and democratize the European parliament (and trade-union federations) with the aim of creating a left majority that could attack monopoly power, lay the foundations of economic cooperation, and catalyze a Europe-wide transition to socialism.[44]

These elements have yet to be synthesized into a comprehensive theoretical framework; they represent the cautious and uneven search for a viable strategy grounded in the changing conditions of advanced capitalism rather than in any fixed model. Interestingly, party theorists rarely discuss this project in terms of the transition to socialism, preferring instead to view it as an opening in that direction made possible by the jettisoning of past myths and obstacles. This last point is crucial, as it indicates the degree to which Eurocommunist departures are shaped by a negative reaction to certain premises of traditional Communist theory rather than a definitive vision of socialist transformation. While "left" Eurocommunists (e.g., Fernando Claudin, Lucio Magri, and Nicos Poulantzas) have tried to fill this void with theoretical initiatives developed independently of the organized parties, it is the "right" that holds actual power and therefore remains in political control of these parties' concrete destiny.

The Politics of the Transition

Yet even if none of the various revisions by itself is completely original, taken together they point toward a reconstituted Marxist theory of the state and party appropriate to certain forms of political struggle in modern capitalism. Leninism assumed that the bourgeois state rests above all upon its coercive mechanisms (the central bureaucracy, military, and police), that it functions essentially as an agency of class domination, and that even the most "liberal" states are but thinly veiled repressive organs that are immune to real democratic transformation. Under conditions of an impotent parliament thrown up against a monolithic state apparatus, the only viable strategy was revolutionary overthrow of the entire bourgeois political system by the intervention of a vanguard party. The Eurocommunists reject this approach, insisting that the political forms of advanced capitalism are in fact more complex and contradictory than Lenin anticipated, their strength based not so much upon institutional force as ideological consensus, or bourgeois "hegemony" in Gramscian terms.[45] They argue that Leninist concepts are today outmoded precisely because their referent points—tsarist Russia, the early phases of European capitalism—are so remote from the conditions of postwar monopoly capitalism.

Bourgeois democracy, according to Eurocommunist theorists, cannot be reduced to a simple instrument of class domination; although this side clearly persists, the system is in part the outgrowth of mass struggles that achieved social and political reforms opposed by the bourgeoisie. The idea of a unified and impregnable state apparatus, controlled by a cohesive ruling class, is a myth. In the first place, many state functions—for example, welfare, education, basic social services—do more than serve the accumulation and legitimation needs of capitalist development. They also constitute real advances for the working class. Second, the state itself (including the military) is increasingly composed of diverse personnel recruited from diverse social groups. Third, the relationship between parliament (and electoral politics in general) and the state bureaucracy is much less direct than it was during Lenin's time. The state in advanced capitalism, therefore, emerges as an arena of class struggle as well as class domination, in which the old separation between politics and civil society is blurred, with power taking on the character of an institutional network of relations between social forces.[46] At certain historical junctures, contestation permeates every sphere of state activity, thus sharply restricting the leverage of the bourgeoisie.

Instead of overturning or "smashing" the bourgeois state, as Leninist strategy dictates, the Eurocommunist parties thus strive for an internal process of democratization on the assumption that representative forms of state power can be gradually infused with socialist content. In this schema, the state becomes a continuous structural element in the transition to socialism; relatively autonomous from ruling class directives, it must now be seen as a potential strategic tool of popular movements seeking to alter the established power arrangements.

Following their interpretations of Gramsci, Eurocommunist strategists point to a shifting of social and ideological blocs within the state—a changing equilibrium of class forces rooted in an expanding socialist consensus and leading to a "gradual modification of structures" that Ingrao defined as an emergent "hegemony in pluralism."[47] The transition is viewed as a long series of steps toward democratization, where a single Marxist party does not actually prefigure the state but develops alongside it, functioning as a mediator between the state and masses.[48] As Carrillo has noted, a breakdown of the postwar class equilibrium in Europe has been under way for some time, as shown by the demise of Francoism in Spain, the erosion of Gaullism in France, and the crisis of the Christian Democratic party and Catholicism in Italy. This process enables the left to insert itself into the political arena more effectively, for it can now "turn around the ideological apparatus" and employ it against monopoly capital.[49] The greater the degree of popular involvement in the established structures, the more intensified becomes the contradiction between democracy and capitalism. Carrillo's analysis can be expressed in different terms: With each stage of democratization, with each socialist advance through the forms of bourgeois democracy, there is an anticipated mounting of the legitimation crisis centered around the state.

Here a certain ambivalence concerning the role of the state becomes visible. On the one hand, the theory of structural reforms has always looked overwhelmingly toward the central state institutions as the sphere in which socialist transformation would be carried out. At the same time, much recent Eurocommunist theorizing has sought to incorporate not only the state but also the church, education, the family, and other spheres of civil society into the strategy of democratization. This tendency (most notable in the PCI and PCE) has encouraged a break with the statism of both the Leninist and social-democratic traditions, emphasizing instead political decentralization, neighborhood movements, "democratic" rather than state-command planning, and a balance between a nationalized and a market-oriented economy. How such conflicting perspectives and pressures are being concretely worked out by the Eurocommunist parties will be explored in succeeding chapters.

Despite these conflicts, the Eurocommunist theoretical-strategic framework is already more coherent and visionary than the rationalist schemata of classical (Kautskian) social democracy. Although it shares the same commitment to electoral politics, it is less inclined to accept a scenario of catastrophic crisis leading to socialism and therefore rejects a crude two-stage theory of transition—a precataclysmic (adaptive, fatalistic) period followed by a postcrisis (utopian, indeterminate) phase of revolutionary development. In contrast to the orthodox "before" and "after" model, it presupposes an organic, evolutionary transformation in which bourgeois democracy shades gradually into socialist democracy. A theory of process rather than rupture, it denies the likelihood of capitalist collapse leading to insurrectionary upheaval.[50] Carrillo suggested, for example, that "economic and political catastrophes" are difficult to imagine today in the developed countries.[51] Eurocommunism does proclaim its continued faith in class struggle, but in fact it foresees no intense or prolonged phase of popular mobilization within the Euro-

pean capitalist societies. In effect, it rules out the possibility of any conventionally defined revolutionary situation.[52]

The Eurocommunist parties have at least as much kinship with the
Comintern's Popular Front tactics of the 1930s as with orthodox social
democracy—a legacy that cannot be surprising given the formative impact of frontism upon these parties. Most Western European Communist
parties have internalized, to one degree or another, several components
of frontist politics: a vigilant posture toward fascism and reaction, electoralism and defense of the bourgeois political-institutional sphere, a
broadened notion of class and organizational alliances, and definition of
monopoly capital (rather than the bourgeoisie as a whole) as the main
strategic target. But insofar as frontism remained a primarily defensive
maneuver to halt the spread of fascism, it could never offer the comprehensive strategic vision that Eurocommunism in the 1970s seemed to
require for political success. In other words, the Comintern did not introduce frontist policies as the basis of a distinctive European road to
socialism but as a temporary tactical departure from Leninism, which
was still regarded as the universally valid model of transition. In the
postwar period, therefore, the PCI's theory of structural reforms went
beyond frontism at the very moment that it looked to preserve the same
operational principles within a reconstructed third path strategy. The *via
italiana* and later Eurocommunism represent the continuous redefinition and transformation of frontism to suit an evolving Mediterranean
socialist strategy.[53]

The sketch of a new theory of transition that emerges, in whatever
fragmentary and unfinished form, recalls the guiding logic if not the full
essence of Bernsteinian social democracy—notably in its assumption of a
linear, evolutionary process characterized by gradual structural transformation and internal democratization of the bourgeois state. In both cases
the explosiveness of class contradictions is de-emphasized if not ignored,
while the anticipation of a new kind of state created through popular
self-emancipation fades away. What simultaneously disappears is the
classical Marxian idea of a class-conscious proletariat as revolutionary
subject. Yet Eurocommunism amounts to far more than a recycled Bernsteinian theory. A range of diverse influences can be detected—frontism,
neo-Marxism, the new left, and even residues of Leninism.[54] The result is
that Eurocommunism has taken up tasks and objectives, at least in
theory, that classical social democracy virtually ignored: democratic process, social and cultural struggles, feminism, and *autogestion*. If the
emancipatory potential of such tasks and objectives has been limited by
the efforts of party leaders to channel them into the electoral-
parliamentary arena, the very fact that they are championed produces

new space for conflict and change. At the same time, the Eurocommunists have paid a strategic price for both their eclecticism and their narrow electoralism. Their vision of socialist transformation still lacks coherence and specificity, as it is often deflected and submerged by the instrumental demands of pluralist bargaining. It is revealed by vague concepts like "renewal," "advanced democracy," and "democratic planning" and by a hazy schema in which "elements of socialism" are somehow expected to gain ascendance in the absence of any direct class confrontation.[55] This and related issues will be explored in subsequent chapters.

The viability of this Eurocommunist theory of structural reforms depends upon a number of crucial interrelated premises: (1) that European capitalist systems will experience prolonged phases of relative economic and institutional stability even where chronic production and legitimation crises persist; (2) that a relationship of political coexistence between rival social forces is possible during the transition, allowing socialist movements to flourish in a generally nonrepressive atmosphere; (3) that the material and institutional basis of capitalism can be overturned without recourse to large-scale revolutionary mobilization involving some form of armed insurrection; (4) that democratization can occur through the state bureaucracy (and military) rather than against it at a time when pressures toward bureaucratization within the bourgeois public sphere seem irreversible; and (5) that a dynamic socialist hegemony can be established within the give-and-take framework of multiparty politics or, conversely, that institutionalization (signifying loss of Marxist identity) can be resisted after long years of adaptation and compromise.

Of course these assumptions cannot be conclusively tested until the Eurocommunist parties have been able to sustain electoral successes over a lengthy period — something accomplished so far by only the PCI — and to convert these gains into hegemonic institutional power. But even if we accept the probability of further gains, an even more problematic assumption remains — namely, that the strong Eurocommunist commitment to political, administrative, and economic rationalization can be actualized without subverting the principles of democratization vital to the third path strategy.

3

The PCI:
A Party of Modernization?

Most forms of economic development in the twentieth century have been embedded in the process of rationalization, that is, the expansion of productive efficiency and administrative control through the implementation of new scientific, technological, and organizational methods. Rationalization, whether carried out by the bourgeoisie, social democracy, or Soviet-type Communist regimes, has generally satisfied three basic economic and political requirements: accumulation, domination, and legitimation. Bureaucracy, and increasingly state bureaucracy, is the core structural element for reproducing the material and cultural bases of rationalization; the ideologies it generates (secularism, technological and bureaucratic rationality) constitute the main hegemonic belief systems of late capitalism, serving in various ways to justify the social division of labor. As the neo-Marxist tradition has stressed, new modes of domination typical of mature industrialism produce an instrumentalized world view (extreme pragmatism, strict rule orientation, worship of expertise, and so on) that strives toward universality, cutting across class boundaries. To the extent that it establishes a social order based upon multiple hierarchies and reinforces a depoliticized public sphere, rationalization inevitably conflicts with the prospects for democratization.[1]

Although Marx himself never thought that socialist transformation would be accompanied by rationalization of this sort, the fact is that the twentieth-century Marxist tradition has on the whole adapted to it. Marx in fact had a rather complicated, two-sided approach to this question. On the one hand, he assumed that capitalist production techniques would themselves lay the material foundations of an evolving communist society. As science and technology permitted greater and greater control over productive forces, in turn production would open up new areas of (popular) control over social life and, ultimately, over political struggle.

This "technocratic" component of Marx's thinking, which can be found in parts of both the *Grundrisse* and *Capital,* looked to a developmental process that would eliminate all barriers to economic growth and favor a restructuring compatible with the principles of scientific rationality. It was a theory linked to a vision of progress rooted in clearly defined historical laws. On the other hand, Marx recognized that these same techniques were the source of an alienated work process and that they would have to be overturned through entirely new forms of social organization, work, and culture. Technology in this sense is also repressive, insofar as it functions to routinize and fragment the work process, thereby making the worker more dependent upon capital. The key element here is proletarian control over the system of production. Under conditions of social equality and workers' self-management, there would be no contradiction between the needs of economic efficiency and those of workers' self-management, as the *forms* of production through which science and technology are concretized would be fully trans- formed.

But Marx apparently viewed the transition to socialism as a very lengthy process that necessarily combines capitalist and revolutionary elements in a tense equilibrium, shifting gradually toward the latter. Democratization too would be a protracted and uneven series of changes requiring, in the final analysis, the destruction of bourgeois productive forces. Although presumably engineered by a leading force (party, revolutionary intellectuals), this transformation would ultimately depend upon the self-conscious activity and political initiative of the proletariat. From this standpoint, the actual role of leadership, the particular forms of socialized production, and the mechanisms through which the division of labor might be subverted were questions left largely unexplored. Still, however vague this conceptualization, Marx did at least develop the kernel of a critique of capitalist rationalization.

At the same time, this critique, and with it the emancipatory side of the transition that Marx envisaged, has been largely repressed and distorted in the historical reality of Marxist movements, parties, and regimes.[2] As Marxist politics has generally stressed economic modernization as the prime mover or "main lever" of development, it is also likely to succumb to the logic of productivism and statism that also underlies capitalist ra- tionalization. In the Soviet Union, this meant full-scale mobilization of resources behind a "scientific-technological revolution," centralized state planning, hierarchical organization of production and administration, streamlined "one-man management," and labor discipline imposed from above. In more developed countries where social-democratic parties have come to power (e.g., Sweden), the result was industrialization through a "mixed" system that merged public and private ownership, monopoly control and competition, and plan and market within a welfare-state capitalism stabilized by institutionalized class conflict. The consequences for both types of society were in some respects similar: the emergence of a privileged managerial stratum, economic decision making oriented toward productivity and competitiveness in world markets, material incentives, and the perpetuation of commodity production and wage labor. In sum, through whatever variants of bureaucratic centralism and state capitalism, rationalization has typically reproduced — behind the legitimating facade of "socialism" — the very tendencies toward economic concentration, state planning, and uneven development present within advanced monopoly capitalism itself.

Eurocommunism, however, appears to offer a way out of this authoritarian impasse — the democratic road. It claims to restore the participatory, antibureaucratic side of the transition that disappeared after Marx. It articulates a comprehensive vision of pluralistic socialism that converges with the cultural and political traditions of bourgeois society at the very moment it seeks to transcend them. And, in moving some distance along the "new course" originally charted by Togliatti, it has won the support of large sectors of the working class, established new positions of institutional power, and attained a broad popular legitimacy. Yet the postwar experience of the Western European Communist parties suggests that these strategic gains have been possible only through basic compromises of ideological commitment and identity. A central thesis of this book is that Eurocommunism seems unable to break the chronic Marxist impasse, in great measure because its concept of socialist transformation (and also of democracy) is in the end limited to bourgeois categories of economic and political development. The third way, however successful it might be on its own terms, contains no revolutionary project for overcoming the social division of labor, that is, for transforming society as a whole through a democratized system of production, authority, and social relations.[3]

Capitalism and Rationalization

In the advanced capitalist countries, where new structures and techniques of production have made possible a second industrial revolution, rationalization involves a preoccupation not only with economic efficiency but also with the imperatives of social control and political legitimation. In extending the social division of labor, it (ideally) stabilizes new forms of domination that rely increasingly upon the working of bourgeois ideological hegemony — technocratic rationality, the culture industry, consumerism. Rationalization thus incorporates much more than the physical appropriation of science and technology. Where it prevails in the absence of significant counterforces (e.g., traditional residues, strong working-class opposition), as in the United States and West Germany, it serves to bureaucratize the entire system of authority and social relations in a way that fundamentally reshapes the nature of political conflict.

As the main instrument of this process, the bourgeois state occupies larger and larger spheres within the productive apparatus and within civil society as a whole. With the earlier collapse of competitive capitalism, the state began to act upon and transform the system by means of its directive role in the economy, education, the military, and social programs. To one degree or another, the state has also become more actively involved in production itself (through nationalization, holding companies, and so on), marking the rise of "social" or "collective" capital. In this respect, the political system appears as the only repository of systemic rationality, the key mechanism of crisis management to protect special interests where those interests—fragmented and lacking in resources—are collectively too weak. Because economic development requires an organized system of planned innovation, the state intervenes not only to break down obstacles to productivity but also to regulate social existence; rationalization thus leads to the imposition of bureaucratic organization over the "anarchy" of both market relations and everyday life as it expands the sphere of administered commodity production.[4]

For the countries of Western Europe, this process represents a trend toward bureaucratic state capitalism that defies conventional Marxian analysis. Historically, capitalist planning has been largely "indicative" in its attempt to set broad national priorities, structure markets, provide investment incentives for private enterprises, regulate industry, and manipulate fiscal policy. Insofar as rationalization has brought the public sector more directly into the area of capital accumulation, the state has become much more than a simple instrument of monopoly capitalist interests.[5] The relationship between the state and the economy now assumes a more dialectical character, rendering the old base-superstructure distinction obsolete. It follows that in late capitalism the state no longer merely expresses class interests but also embodies a political-bureaucratic logic that converges with the class principle of property relations, while shifting the contradictions between wage labor and capital in part to the sphere of state activity.

With advancing levels of rationalization, social forms of investment and consumption take on new meaning beyond the limited Keynesian welfare-state policy of income transfers. Social programs and services—education, scientific and technological research, transportation and communications, urban development, health, even welfare—feed into the expanding accumulation needs of the system, which embrace not only the technical requirements of capital but also the reproduction of labor power and the maintenance of political order. This growth of the public sector has been to some extent a response to popular struggles and demands; it nevertheless constitutes a vital part of the monopoly capitalist infrastructure itself. No longer can it be understood as an appendage to or "parasite" upon the market economy. Stabilized and effective accumulation functions absolutely require state initiative, extension of the public sector, and social services.[6] At the same time, the dictates of capitalist rationalization increasingly affect the patterns of state activity.

To carry out the tasks of capital accumulation (and legitimation), a dynamic technocratic intelligentsia appears within the state apparatus, the military, the corporate sector, and the universities, as well as the political parties and trade unions. Though clearly not a ruling managerial class as such, this stratum operates within the milieu of bourgeois domination through its control of bureaucratic roles and manipulation of knowledge; it thus occupies a privileged sphere within the social division of labor.[7] Rationalized production intensifies the fragmentation of the work force around divisions in knowledge, skills, and job categories, and this fragmentation in turn is compounded by fundamental sexual and racial conflicts. The technocratic intelligentsia—technicians, managers, professionals, academics, top-level bureaucrats, cultural workers—constitute a diverse and highly educated "new middle stratum" of salaried mental workers that is partially independent of both the bourgeoisie and most sectors of the working class.[8] In contrast with the role of intellectuals in preindustrial and early capitalist societies, which was essentially ideological and cultural, the modern intellectual formations carry out necessary and even central activities within the productive apparatus. As wage earners, therefore, they share interests and outlooks not only with the ruling class but also with workers; objectively torn between two poles, the technocratic intelligentsia often finds itself drawn toward the workers as it too experiences proletarianization.[9]

A major consequence of rationalization is the appearance of new forms of structural and ideological domination that operate to confine or absorb political opposition. Highly bureaucratized mechanisms develop to institutionalize class conflict, often transforming popular or working-class movements into stable fixtures within the legitimate political system. One recent expression of this trend in Western Europe is a formal tripartite relationship among corporations, the state, and the trade unions based upon standardized norms of contractual bargaining. The new labor force is more committed to upholding formal-legal processes and preserving harmonious class relations, whatever ideological claims it presses. In this context a once-combative Marxist party is likely to be forced to either abandon its subversive identity or end up resorting to desperately utopian and adventuristic attacks against the integrative structures of the bourgeois state.

In ideological terms, the rationalized system of accumulation and control calls for new modes of legitimation to replace the old market-based ideologies (e.g., liberalism) as well as the "archaic" expressions of traditionalism and religion. Bourgeois hegemony in late capitalist societies becomes more administered and instrumentalized, more tied to the generalized aims of efficiency, growth, and organizational stability. As an expression of technocratic rationality, the managerial fetishism of technique, expertise, discipline, and routine strives toward a mass ideological passivity that reinforces what Marcuse labeled "one-dimensionality" and what Habermas referred to as "civil privatism."[10] To the extent that this process is reproduced, the result is a workplace that is emptied of creativity and self-consciousness,[11] a social and cultural life that is commodified,[12] and a public sphere that is depoliticized[13] — all leading toward a situation where effective political opposition is either isolated or integrated and where the working class is driven toward economistic and corporativist strategies.

Yet in repressing democratic impulses, rationalization generates new contradictions that give rise to new resistance and popular struggles; the smooth and inexorable pattern of bureaucratic development foreseen by Max Weber has been realized in few if any countries. The locus of the new contradictions is primarily the state insofar as systemic conflict previously rooted in the private corporate sphere has been transferred into the administered public sphere. If this process has created a more streamlined bureaucratic state capitalism, and with it a certain containment of the old contradictions, it has simultaneously produced unanticipated crises of the state and legitimation — for example, the shortage of material and political resources to meet growing social demands upon the state (the "fiscal crisis"); the narrowing cultural and ideological basis of legitimation;[14] the promises of technocratic elites (to deliver better health care, a more livable urban environment, full employment, and so on) and the capacity of a system that is governed by profit and bureaucratic criteria to satisfy these promises.

The role of this technocratic stratum itself, moreover, is also contradictory. On the one hand, as I have suggested, it has a privileged status as well as commitments (however ambivalent) to bourgeois forms of rationalization. On the other hand, large sectors of this same stratum value the kind of creativity, open discourse, and occupational autonomy generally associated with high levels of education.[15] Rationalization often awakens this latter (critical) side as the confining effects of proletarianization are felt, thus revealing in different terms the fragility of bourgeois hegemony. A dynamic of this sort underlies the radicalization of the new middle strata in countries like France and Italy[16] — a process analyzed by Low-Beer in his investigation of class consciousness and political activity among highly educated technical and scientific workers in northern Italy. He found that a large proportion of these workers supported either the PCI or groups to the left of the PCI and explained their preoccupation with struggles for self-management and job autonomy as a predictable response to workplace bureaucratization that degrades production and blocks creative involvement.[17]

The impact of rationalization depends upon several factors: the strength of the state apparatus, the degree to which bureaucratic norms are congruent with particular national traditions, the scope and intensity of political opposition, and the like. A pervasive technocratic consensus is likely to be achieved in societies where the obstacles to capitalist development are minimized, in the first phase by breaking down the residues of feudal or precapitalist formations (e.g., the ideological influence of the church), in the second phase by organizing a state-directed planning infrastructure designed to manage crises. The key to both phases, but particularly the latter, is the capacity to enforce labor discipline. A century ago Marx was able to analyze the debilitating consequences of machine technology for proletarian social relations and consciousness. So too at a later point did Gramsci, who saw in "Fordism" — the drive toward a comprehensively administered system of production — a process in which "subaltern forces are manipulated and managed to meet new ends."[18] With the routinization and submission to authority demanded by capitalist rationalization appeared a new working-class personality, that of the "trained gorilla" whose "regulated social life" necessitated repression of desire, passion, and self-activity.[19] Gramsci was describing a transitional stage of bourgeois development whereby modernizing forces (led by the large bourgeoisie) were struggling to prevail over traditional forces (the church, large landholders, the petty bourgeoisie) who stubbornly clung to the "great traditions" of the past. In the postwar period, Togliatti arrived at basically the same conclusion: "The uniformity of technology is creating an artificial uniformity in the lives of men, a uniformity that is progressively invading even their consciousness, humiliating them, making them strangers to themselves, limiting and suppressing their initiative, their freedom of choice and development."[20]

Since the "past sedimentations" of feudalism were still strong in Italy even after World War I, the northern bourgeoisie was never able to secure firm hegemony. In seeking to fill this void, fascism set out to destroy traditional barriers to economic modernization, relying initially upon an ideology of anticapitalist romanticism and populism as a springboard to power. The overriding goal of Mussolini's corporate state was to establish a forced integration from above, stressing rigid labor discipline, state initiative in capital accumulation and planning, and rapid industrial development. But fascism generated its own contradictions — one being that it was still tied to the past (through its *modus vivendi* with the church, among other things) — which undermined its efforts to rationalize the economy. Italy remained a dual and extremely contradictory society, divided between "modern" and "traditional" elements, well into the post–World War II period. Moreover, in the absence of an efficient bureaucratic administration, and compromised by widespread corruption, parasitism, and patronage, the Christian Democratic–ruled state possessed neither the will nor the means to shape capitalist development.

In the United States, on the other hand, the collapse of market capitalism in the 1930s triggered a movement toward rationalization first embodied in the New Deal and then, more dramatically, in the project of wartime mobilization that became the stimulus to postwar monopoly consolidation. More successful yet was the "progressive" model of European social democracy, which tackled the old contradictions by enlarging the public sector through nationalization, state planning, and social welfare programs, thus opening up a new dynamic of accumulation and legitimation under the political aegis of working-class formations. Only in the United States did primary initiative for rationalization come from the bourgeoisie; elsewhere, working-class struggles for social reform played a more important role, as the ruling class generally lacked the political resources to carry it out. At the same time, the growth of technology and social investment helped to legitimate bourgeois institutions by creating a new infrastructure for capitalist development, organizing new forms of consumption, and generating consensual ideologies.[21] Everywhere this phenomenon increased the domination of the state over civil society.[22]

The Mediterranean countries, however, have more or less followed the Italian pattern; rationalization has taken place at an uneven and retarded pace in comparison with northern Europe, Japan, and North America. What typifies Italy and Spain in particular is the survival of traditionalism: the Roman Catholic Church, a strong patriarchal and family structure, a deeply rooted peasant culture, a fragmentary system of agricultural production, the predominance of small and medium-sized family-owned enterprises, patronage-ridden public bureaucracies. Although industrialization has undermined much of this—as seen, for example, by the visible erosion of Catholicism—the distinct character of Mediterranean capitalism remains an uneasy mixture of industrialism and tradition, rationalizing impulses and preindustrial residues. To one degree or another, the bourgeois transformation has not been fully completed. An outgrowth of this is recurrent legitimation crises, expressed on the one hand by a precarious bourgeois hegemony and on the other by combative working-class movements and strong leftist oppositions. Moreover, as the global crisis of capitalism worsens the Mediterranean systems suffer disproportionately because of their weakened and dependent economic position relative to more developed countries like the United States and West Germany.[23] Long-term structural crisis generates a vicious cycle of declining productivity and reinforced international dependency, which further erodes bourgeois domination and lays the basis of popular radicalization. It is this logic that shapes the rise and development of Eurocommunism.[24]

The immediate economic and social impact of the crisis is thus particularly acute in southern Europe. Inflation rates have exceeded 20 percent; unemployment levels have approached 10 percent and have precipitated Europe-wide demonstrations; currencies have been extremely unstable; balance-of-payments deficits have soared, creating a precarious reliance on both the oil-producing nations and the International Monetary Fund; and municipalities are experiencing severe fiscal crisis—to identify the most graphic signs of paralysis. This decline has intensified since the early 1970s, partly owing to the reversal of Europe's long period of postwar industrial expansion, partly because of trade-union gains, and partly because of the explosion of new social needs and demands. The economic "miracles" of the 1950s and 1960s, made possible through U.S. Marshall Plan aid, cheap labor, and the foreign demand for commodity goods, gave way to the stagflation of the 1970s, which reflected the exhaustion of the old (commodity and export-based) accumulation model.[25]

The crisis has been met, on the political side, by an immobilism typical of fragile bourgeois states. In Italy, the Christian Democratic party (DC) has yielded its once-commanding position, giving way first to a series of patchwork, futile center-left coalitions and then to an "imperfect bipartism" that has put the DC face to face with the resurgent Communists.[26] Grand promises never fulfilled, the constant shuffling of cabinet posts and leadership roles, and the massive extension of patronage networks have substituted for a viable rationalizing force that could implement effective social reforms and avert an acute crisis of legitimacy. By the mid-1970s, the collapse of bourgeois hegemony in Italy compelled the DC to either resort to a shaky *monocolore* (single-party) regime or join the historic compromise with the PCI, neither of which would present durable solutions.

The political situation in Spain is even more tenuous. On one level, the "Prussian" model of industrialization adopted by Franco produced an entirely new economic infrastructure and a thriving urban culture that can no longer be contained by the old authoritarian forms. As the Spanish bourgeoisie looks for new space to maneuver, important traditional groups (the Falange, landholders, the church) that propped up Francoism have lost popular support; the Prussian model has generated social forces that will inevitably lead to its own unraveling, while the modernizing capitalists are finding little political terrain for advancing their interests. This is largely because popular movements have grown remarkably in the last several years, not only challenging Juan Carlos's "liberal" monarchy but also threatening bourgeois efforts to create a rationalizing momentum.[27] By 1980, with electoral reforms, legalized opposition, and a new constitution, Spain appeared to be well on its way toward the liberal democratic stage of its bourgeois transformation, but the social forces striving to actualize it are squeezed into a narrow space between traditional resistance and left opposition.

The French case differs somewhat from the Italian and Spanish, as France has both a more developed capitalism and a weaker legacy of traditionalism and fascism. The French bourgeoisie has therefore been able to initiate a rationalization of the state and economy (in certain areas of planning, for example) far surpassing that of other Mediterranean countries. But in the absence of any real social-democratic formation, the consensus behind the capitalist-directed rationalization has always been frail, marked by widespread working-class disaffection. This helps to explain the French bourgeoisie's postwar "Jacobin" embrace of Gaullist authoritarianism. Gaullism was a hollow solution, however, and in the wake of the May 1968 events its hegemony waned while the left (Communists and Socialists) expanded its strength to roughly half the electorate.[28] As in Italy and Spain, the crisis of legitimacy narrowed the options of a ruling stratum struggling to consolidate its power in a period of crisis.

Crisis, Immobilism, and Opposition

How do the Eurocommunist parties fit into this picture, and what is their ideological and programmatic stance toward the crises? The answers we provide to these questions are absolutely crucial, for they set the contours of the general assessment of Eurocommunism presented here. Viewed in this way, the central argument I wish to advance is as follows: While allowing once again for differences in emphasis and political context, as well as for the best intentions of party leaders, the overall Eurocommunist strategy clearly entails a commitment to rationalization, although from a "left" approach that stresses social and welfare reforms, decentralization, and greater working-class involvement within bourgeois political structures. It is a rather self-conscious but not altogether worked-out design that follows the "state-capitalist" (northern European) rather than the "bureaucratic-centralist" (Soviet) model of rationalized development. The Eurocommunist logic is shaped above all by a faith in science and technology as the prime mover of the transition—an emphasis that takes on added meaning in the southern European context where the traditional foundations of bourgeois domination are peculiarly weak and destabilizing.

What in effect this strategy proposes is an "intermediate" solution—overcoming the economic crisis, laying the material basis of the transition—that would in time allow for a more far-reaching socialist transformation. The stabilization of capitalism on a new footing would be a necessary first step, as in destroying the parasitism, inefficiency, corruption, and waste associated with traditionalism it would dispose of the barriers to further (emancipatory) social development. In political actuality, however—assuming of course that the parties can achieve their power objectives—no such rupture between stages is likely to occur, nor has one been theoretically specified by any of the party leaderships. The probability is that the strategic premises of the "first stage" cannot be arbitrarily overturned at some future moment in the transitional process; on the contrary, the initial pattern of change (in this case, toward a rationalized capitalism) can be expected to define every phase of transformation, as the Soviet and Eastern European experiences have shown. Hence, where the dynamic of rationalization is already set in motion, it is bound to shape development for the future.

How does this general conception translate into specific programmatic goals? Setting aside temporarily the question of whether such a rationalizing project can actually succeed under present conditions, the main features include (1) stimulating industrial productivity through technological innovation as the first step toward redressing the balance-of-payments deficits, combatting the oil and energy crisis, and improving the position of the Mediterranean countries within the international capitalist division of labor; (2) expanding public intervention in the economy by means of consolidating the state ownership of large enterprises, new forms of democratic planning and coordination, and revitalized public investment to reverse uneven development; (3) modernizing state and corporate institutions by professionalizing the civil service and industrial management, abolishing patronage, and simplifying the ministerial systems; (4) enforcing a labor discipline that is rooted in established modes of contractual bargaining, the primacy of trade-union and party agendas, and austerity measures imposed to combat inflation; and (5) developing the countryside through state investment programs, stimulated agricultural productivity based upon more effective use of technology, and reclamation of abandoned land.

It will help to look more closely at the Italian situation, where the crisis of capitalism seems most acute and where the PCI for years has pursued a course that might be labeled the "Eurocommunist road." An analysis of Italian development must first of all come to grips with the fact that past rationalizing initiatives came almost exclusively from the northern bourgeoisie along the lines of the private consumption-oriented "Fiat" model (with the assistance of a feeble state infrastructure). This model, as is well known, was associated with a lack of overall economic direction, privatized and fragmented forms of social life, and uneven development within the country as a whole—producing, among other things, an enormous gulf between the northern and southern, industrial and agrarian, "modern" and "traditional" sectors. Although highly advanced in some areas, rationalization was never systematic or planned in a general sense; it therefore only exacerbated the contradictions of Italian capitalism.[29] At the same time, the historic task of the PCI dating from the 1920s has been to dialectically insert itself into this extremely complex situation. It has done so with considerable success as part of its broad electoral strategy. Thus, to the extent that the PCI already began to establish a local power base in the early postwar years, the party leadership has had more time and maneuverability to elaborate its structural reformism than either the PCF or (for different reasons) the PCE. The PCI's "modernizing" response to Italy's uneven development, inspired by efforts to overcome the limits of both Leninism and social democracy, turns out to be a moderated statism, that is, reliance upon a (decentralized pluralistic) state apparatus to carry out the main functions of rationalization.

The PCI's schema rests upon a compelling logic. From the time of the Risorgimento (1860s and 1870s) to the post–World War II period, the Italian state always lacked political cohesion; compromised by the pervasive dualism mentioned above, the central bureaucratic structure reflected the disaggregation and immobilism typical of the society as a whole. Organizational formalism and traditional clientelism existed side by side. As Henri Weber has noted, Italy became an "under-administered country with a behemoth bureaucracy."[30] A series of center-left governments sought to break this impasse in the 1960s and early 1970s. Built out of fragile coalitions that included the DC, the Socialists, and some minor parties (the Republicans, Liberals, and Social Democrats), these governments stimulated growth of the public sector, created new state holding companies, and initiated social reforms that promised a reversal of the spiraling crisis. By 1973 roughly 55 percent of the Italian economy was nationalized in some fashion. Yet such efforts inevitably wound up mired in political quicksand, as the public sector itself was thoroughly colonized by private interests and traditional patronage networks.[31]

From the standpoint of rationalization, then, the most developed sector in Italy is that of the capital-intensive, technologically advanced, export-oriented monopolies of the north. Fiat, for example, has introduced the most completely automated and computerized assembly line in the world. One result has been the kind of dehumanized work process foreseen by Gramsci and analyzed by Harry Braverman. Management has seized upon this technological restructuring as a means of "exporting" contradictions from the factory, first, by imposing new levels of labor discipline as a way of reclaiming control lost to the workers in the 1960s and second, by reducing more and more operations to machine functions with the aim of eliminating the self-conscious human element. But it is precisely this sector over which the state now has least control. The central economic plan has no real sanctions, regulating policies are either weak or do not get adequately enforced, the taxation system works erratically, and no effective fiscal program has been instituted.

On the other side, the persistence of small, labor-intensive enterprises with fragmented, nonunionized work forces and lagging productivity poses obstacles to planned development and social reform. Unlike most northern European economies, Italy has a strong tradition of family-based firms with origins in artisan production; not only small-scale operations but medium-sized ones like textiles and wine fit such a pattern. The traditionalism of this sector has resisted the technological innovation and managerial restructuring that might allow for sustained investment and growth, thus exacerbating the problem of marginality.[32] Government has often intervened (through credits and other stopgap measures) to bail out faltering enterprises, but in the absence of basic structural changes these solutions could never be more than patchwork.

The Italian agricultural economy, for similar reasons, remains a bastion of opposition to rationalization. Italy has been locked into a system of small, unproductive farms that lack the necessary capital for mechanization, requiring the import of vast amounts of foodstuffs and raw materials. In the south and Sicily, where until recently there was little capitalist penetration, social fragmentation and economic underdevelopment are even more pronounced. And with the postwar collapse of precapitalist production and social relations, large farming areas have been abandoned while the majority of young people go north in search of jobs. Meanwhile, the extensive patronage and clientele networks live on — the fiefdoms of landed and commercial interests and in some cases of party machines[33] — as formations hostile to social transformation. Efforts through the public sector to modernize the south, by setting up the Cassa per il mezzogiorno and a few state corporations like Alfa Sud, have generated only small pockets of growth and just the initial signs of a modern industrial labor force. What they have produced, however, is the first expansion of bourgeois state power into the most backward agrarian regions.

This situation brings up once again the crisis of the public sector itself. It is clear that, under successive DC-controlled administrations, the sizable growth of state functions has merely served to aggravate long-standing social contradictions while partially transferring them into a new arena; the state has tried, but failed, to absorb and deflect the mounting conflicts within Italian society. Evidence of such failure is provided by the continuing political crisis and impasse, which in turn reflects worsening economic stagnation.

First, the state holding companies (including steel, shipbuilding, telephone and communications, banking, oil and chemical, electronics, and computers) have suffered enormous losses in recent years. This is less a technological than a political and administrative problem: Many of the holding firms have evolved into bureaucratic empires controlled by corporate magnates and subsidized by the mass of taxpayers. Moreover, although holding companies are nominally subject to ministerial supervision, in practice they are governed by joint private-public investment structures, resulting in bureaucratic rivalries and muddled systems of authority.[34] Second, the planning structures established by the center-left have been little more than hollow shells. Many national targets and priorities have been set, but they can never be reached because administrative control over private enterprises is lacking, the public bureaucracy obstructs their implementation, or in some cases political consensus is lacking. Not surprisingly, social and welfare services fall distressingly short of even limited objectives in many areas. One long-range consequence of this is the largely chaotic, unplanned, and environmentally disruptive nature of Italy's rapid postwar urban growth, even in cities where left-wing coalitions hold power.

The general problem is that, although the Italian state has experienced massive growth over the past two decades (taking over more and more accumulation functions in the process), there is no integrative mechanism to direct national economic development. "Planning" is shaped overwhelmingly by market processes. Moreover, aside from being poorly organized, patronage-ridden, and penetrated by corporate interests, the state apparatus is remote from the scrutiny of representative assemblies and thus relatively free to pursue its own bureaucratic logic.[35] Under DC hegemony the practice of *clientela* has led to an institutionalized tripartite relationship between government agencies, private interest groups (e.g., Confindustria, Catholic Action), and the party machine. The DC has also preferred to recruit from traditional strata rather than from the ranks of the technocratic intelligentsia to fill leading civil service posts. Insofar as the church too, either directly or indirectly through the DC or Catholic Action, has succeeded in imposing its economic and ideological claims on the state, it has solidified the social forces of traditionalism against those of modernization, even if Catholicism itself has suffered political erosion. The entire public sector, then, expresses the larger contradictions of Italian capitalism, diminishing the prospects of rationalization under existing conditions.

The PCI's Rationalizing Ideology

The PCI strategy anticipates the possibility of an essentially political solution to this stalemate—that is, it looks to an institutional restructuring that would liberate the rationalizing potential arrested by a faltering bourgeois regime. If the Communist program contains many ambiguities and vague references to "renewal," it is still more coherent than the programs of other Italian parties. With Italy caught in the midst of a debilitating vicious cycle involving economic stagnation, political immobilism, and terrorism, the PCI leadership has been preoccupied with finding intermediate measures that would reverse the crisis tendencies and restore a dynamic economy within the parameters of international and domestic capitalism. Initial steps are viewed as organically linked to socialist objectives in that they would presumably lay the groundwork for the transition.

For this process to unfold, however, it will first be necessary to reverse the marginalization of the Italian economy within global capitalism. Here efforts to encourage industrial stability and growth are central to the PCI's outlook: the basic precondition for even a modest opening to the left is a break with Italy's costly dependency upon the advanced capitalist powers, which would require a reduction of foreign debt, curtailment of protectionism, strengthening of the monetary system, and expanded involvement in the EEC (meaning greater self-sufficiency in commodity production, especially agriculture). The cycle of dependency and crisis cannot be overcome, according to PCI theorists, by simply relying on conventional protectionist and autarkic responses that "ignore Italy's need to maintain full relations with other economic areas and especially with the advanced capitalist bloc." What it does involve is reliance upon positive rather than negative restrictive measures. According to Giorgio Napolitano, it means "correcting the domestic causes that aggravate the deficits in foreign payments — the structural and productive insufficiencies of our agriculture, the expanded consumption of imported goods, the flight of capital — and [thereby] seeking to strengthen Italy's international presence and initiative." Napolitano added that it is necessary "to redesign our export pattern to achieve more advanced positions within the international division of labor." To accomplish this, "Italy must prepare itself to withstand both American maneuvering to shift the weight of the world crisis onto other countries, including those of Western Europe, as well as the trend toward heightened competition and conflict among European capitalist countries themselves."[36]

Consistent with this strategy, which demands close linkage between international and domestic responses to the crisis, is the development of national (and ultimately Europe-wide) mechanisms of rationalization. The dynamic element here is the state, beginning with the bourgeois democratic state into which the PCI strives to introduce its "elements of socialism" as part of a gradually enlarged (but still limited) public sector.[37] As the existing state is too fragmented and immobile, too plagued with "sectoralism" and inefficiency to promote a rationalized solution, the best possibility would be a transitional system (governed by a left coalition) prepared to introduce "global" planning and coordination. A PCI-dominated state would stimulate institutional "renewal" and become what Ingrao has referred to as the "protagonist of the masses."[38] It would possess enough binding authority to whittle away at the obstacles to social transformation (monopoly power, the old bureaucracy, interest-group politics, parochialism) and thus counter the "anarchic character of capitalism."[39]

But such a reconstitution of the state apparatus would obviously fall rather short of the Jacobin aspirations typical of most Communist movements and regimes. In hoping to avoid the *dirigismo* (bureaucratic centralism) of the Soviet model, the PCI has opted for the Yugoslav approach that combines centralized direction with local initiative, decentralization, "democratic" planning, and a mixed economy involving private ownership of small and many medium-sized enterprises.[40] The idea of nationalizing the entire system of production is rejected as a harmful return to Marxist orthodoxy; in its place the PCI has substituted what party economist Luciano Barca calls "socialization of the rewards, not socialization of property,"[41] according to which central economic planning would be supplemented by the market, profit criteria, and material incentives. Of course, this approach coincides with the PCI's long-established alliance strategy, originally introduced by Togliatti, which sees the *ceti medi* (shopowners, artisans, professionals, and even owners of medium-sized industries) as part of the social bloc objectively favoring socialism.

More recently, the PCI has carried its acceptance of the private sector much further — to levels that even the Togliatti leadership would surely have found objectionable. The party is no longer opposed to the principle of large-scale corporations continuing under private ownership; nor does it reject the presence of foreign multinationals, of which there are many, as it views them as a source of important capital investment and a possible solution to the balance-of-payments deficit. Indeed, one component of the PCI's rationalizing ideology is to establish an economic climate in Italy conducive to new (foreign and domestic) business ventures. It is not really the matter of ownership itself, or even the profit motive, that is crucial, but rather the extent to which production actually contributes to the public welfare. Thus, when in 1977 the PCI outlined its plans for heavy investment in public transportation systems it looked to Fiat instead of the state as the locus of development.[42] At the same time, the PCI insists that the state exercise a degree of regulatory supervision and control over private firms to ensure compliance with general social priorities — although how much is unclear.

Although the Communist transitional program encourages a large and dynamic private sector and is hostile to the illusions of statism, it still relies heavily upon state administration for its rationalizing objectives. The reconstructed state envisaged by the PCI cannot appear until the "crisis of institutions" is first resolved — until, in other words, DC control over the public sector is dismantled. This will mean a more or less complete revamping of the civil service and public management. The PCI's aim is to eliminate the political clientelism and conservative obstructionism that have been so deeply entrenched in the Italian public bureaucracy since the fascist period and to replace it with a professionalized meritocracy independent of any single political formation. Accordingly, technocratic civil servants would supersede patronage appointments along the lines of northern European systems, thus presumably facilitating the administration of legislative reforms and programs that have regularly been opposed by bureaucratic interests. In the PCI's view, socialist transformation depends upon the triumph of "clean" and efficient government over the mismanagement, corruption, and waste long associated with DC rule. This is precisely what the Communists try to exemplify where they have established control over provincial and municipal governments in the "Red Belt" area of central Italy (which includes Bologna). And they have achieved some impressive successes, within the limits of local resources, but not without taking on many of the trappings of an urban political machine fueled by the exchange of favors for votes.[43]

The second priority is a broad structure of democratic planning that would mobilize and channel the country's material resources according to a transitional national program, with the state initiating a "series of industry-wide plans that give a new orientation to investment and at the same time prepare new market outlets" and social priorities.[44] How such a plan would operate has yet to be specified in PCI programs. Clearly, however, PCI theorists see the state as the indispensable lever of enhanced productivity and the focal point of guided economic development where the various sectors, motivated only by their own narrow profit drives and often pitted against each other, would only reproduce the existing condition of planlessness. State planning is viewed as a necessary mechanism for reallocating resources, not only to avoid waste and parasitism but also to instill new models of social consumption.[45] To operate effectively, it would require more state-directed scientific and technological research (and hence educational modernization) than now exists. For example, the PCI wants to build new research centers and create a more standardized and production-grounded university curriculum. It would also demand firm ministerial control over the state holding sector and complete reorganization of the state apparatus in order to streamline decision making.

What makes the PCI approach more "democratic" than, for example, traditional capitalist or Soviet planning is greater working-class participation — through trade-union "co-management" within the state, greater accountability to parliamentary assemblies, and stronger local and regional involvement (although here again one encounters a lack of specificity in the Communist planning schema).[46] In other words, the nonbureaucratic system of planning is expected to evolve within the framework of the PCI's overall vision of political democratization.[47] For the model to succeed, however, monopoly power — and class domination of the state in general — must be broken, but the PCI leadership remains vague about how this too will be accomplished.

PCI-engineered rationalization would also involve the transition from private to social forms of consumption, congruent with a reorienting of the public sector. Whereas the "Fiat model" produces essentially export goods and personal commodities, the PCI plan would utilize the state to fulfill a variety of societal needs—health care, public transportation, education, low-cost subsidized housing, and energy development. The intent is to go beyond capital transfers of the welfare state type, from one sphere to another, and establish an entirely new infrastructure of investment and consumption that involves more than a mere shifting of resources or a redistribution of income. According to Berlinguer, continued Italian emphasis on consumerism will devour the economy without ever raising the question of social needs and services.[48] The shift to social consumption (use-values) therefore necessitates a complete redefinition of working-class politics, away from asserting the claims of one sector against the total economy and society. For the long run, this means a fundamental departure from the customary "corporative-economistic tendencies" and the wage demand–consumerism syndrome that feeds inflation, dissipates resources, and encourages privatized social relations.[49]

But for the short run, it means a "politics of austerity" that calls upon organized workers to restrict their demands to help restabilize the Italian economy. The PCI's "austerity with a socialist face" would ideally differ from the capitalist stratagem of imposing labor restraints on behalf of a fictitious "national interest." First, it would be tied to a general program of economic planning and social investment that is designed to advance the future interests of the working class. Second, in return for its vigorous support of austerity measures, the major leftist trade union organization, the Italian General Confederation of Labor (CGIL), can expect greater managerial representation within state-operated industries and probably also within the private sphere. Third, austerity is understood as part of the PCI's larger attack on privatized consumerism as an obstacle to social transformation.[50]

Although the Eurocommunist version of austerity politics is presented as an imaginative strategy linked to long-range socialist objectives, it is really a defensive policy aimed at curtailing labor costs and inflation as a means of bolstering Italy's position within the global capitalist division of labor. From the standpoint of the labor movement, the resulting sacrifices (both material and ideological) have been severe, insofar as austerity measures function concretely to restrain class confrontation. Indeed, CGIL leader Luciano Lama has argued that the long-accepted premise of the class struggle as the basis of union activity must be rejected, as it can produce only economic chaos by accelerating the effects of consumerism, inflation, and fiscal crisis. The CGIL is willing to ensure labor stability and wage restraints (to the extent it can) in exchange for greater union "control" in the managing of state and private companies. To this end Lama has conceded the right of industry to lay off workers and to discipline those engaged in "spontaneous" forms of opposition.[51] Legislation harmful to labor interests has also been allowed to pass. In the spring of 1977, at the peak of historic compromise sentiment, parliament endorsed (with PCI support) the dismantling of the *scala mobile* (cost-of-living wage scale) that had protected workers against the most extreme consequences of inflation. The PCI received nothing from the DC government in return for this concession.[52]

A further priority of the PCI's rationalized state intervention would be reversal of the Italian pattern of uneven development, starting with modernization of agriculture and of the south. The overriding task here is to break the extreme subordination of agriculture to industry, of countryside to urban areas, and of south to north. Such unevenness makes Italy less self-sufficient in production of foodstuffs, creates a divided work force, and blocks the country's full integration into the EEC. The PCI plan is to utilize "public instruments" and "combined technologies" in order to integrate the industrial and agricultural sectors for the first time. Ingrao has defined this as a system of "agro-industrial production" designed to increase farming efficiency and transform social relations in the less developed regions.[53] It would demand a massive program of technological development and capital investment in the *mezzogiorno*, possibly assisted by the European Investment Bank, that, among other things, would create the basis of a proletarianized work force. Traditional survivals—for example, the fragmented, labor-intensive system of land tenure typical of what the PCI calls the "anarchism of rural markets"—would gradually yield to larger, more mechanized operations. And with this would presumably evolve new methods of social and political organization, including a "modern," nonclientelistic party system. Thus the PCI's strategy of democratization is logically based in its efforts to reverse uneven development.[54]

Here we find perhaps the clearest instance of the Eurocommunist reliance upon the methods of capitalist organization in its pursuit of social transformation. The PCI's remarkable shifts of position on the issue of European integration and, more recently, on the role of multinational corporations needs to be understood in this context. The multinationals, as previously mentioned, are no longer viewed as the simple agents of international monopoly capital but as potentially positive forces in bringing to the less developed areas of Europe the virtues of science, technology, expertise, and capital. Of course there are "good" and "bad" multinationals, with the "good" ones assigned a modernizing role in agricultural mechanization, industrial restructuring, and overall technological expansion. Therefore the PCI rejects the "ritual condemnation" of the multinationals as the embodiment of total evil, suggesting instead that they are really the most productive and unifying sector of advanced capitalism.[55] For example, Lucio Libertini wrote, "We do not believe that the multinational corporations are the creation of the devil. On the contrary, they are an essential structure of capitalism in its present phase of development," particularly insofar as they contribute to the "unification of world markets."[56] But although the PCI urges the multinationals to invest more capital in Italy, its orientation nonetheless remains critical; it would like to establish a uniform code of operations for the EEC, curtailing the excesses of the multinationals by making it more difficult for them to evade taxes or move quickly from one area or country to another.

These various components of rationalized development—institutional renewal, democratic planning, social investment, austerity, and agricultural modernization—reflect an essentially unified Eurocommunist political impulse. Taken together, they constitute the vision of a stabilized system of production and administration built through a mixture of state and private initiative in a context where a tradition-bound capitalism has become unworkable. For the PCI, the first stage in the transition to socialism is to expand and consolidate the existing material forces while attacking the cycle of uneven development—an approach that it views as the only one possible in the midst of a perpetual crisis within world capitalism. Yet this effort appears to be as contradictory as those it has superseded. The new form of accumulation might sweep away some of the archaic features of Mediterranean capitalism, but its very logic will reproduce rather than undermine the bourgeois division of labor.

New Strategic Dilemmas

The historical and geographical uniqueness of the PCI's structural reformism has not discouraged other Communist parties, in Europe and elsewhere, from looking to it as a model. Indeed, it is often viewed as an "advanced" perspective that maturing Marxist parties, having outlived their Leninist fantasies, are expected to adopt sooner or later. What is significant about the Eurocommunist departure is its attempt to build upon the most progressive traditions of bourgeois democracy as a countervailing force to the authoritarian features of rationalization. It is a strategy that appears feasible within a relatively stable bourgeois democracy, where there is political space for large-scale reform intervention but where revolutionary goals seem remote. When evaluated as a methodology of socialist transformation, however, its limitations and contradictions become apparent.

A fundamental problem is that, whatever its contrasts with traditional capitalist and bureaucratic centralist approaches to rationalization, Eurocommunism relies on many of the same bourgeois and statist premises. Beneath their proclaimed "Marxist" and "socialist" ideologies, the parties champion programs that are compatible with the evolution of a progressive state capitalism. For in the final analysis they assume a basic structural continuity in the global and domestic capitalist economy. Thus ambitious efforts to streamline state and industrial organization, to enhance the competitive standing of particular national economic systems, to accelerate scientific and technological progress, to broaden labor input in managerial decision making, and even to expand the public sector do not in themselves point toward an overturning of the social division of labor or a reversal of uneven development. On the contrary, they end up reinforcing on new foundations the forms of bourgeois domination that have become institutionalized in the advanced societies. This is no incidental or temporary phenomenon, but rather a function of deeper theoretical and political assumptions, some of which have roots in earlier Marxist strategies.

In the first place, PCI strategy assumes the coexistence of a national planning mechanism with a large, even predominant market sphere (including the multinationals) that functions according to the imperatives of monopoly capital. But such a planning infrastructure, which seeks new modes of investment, consumption, and regulation within a capitalist framework, is contradictory from the start. Planning for new social priorities necessarily runs up against the logic of corporate power. Moreover, the internationalization of capital has eroded the capacity of national governments to effectively control their own economies; without a sustained assault on this dependency, any movement beyond a limited Keynesian intervention will soon be neutralized—as the decline of social expenditures (through cutbacks, reprivatization, and so on) in many of the advanced countries has already shown.[57] With theorists like Amendola taking the lead, the PCI has more or less uncritically endorsed the role of market relations, private property, and the profit incentive in any future economic transformation. To the extent that investments will have to be profitable, however, there is no indication how the PCI's new planning scheme could maximize social priorities and commodity production simultaneously.

This contradiction is related to another highly problematic PCI notion—that in certain respects the present crisis can be understood as the result of "inefficiency" and "mismanagement" on the part of the Christian Democrats and some especially backward corporations. The emphasis on problems like institutional decay, corruption, tax evasion, protectionism, and technological backwardness reflects an overriding concern with proper leadership and administration. Crucial as these problems are in the case of Italy, the real issue is one of capitalism itself and the exploitative presence of the multinationals, rather than the way in which capitalism is managed or planned. And parallel attempts to restructure the EEC, which operates behind a facade of European unity that conceals the real purpose of monopoly integration, only transfers the problem to another level. The same impasse exists.[58] As a framework of regionally planned capitalism, the EEC itself reproduced dependency and unevenness by favoring the advanced countries, areas, and sectors over the retarded—that is, by favoring the development of monopoly interests. (In 1980, there were more than two hundred multinational corporations in Italy; situated mainly in the north, they were in a position to decisively influence the country's economy.) For this reason, the familiar consequences of structural crisis—inflation, unemployment, decline of social services, debt-ridden governments—have only worsened in the Mediterranean countries.

The PCI's strategic dilemmas reflect a deeper theoretical quagmire that results from the commitment to rationalization: There is no radical critique of the social division of labor and thus no challenge to the bourgeois forms of domination that shape economic, political, and social life. One outgrowth of this is the uncritical Communist acceptance of science and technology as the main engine of "progress"—a neutral force that winds up detached from its capitalist origins. This acceptance sidesteps the role of technological innovation and routine in legitimating the separation between intellectual and physical work, skilled and unskilled tasks, management and wage labor, urban and rural sectors.[59] The PCI has yet to formulate a concept of economic development that incorporates science and technology into new modes of social and political organization—for example, into forms of direct community and workplace democracy. Another consequence is failure to confront the issue of social and cultural transformation, which has preoccupied a variety of feminist, youth, and environmental movements for the past two decades, in a way that could advance the democratization of everyday life. Here the economistic logic of rationalization is especially visible.

The failure to attack the social division of labor is further linked to the problem of statism. For Eurocommunism, whatever its contrasts with classical social democracy and Leninism, the state constitutes the primary locus of political initiative, legitimation, and economic planning. Of course the PCI's statism is moderated by clear democratic impulses and by a willingness to preserve a large market sphere; still, in the absence of a critique of the bourgeois state, this is hardly enough to counter the dynamic of bureaucratization. Statism is the natual product of rationalization, which entails more global methods of economic planning, administrative control, crisis management, and technocratic integration. Even within existing capitalist societies there is a marked shift toward concentrated state power, toward the predominance of executive bureaucracies over legislative bodies, and toward hierarchical authority relations in all areas of social existence. Rationalization under the auspices of Eurocommunist parties can only accelerate these tendencies. (This predicament will be discussed more fully in the next chapter.)

It follows that although the PCI remains a mass party in the sense that it has a large membership and appeals to many voters, there is no longer a commitment to mass mobilization against the structures of bourgeois society. Direct action, collective struggle, spontaneous political intervention—any form of popular intervention—are anathema to the party leadership. And if the PCI claims to be a *partito di lotta* (party of struggle), its rationalizing goals compel it to be a party of order that aspires to be a *partito di governo* (party of government). In this context, the distinctions between opposition and the status quo, working class and bourgeoisie, Marxism and liberalism have become blurred. Indeed, the Eurocommunist strategy has assumed a thoroughly class collaborationist (or interclassist) character in that it has finally abandoned the premise of class struggle, despite its long historical identification with the labor movement.[60] True to its Bernsteinian inspiration, the PCI has substituted a nondialectical linear process of economic modernization for a transition grounded in totally conflicting political forces.

Because rationalization corresponds to the rise of a planned or "social" capitalism, it also produces a new phase of class struggle characterized by integration of the most advanced strata, marginalization of the technologically displaced, and rebellion at all levels against the new authoritarian work structure. The PCI's political base is concentrated in the best-organized, most highly skilled, and best-paid workers, situated in the large northern industries (e.g., Fiat)—the sector that is the most thoroughly absorbed into the rationalizing process. This development is crucial, for it signifies a congruence of the Communist program with imposition of an increasingly rigid labor discipline, accompanied by three major phenomena: technological and bureaucratic routinization of the workplace, the planning requirements of the party, and the emergence of corporatism.

Capitalist restructuring in Italy is already transforming the nature of work and authority in industrial enterprises. For example, at Fiat the new "post-Taylorist" computerized techniques and automated assembly lines have subjected workers to nearly absolute managerial control. More than that, they have emptied the work process of creative mental activity and have broken down the cohesion and class consciousness of the labor movement as a distinct anticapitalist force. As more and more initiative comes from above, in the form of managerial commands, the workers are detached from their political subjectivity—a condition intensified by the diminishing presence of human labor power within industry and by the growing obsolescence of the factory itself as the main sphere of economic and political contestation.[61] In part this can be seen as a logical tendency of late capitalist development; but it must also be understood as a conscious managerial design to restore "governability" (Fiat owner Giovanni Agnelli's term) to production by stifling the struggle for workers' control.[62]

The PCI's strategy reinforces this dynamic, structurally and ideologically. To effectively pursue rationalizing objectives—that is, to carry out a policy of structural reforms, implement a system of planning, and establish a legitimate claim to govern—the party absolutely must be able to guarantee labor discipline. And of course as a "working-class party," the PCI can ensure such industrial stability better than the traditional capitalist parties—up to a point. Both the PCI and CGIL have harshly criticized rebellious workers who have carried out autonomous strikes and protests or who have tried to create rank-and-file organizations; indeed, CGIL leader Lama has often tried to link such activities with the terroristic left. To preserve order at the workplace, the CGIL unions are broadening forms of *modus operandi* with industrial management, which gives the unions more power but undercuts their anticapitalist potential.

As the reorganization of labor follows the pace of rationalization, the stratum of unionized, technologically skilled workers comes to occupy a privileged position vis-à-vis other strata, especially the marginalized and displaced. In Italy, as in other developed capitalist countries, what has emerged is a tripartite collaborative relationship involving industrial management, the state, and the trade unions that gives the labor movement a formal share of managerial power and thus greater capacity to influence decisions regarding investments, wages, and so forth. What the labor movement yields in return is its commitment to direct class confrontation and to the building of independent structures of democratic control. Thus the same unions that earlier were a radicalizing force—and in most cases still proclaim a socialist ideology—now develop within the orbit of capital. The PCI outlook reinforces this trend; should they hold national power, the Italian Communists (using their leverage in the state and trade unions) would probably solidify this corporatist path toward economic order and productivity. Corporatism would further encourage the rise of a sector of workers bound to a narrow interest-group politics in opposition to the labor movement as a whole. Both the PCI and CGIL strive to protect the status of this sector against the less privileged, disenfranchised strata, which do not figure in the Communist alliance strategy. To the degree that it is successful, therefore, the PCI's structural reformism is likely to reproduce the twin tendencies toward corporatism and marginalization inherent in advanced capitalism. Significantly, the popular revolt against these manifestations of crisis has generally been directed against the PCI and CGIL and often through groups identified with the radical left.[63]

The PCI's relationship to the countryside, and to the south in particular, is different and somewhat more complicated. In the long run, the PCI would like to bring industrialization to these areas, mechanize agricultural production, and thereby create a new proletarian work force that would, among other things, broaden the party's electoral base. For the time being, however, the dynamics of this situation remain highly ambiguous. Politically, the PCI's introduction of a bureaucratic mass party apparatus throughout the most traditional regions of Italian society and the accompanying breakdown of *clientelismo* have paved the way toward a network of "modern" organizational forms (including a party structure, local administration, and urban-style machines). In this fashion the PCI would engineer a "bourgeois revolution" in the most remote and least industrialized areas — a process consistent with its overall aim of rationalization.[64] Economically, however, the same Communist goals are likely to be compromised not only by the encouragement of small-scale peasant farming but also, and more decisively, by the PCI's deep commitment to the corporatist politics of the northern organized proletariat. Here again the PCI has in fact adapted to the imperatives of uneven development.

An Economistic Model

The implications of Eurocommunist logic are thus profound: Rationalization not only conflicts with democratization but coincides with the very requirements of capitalist accumulation in its statist phase. Of course PCI leaders assume that socialist transformation will proceed through various "stages," that the crisis must first be overcome before socialism can be a real possibility. Yet the immediate and overwhelming preoccupation with capitalist stabilization generates forms of commitment and involvement — indeed an entire political style — that cannot be overturned at will. The categories of thought and action that prevail at the outset are almost certain to persist throughout all stages, ensuring a continuous bourgeois developmental pattern with its specific contradictions. This is so, moreover, because the PCI (and other Eurocommunist parties) has no conception of a fundamental rupture with the totality of capitalist society. After years of mediating between the interests of the working class and the bourgeois state, after a long institutionalized presence within the legitimate structures of Italian society, the PCI now occupies a historical position that compels it to contain open expressions of militant class conflict, autonomous struggles for workers' control, and efforts to create new social and authority relations. The Eurocommunist vision of democratic transformation thus succumbs to an economistic model of the transition that leads directly to state capitalism.

The triumph of rationalization under Eurocommunist hegemony, therefore, would usher in a neo-Keynesian system characterized by state planning, a shift toward social investment, a possibly more equitable income distribution, and corporatist integration of the most advanced sectors of labor. It would also mean the ascendancy of a technocratic-managerial stratum tied not only to the bureaucratic party apparatus (and to the state) but to the monopoly corporate sphere.[65] Within this schema, parties like the PCI would become a vital driving force behind the goal of economic growth. At the same time, they would emerge as a new kind of crisis manager. Indeed, this has already occurred. During the 1968-69 and 1975-76 upheavals, the PCI put all its political strength behind stabilization of the economic and social order.[66] While this orientation has been justified as a necessary adaptation in the midst of crisis, its premises hardly converge with the requirements of *socialist* transformation. Thus, whatever the precise social composition and institutional features of a Eurocommunist-defined regime, one conclusion seems evident: Most workers would continue to live and work as commodified objects to be disciplined by capital and administered by the state, the victims of a rationalizing process antithetical to human creativity and self-conscious activity. The irony is that such regimes, if not aborted by a Chilean-style coup, economic collapse, or foreign intervention, would in many respects impede democratic and egalitarian possibilities at the very moment that "Marxist" governments were coming to power.

4

The Limits
of Structural Reformism

The emergence of a distinctly Eurocommunist politics in the 1970s actually reflects a very mixed, contradictory, and in some ways volatile situation. On the one side, the electoral gains of leftist parties in the Mediterranean countries and elsewhere stem from a popular radicalization that has deep roots in the present structural crisis. In the context of a declining and partially delegitimized capitalism, Eurocommunism has already begun to pose new challenges, press for extensive social reforms, and mobilize new sectors of the working class into the political arena. This dynamic will no doubt be accelerated should any leftist coalition come to power; under some conditions, it might even intensify systemic conflict to the extent that class confrontation would become more acute. At the same time, insofar as revolutionary change entails ongoing mass struggles against the bourgeois division of labor, the Eurocommunist parties clearly have no transformative strategy or program. They appear (potentially) as twofold phenomena: first, as rationalizing forces that operate to legitimate a reconstructed state capitalism on new ideological foundations and second, as institutionalized oppositions serving to expand the scope of democratic participation, at the same time reducing the public sphere by narrowing the content of that participation.

Future successes of the Eurocommunist type in any of the advanced or semiadvanced capitalist societies will probably raise the conflict between democratization and rationalization to new levels. This has already occurred in Italy, France, and Spain, where the Marxist left has a strong tradition and where Communist and Socialist parties together can regularly expect to win nearly half the vote. With each new series of electoral (and trade-union) gains, new contradictions centered around state activity begin to appear.

By situating our analysis of Eurocommunism within this conflict, it is possible to avoid narrowing the critique to one of two extremes—leadership motives or determination of social conditions. Here, as with any historical formation, it is necessary to take into account the dialectical relationship between subjective and objective, ideological and material factors: Theory and strategy shape political involvements, and social conditions and organizational commitments in turn influence strategic choices. Hence the process of rationalization, once set in motion (and encouraged by decisions of the party leadership), has antidemocratic consequences that are not fully anticipated in Eurocommunist theory. And the theory itself, which embraces an instrumentalist concept of the transition at the outset, restricts the very definition of democracy and hence also the content of socialist transformation. It is a fallacy, therefore, to seek to explain the Eurocommunist retreat from revolutionary goals as simply an opportunist betrayal on the part of "revisionist" leadership, or, conversely, as a shrewd tactical ploy to deceive class enemies before the later unveiling of a full-blown emancipatory movement. Equally short-sighted is the analysis that sees economic and technological modernization as a process that universally engulfs and domesticates Marxist parties in late capitalism. As Lucio Magri has argued in the case of the PCI, the gradual shift toward a moderate politics cannot be understood in terms of lapses, mistakes, or confusion on the part of leaders but must be seen as the "organic limitations of a specific strategy rooted in history," as the "expression of a whole complex of social alliances, electoral links, organizational ties, and official positions."[1]

To expand the analysis of Eurocommunism further, in this chapter I will explore the various forms of party involvement in the bourgeois political system (again with most attention directed to the Italian case) from the standpoint of rationalization elaborated previously. A guiding assumption is that, in the context of late capitalism, the realm of politics is neither autonomous nor instrumentally subordinate to the realm of economics. As an integral part of the social totality, the sphere of the state apparatus, party system, and political ideologies cannot be collapsed into an assumed underlying economic substratum; because politics has a distinct logic, history, and set of internal contradictions, it consists of far more than a cumulative expression of class forces or "objective determinants." The present critique of Eurocommunism therefore goes beyond the mode of production to emphasize the important role of political institutions, practices, traditions, and ideologies, a focus that is often lacking in Marxist literature.[2] It is true that popular movements enter the state and have the capacity to shape its direction in late capitalism, but the temptation to characterize the bourgeois state (as Poulantzas has done) as the mere "condensation of class forces"[3] needs to be resisted because it is too one-sided. If the state apparatus is not an impenetrable fortress, neither does it develop outside the scope of bourgeois hegemony. And although the state has become merged with civil society to a greater extent than ever, it has nonetheless taken on a degree of structural autonomy and historical identity. For our purposes, this identity revolves around the fact that the contemporary state is increasingly the focal point of both legitimation and class conflict.

Legitimation and the State

The legitimation crisis of Mediterranean capitalism is largely the outgrowth of severe strains in the international capitalist economy; yet the specific features of this crisis are deeply embedded in the particular traditions of Italy, France, and Spain. These include the absence of any efficient directive or planning mechanism for mobilizing resources and managing economic crises; the failure of public services to adequately meet popular needs and demands; and the void left by the erosion of traditional social relations and belief systems. In short, these are societies that have not yet completed the transition from liberal capitalism to organized state capitalism.[4]

Under such circumstances, Eurocommunist strategies could lead to the kinds of structural and ideological transformations that might facilitate the transition to a more rationalized bourgeois order, assuming once again that the parties will at some point wield sufficient power to carry out their programs. A Communist or left-dominated bureaucratic state would presumably supersede the most inefficient or chaotic elements of both commodity production and pluralist democracy (overturning the anarchy of the market and of the political system simultaneously). Insofar as the state would take on the functions of a "collective capitalist"—i.e., performing those activities (planning, investment, technological development, and so on) needed for accumulation—it would at the same time require new legitimating ideologies, as the traditional supports (religion, liberalism) are decreasingly cohesive.[5] The postwar secularization of Mediterranean societies has vastly reduced the political and cultural strength of Catholicism, best reflected in the bitter defeats suffered by the church in Italy on the issues of divorce and abortion. For the same reasons the family too has weakened. And as the authoritarian tendencies of the modern bourgeoisie run counter to its historical commitment to democratic ideas, what remains of liberalism is largely the sanctity of private property. But this is an impossibly narrow base upon which to build ideological consensus, the more so in a period of deep crisis. Moreover, the ideological thrust of the old traditions comes increasingly into conflict with the rationalizing demands of capital accumulation,[6] which suggests the need for an entirely new legitimating framework.

Here the Eurocommunist parties, with their large working-class constituencies, could well become the center of a revitalized system of ideological hegemony. If so, it will probably take two forms. One would be technological rationality, with its appeal to what is progressive and "rational": scientific and technological advance, the power of knowledge and expertise, administrative competence, economic growth. The other would be the democratic mystique of "socialism," which promises social equality and political community as part of the historical mission of any Marxist party. Both together would justify a rationalized pattern of development by concealing or distorting its true antidemocratic content. The first would supply a world view that, like nationalism and religion, presents itself as "neutral," above the tensions and contradictions of bourgeois society; the second would furnish a vision of the "common good" rooted in the ethic of democratic collectivity. The clash between rationalization and democratization in social reality does not necessarily undermine this complementary dualism, as the Eurocommunist ideology of democratic transformation is still rather ambiguous and future-oriented.[7]

Technological rationality corresponds to the instrumental requirements of expanded production in late capitalism, at a stage of development where the state, bureaucracy in its different forms, and science and technology are central to accumulation. Its legitimating power derives from an identification with "progress" through economic and administrative innovation, enhanced productivity, and material growth and abundance — all of which appear to confer benefits equally on all groups in the population. It also embodies a certain anonymity of technique, which shrouds the decisions and activities of the power structure in an impersonal, scientific, and "classless" veil; knowledge and expertise themselves are seen as the main principle of authority, operating impartially on the basis of universal norms rather than dominant class interests.[8] For Marxist parties and regimes, moreover, technological rationality has typically reinforced the common positivist assumption that all socialism needs for its realization is to inherit the material achievements of capitalism.[9]

Beneath this ascribed neutrality of science and technology, however, are sophisticated dynamics of control through which the social division of labor is reproduced. This occurs in three ways: (1) justifying the privileged role of a technocratic intelligentsia, whose power in crucial spheres — economic planning, education, social services, the military, health care — relies on the claim to specialized, nonpartisan knowledge;

(2) legitimating the hierarchical and fragmented character of production relations that, insofar as it appears "natural" or rational (i.e., necessary for efficiency purposes), stifles the development of class consciousness; and (3) reproducing the liberal-pluralistic ethos in both its formal-democratic and its bureaucratic dimensions, thereby reinforcing a narrow institutionally defined politics that blurs existing class and power divisions and limits the space for growth of a radicalized opposition. What these tendencies could mean, given Eurocommunist hegemony, is, paradoxically, a shrinking of the public sphere, even with enactment of progressive social reforms.[10] In other words, it is quite conceivable that the political framework within which popular struggles are carried out would be narrowed rather than expanded—precisely the opposite of what structural reformism presents as the basis of its strategy.

To argue that technological rationality has such a confining impact, however, is not to suggest that the end result is likely to be Soviet-style bureaucratic centralism or that the Eurocommunist model contains no participatory thrust whatsoever. The historical situation is more dialectical. What in fact distinguishes the Eurocommunist from the Soviet approach, as I have suggested, is the actuality of conflict between the logic of rationalization and the aim of democratization, a conflict that in the USSR was long ago "resolved" by the authoritarian party-state. The point is that so long as the Mediterranean parties do not really confront the capitalist division of labor, this conflict will probably be limited to the boundaries of bourgeois democracy.[11]

The symbolic value of Marxism, on the other hand, derives from the long substantive legacy of the European Communist tradition and the capacity of party leaders to generate a vision of a future socialist order. If technological rationality provides the instrumental basis of legitimation, Marxism supplies the purposive basis—the broader political and cultural meaning—that would otherwise be lacking in even the most progressive form of state capitalism. For this reason the Eurocommunist parties, whatever their actual programmatic deviations from past Marxist experience, cling tenaciously to the conceptual heritage: proletarian internationalism, world revolution, socialist democracy, the classless society, and so on. And for much the same reason, despite their "catch-all" or multiclass composition, they continue to define themselves as "parties of the working class." But Marxism, as we have seen, possesses a rationalizing as well as an egalitarian side—a celebration of technological rationality and at the same time a transcendence of it. To what degree the Eurocommunist variant of Marxism, given its particular modernizing commitments, can avoid drifting away from the egalitarian-purposive side toward a one-dimensional approach is unclear. As a diffuse world view Marxism would in any case no doubt preserve its "democratic" legitimating role, as it has in even the most closed single-party Communist systems, but in the Western European context this role would be more likely to be compromised if Marxist objectives were associated with a real authoritarian-statist regime.

Of course this predicament is hardly new within the Marxist tradition. Going back to the earliest development of social-democratic and Leninist parties, the theory has been identified with one or another form of statism—what Stojanovic called the "statist myth of socialism."[12] Although Eurocommunism reflects an awareness of the problem and claims its third road strategy does not fit the historical pattern, its rationalizing function nonetheless means extensive reliance upon state initiative. This dynamic is reinforced, moreover, by the fact that in late capitalism an expanded and organized state apparatus has taken on qualitatively new tasks: on the accumulation side, nationalization of many large and failing enterprises, economic planning, fiscal and monetary management, public services, and research and development; and on the legitimation side, social welfare, educational and cultural programs, institutionalization of class conflict, and "patriotic" mobilization. As the Mediterranean bourgeoisie (the French partially excepted) has not systematically pursued these tasks, the Eurocommunists, probably in alliance with socialists or other center-left parties, would be in a favorable position to implement their own modernizing goals in a period of economic stagnation. Insofar as the imperatives of accumulation and legitimation would now converge within the sphere of state activity, technological rationality (embellished and reinforced by Marxist language) would emerge as a potentially cohesive ideology unifying the two realms and establishing the needed "global" dimension.[13]

Structural reformism, if successful in its power aims, would thus give fuller expression to those centralizing and bureaucratic trends already visible in the advanced capitalist countries. (Such trends, incidentally, are even more visible in Italy and Spain, where the residues of fascist corporate centralism are still powerful.) Under these circumstances, the state might constitute a new directive force that penetrates and transforms the larger society in new ways. To achieve this, however, a reconstructed bourgeois state would require broad consensual support anchored in social groups outside the traditional proletariat.[14]

Class Struggle or Corporatism?

Eurocommunism therefore predictably assigns a critical strategic role to the new middle strata of technicians, professionals, intellectuals, and service and public-sector workers. With varying emphases and degrees of success, the PCI, PCF, and PCE have been trying to incorporate these strata into a social bloc that, in a new governing structure, would carry out both the technological and ideological functions mentioned above.

This shift from an essentially proletarian outlook involves a twofold logic. First, because of the importance of mental labor in a rationalizing capitalism, the new middle strata are growing both in numbers and in social and institutional importance. This growth significantly alters the conditions of electoral mobilization. As the old alliance between workers and peasants (envisaged by theorists like Gramsci) breaks down with advancing levels of urban development, Marxist parties are increasingly forced to look to the middle strata unless they wish to endure political isolation. Second, because the state assumes a more complex, specialized, and ideological character, efforts to transform capitalism will require the contributions of social groups with particular knowledge, skills, and training. Here the new middle strata are likely to become the vital social link between the existing state and corporate bureaucracies on the one hand and the Eurocommunist commitment to a new phase of accumulation and legitimation on the other. And this constituency represents a larger proportion of the membership and mass base of the parties (especially in the PCI) with each passing year.[15]

Palmiro Togliatti understood the strategic possibilities of the *ceti medi* (middle strata) as part of a projected antimonopoly alliance as early as the mid-1930s, and the PCI integrated this into its theory of structural reforms in the late 1940s. The PCI was one of the first Communist parties to move away from its strict *ouvrierist* beginnings. The party leadership conceded that the middle strata had internalized very little socialist consciousness, but its viewpoint was that their objective antimonopoly position made them amenable to radicalizing swings, especially during crises, when their demand for economic security and job autonomy would naturally ally them with the industrial working class. This sensitivity, enhanced by Togliatti's fascination with the problem of ideological hegemony, opened up space for the PCI's postwar electoral successes and its durable local governing coalitions with the Socialists. If the *via italiana* was to have any chance of success, it would have to attract new bases of moderate support. Underlying this approach were two basic political moods: an optimism that the middle strata would respond positively to Marxist symbols (because of the Resistance experience) and fear of a right-wing resurgence.[16]

Meanwhile, only with their departure from Leninism did the French and Spanish parties seriously look toward the middle strata—the PCF after a long period of orthodox attachment to the industrial proletariat, the PCE after four decades of underground refuge during fascism. In the case of the PCF, this reorientation was spurred by the May Events of 1968, which for the first time revealed the explosive radicalizing force of professionals, technicians, and white-collar workers, many of whom joined intellectuals and students in militant revolt.[17] In the case of the PCE, it reflected the party's greater isolation and desperate need for new allies in the struggle to establish a pluralist democracy.[18] For Eurocommunism in general, appeals to the new middle strata are intimately connected with the goals of rationalization. Change within the PCF, however, is taking place slowly and ambivalently because of strong *ouvrierist* tendencies in its ranks; the PCI and PCE, in contrast, have actually broadened their definition of social bloc to include "progressive" sectors of the bourgeoisie (for example, some middle-level business interests that are being squeezed by the monopolies).[19]

To the extent that the new middle strata are pivotal in the development of late capitalism, their contribution to a modernizing and socially conscious Eurocommunism would be indispensable. These strata (or certain groups among them) could form the nucleus of an expanded technocratic intelligentsia whose mission would be to preside over the transition to a new system of rule. A growing force within the party itself, they could be expected to provide organizational cohesion, facilitate harmonious relations between party and state, and articulate the normative rationale for modernization.[20] Once having loosened their dependency upon monopoly capital, the new middle strata, at present essentially a mediating force between the bourgeoisie and the working class, would be freer to extend their imprint on authority and social relations, work patterns, culture, and lifestyles. Their political role and social identity within the division of labor would be more firmly established at the core of a newly evolving structure of domination. As I have argued, there is little in either the theory or programs of the Eurocommunist parties that explicitly challenges this form of power or ideological control.

The conflict between this prospect and the aims of democratization, however sincere those aims might be, is obvious enough. One possible outcome—assuming a fairly long phase of political stability—would be institutionalization of the separation between mental and physical work, in effect solidifying technocratic domination over the mass of wage earners as well as others subjected to the same bureaucratic regimen.[21] This would converge with the process of corporatism discussed earlier. And it would be ideologically reinforced by a Marxism that, conceived as a tool of workers' struggles, might instead legitimize technocratic monopoly of "theory," knowledge, and skills over the labor force. To what extent any structural reformist party in power could actually impose such binding control over its own constituencies is unclear, as the democratic claims and promises of Western parties are taken more seriously than those of the Soviet and Eastern European regimes. In any event, the possibility that a broad leftist government might emerge as a distinct new ruling stratum (based on the ascendancy of the middle strata) cannot be discounted. Some critics of the PCI have suggested that the party is on the road to becoming a "new bourgeoisie," that its historical role is to transform a corporate-entrepreneurial system into a bureaucratic state capitalism, with accumulation located more squarely in the state and directed by a *political* formation.[22] For this to occur, the state would have to dominate the private sphere and civil society in general, with the operations of the market subordinated to a systemic plan.[23] From the viewpoint of analyzing such a phenomenon, which has only partial historical antecedents in the rise of European social democracy after the 1930s, the logic of bureaucratic hierarchy would sooner or later become merged with that of capitalist economic rationality.

The Eurocommunist reliance upon the new middle strata creates new problems, however, at the very moment that it maximizes power opportunities. What must be resolved is how, given the cleavages produced by rationalization, both the middle strata and the working class can be effectively represented within the same party. Although a tendency toward convergence can be detected at the level of economic interests, especially around their mutual hostility to the large monopolies, cultural differences between the middle strata and industrial workers have generated tensions paralleling those of the ill-fated alliances between workers and peasants in the past. In the PCI, where the middle-strata presence is by far the strongest,[24] disruptive internal strains have already surfaced over this antagonism—for example, in the widespread demonstrations since the mid-1970s against austerity and the historic compromise and in the rank-and-file worker revolts (directed in part against the PCI and the trade unions) at Fiat and elsewhere. Indeed, these strains probably go back as far as the "hot autumn" of 1969, which triggered a wave of working-class radicalism that ultimately gave rise to the PCI's own "interclassist" contradictions.[25]

The fact is that if the middle strata have been moving leftward in recent years, their much-heralded "radicalization" is both contradictory and limited. It is true that large numbers of intellectuals, professionals, and students have been mobilized or at least touched by the social and cultural struggles of the new left; at the same time, many technicians, scientists, and civil servants—the more narrowly technocratic groupings—have come to oppose capitalism, but their "socialist" leanings are often motivated by the desire for job or professional autonomy, social reform, and rational planning *within a bureaucratic framework*. This latter dynamic is particularly strong in countries like Italy and France, where technical and scientific workers, for example, have resisted the confining effects of proletarianization.[26] And this is the sector most closely identified with Eurocommunist politics in its concern with expanding social production and democratizing the state under an umbrella of institutional stability. In contrast, those groupings within the new middle strata closest to the universities and cultural institutions have been the terrain of the "emergent movements" (including feminism) and the radical left. To the degree that this generalization applies elsewhere, it validates Poulantzas's thesis of a growing polarization within what he calls the "new petty bourgeoisie."[27] This situation, along with the inevitable clash of interests between the new middle strata as a whole and sectoral working-class demands for higher wages and better workplace conditions, especially if the economic crisis intensifies, creates a predicament for Eurocommunist alliance strategy.[28]

At the same time, there is still the possibility that Eurocommunist programs for a revitalized public infrastructure, new social services, and an expanded trade unionism might offset this antagonism and create the terrain for a political merging of new middle-strata and industrial workers. That the parties will struggle mightily to achieve such a social bloc as time passes seems inevitable; without it they are faced with a desperate choice—either isolation or the Chilean path (a shaky left government with a narrow proletarian base). The realization of a broad alliance of interests, however, would not change the subordinate position of the working class in the capitalist division of labor; it would only legitimate it in an even more rationalized form. This in turn would impose new obstacles to working-class solidarity and self-activity.

The party leaderships have never really addressed this problem or confronted its long-term depoliticizing effects. Of course worker militancy in Italy and Spain—and to a lesser extent France—is quite widespread, but the parties and unions generally find themselves trapped in an ambivalent position: They must try to build upon such militancy in order to sustain their credibility within the labor movement; yet to carry mass radicalism too far would clearly jeopardize their alliance efforts, their austerity policy, and, most important, their institutional power. One result is that, in Italy, the vacillation of PCI and CGIL leaders around issues of direct action has driven many workers away from the Communist left and into sympathy with radical antiparty and antiunion groups like Autonomia Operaia (Workers' Autonomy). The PCI insisted, with particular fervor during the period 1975–1979, that popular revolt at the workplace had to be muted if Italy were to emerge from the structural crisis. Thus, in the fall of 1979, Amendola harshly attacked the CGIL when it wavered on the question of austerity; he called for a more resolute sense of sacrifice and "self-discipline" in the labor movement.[29]

Underlying this predicament is the deradicalizing process that has been at work throughout the postwar evolution of the Western European parties. In France and Italy, a long period of electoral politics set in motion forces dividing parties and unions, and elections and contract struggles over the themes of labor "autonomy" and the "incompatibility" between party and union leadership roles. The task of winning general reforms in the political sphere is viewed as the responsibility of the party apparatus, while the important leftist unions (the CGT [General Confederation of Labor] in France, the CGIL in Italy) are expected to utilize their growing independence to push for contractual bargaining at both plant and industry levels, with wage demands (limited by austerity concerns) tied to maximizing output and efficiency.[30] This separation between politics and economics, clearly more appropriate to a modernizing strategy than the old Leninist "transmission belt" notion, nonetheless tends to distance the party from its working-class constituency. On the one side, the parties cannot assume any kind of mobilizing or real politicizing role at the workplace; they approach workers primarily as voters, offering legislative reforms, local social services, and the promise of future renewal in exchange for electoral support. On the other side, the unions have built closer ties with the workers at the point of production, but their control is increasingly bureaucratic and economistic—that is, corporatist.[31] What this kind of dualism has produced, especially in Italy, is the insulation of labor struggles from popular movements (e.g., those of students, women, and the unemployed) centered outside the factories.

What the Eurocommunist parties offer to their constituencies is an ideology of social change, a broad framework of political community, and, in many local areas, a machine-style organization that provides jobs and a variety of services. In a party like the PCI, however, with an electoral base of roughly 13 million and a membership of 1.8 million, the ideological side of this attachment has eroded over the years, as reflected in a declining grassroots activism (atrophy of cells, near-collapse of the sections in many areas, poor turnout at rallies and demonstrations). The unions, on the other hand, have a powerful and established organization that can protect workers' immediate interests, negotiate better contracts, and more recently, strengthen labor's role in management within a framework of co-management. Throughout the 1970s, the CGIL also assigned priority to goals of full employment and investment in the south, although the confederation did not commit a large amount of resources to this end. What the unions expect from the workers in return, however, is both containment of militancy and compliance with norms of productivity and discipline—a position compatible with the drive toward co-management. In periods of economic downturn, such as the late 1970s, a policy of wage moderation has also been stressed, purportedly to control inflation and stimulate new investment, with mobilization around concrete short-term demands to be deferred in favor of an overall restructuring of the economy. Like the PCI, the CGIL insists that only by holding down the high cost of labor can Italy hope to improve its position within the international capitalist economy and emerge from the crisis strong enough to advance further structural reforms.[32]

The problems with this approach to class issues, from the viewpoint of a unified socialist politics, are many and deep-rooted. What has not yet been explained by either PCI or CGIL leaders is how worker restraint at the point of production—especially at factories like Fiat, where rebellious attitudes are widespread—can be reconciled with the imperatives of the anticapitalist struggles that Eurocommunism still claims to support. How can a lessening of combativeness at the workplace build toward fundamental changes in the economy, in social and authority relations, and in the state? Other questions arise: To what extent is the further integration of Italy into the world capitalist system, and the consequent strengthening of its existing domestic economy, likely to pave the way toward *socialist* transformation? Is the stability projected by Eurocommunism more apt to generate heightened forms of class struggle than would crisis and polarization? Is the division of labor between the political parties and trade unions compatible with a unified and general strategy necessary for society-wide changes? Eurocommunism inevitably runs aground on such questions. Its moderating and corporatist thrust has not only met with resistance from unskilled and marginal workers, it has simultaneously created a new range of problems.

Perhaps the largest of these problems is a failure to grasp the new social contradictions and class configurations of European monopoly capital in a period of technological restructuring, multinational deployment of resources, and changing work patterns. The PCI orients much of its rationalizing strategy toward large-scale manufacturing enterprises and the unionized labor movement rooted in this sector; thus Fiat, which is the biggest enterprise in Italy, has become the chronic battleground of working-class struggles, the focal point of CGIL activities. But the changing structure and composition of the total work force has called such a strategy into question. As technology destroys the human component of labor power—that is, as production becomes more computerized and "robotized"—employment in the traditional manufacturing sectors (autos, steel, chemicals, electronics) has stagnated, while the dispersed and fragmented marginal sectors (service work, some areas of public employment, the underground economy) are expanding. Whereas the former is composed of highly skilled blue-collar and well-paid technical workers, the latter includes the unskilled, youth, women, and seasonal or temporary workers—a distinction that corresponds to the contrasting social bases of the PCI and the emergent movements of youth, students, feminists, and the unemployed.

In its commitment to the established trade-union movement as a cornerstone of its modernizing approach, the PCI is compelled to protect the interests of a declining labor force against the totality of class politics that is now centered outside the factories, outside the classical site of proletarian wage struggles.[33] Austerity or not, this is essentially a defense of privileged sectors against the marginalized strata—one basis of the Communist antipathy toward the popular movements (and hence its unwillingness to more seriously confront issues that are directly relevant to these strata, such as housing, unemployment, and environmental concerns).[34] In this context, as layoffs and technological unemployment mount, the official PCI program calling for full employment and social equality becomes abstract. Likewise, at a time when the "societal worker" poses new contradictions for monopoly capital, continued preoccupation with the factory serves only to reproduce divisions within the work force and the system as a whole, meanwhile blocking efforts to take advantage of new opportunities for mass mobilization.

Consequently, even as the PCI continues its appeals to diverse strata, it is really more a sectoral party tied to specific interest groups than a class party rooted in broad anticapitalist struggles. As it seeks to legitimate itself within technical groupings of the new middle strata and unionized urban workers that are attached to institutional stability, the PCI's capacity to build any real presence in the new popular movements based in the marginalized strata is correspondingly undercut. This predicament can be traced back to the logic of rationalization and to the split between politics and economics that stems in part from the electoralism of the *via italiana* strategy.[35] It is a predicament expressed at the most general level through alienated politics in the sphere of the party and economism in the sphere of the trade unions. Bureaucratized and increasingly detached from social struggles outside the legitimate institutions, both deny the transformative potential that their Marxist ideology proclaims.

Whether Eurocommunists in power could ever effectively govern on such a basis is another question. The attempt to establish a new system of rationalizing and corporatist priorities (including austerity measures) on whatever ideological basis, given the history of combative working-class and popular movements in the Mediterranean, can only generate new contradictions.[36] For the present, it is clear that neither the parties nor the trade unions envisage a democratization of the workplace or the growth of self-management forms in the community. Neither looks, in other words, to a reunification of politics and economics that would permit a generalized attack on bourgeois forms of domination.[37]

The Logic of Institutionalization

The political strategy of the Italian and French parties has revolved largely around parliament, local government, and trade unions. In these arenas significant advances have been made, but not without reliving the dilemmas experienced by classical social democracy. Perhaps the most serious dilemma is that associated with the single-minded pursuit of electoral politics and the threat of institutionalization it poses. After more than four decades of stable Communist involvement in the bourgeois political system, it is necessary to ask how much, and in what way, a deeply ingrained parliamentarism has stifled the parties' capacity to fulfill their democratizing intent.

Both the PCI and the PCF were born out of hostility to the liberal democratic tradition, consistent with the early Comintern position that regarded parliaments as instruments of capitalist rule and mystification. They viewed electoral campaigns and legislative reforms as limited propaganda and tactical maneuvers, never as strategic mechanisms for the overthrow of capitalism; for the latter, only competing forms of social and political organization would suffice. Although from the beginning most European Communist parties took seriously bourgeois elections and parliaments and often won a sizable proportion of the vote, their ideological stance toward representative democracy was ambivalent until well into the postwar years. Togliatti's cautious introduction of structural reformism in the late 1940s was the first real departure from Leninist theory but it was not until 1956, when the Soviet leadership endorsed "peaceful roads to socialism," that the PCI and PCF finally adopted electoral politics as a positive factor in socialist transformation. Once this dynamic was set in motion, electoralism rapidly developed into a central and guiding factor of Communist strategy. The PCI, for example, has throughout the postwar years devoted most of its resources to electoral politics, hoping to move toward hegemony within this arena of competition.[38]

If the PCI has yet to achieve parliamentary hegemony, its electoral success has enabled it to establish a presence within the national political system rivaling that of the Christian Democrats. As it became a fixture within bourgeois structures, the PCI realized new levels of both power and legitimacy. This reflects a massive change in Italian political culture, one result being that by the late 1970s the left was capable of exerting real influence and challenging the domination of the DC. Once the PCI adapted to the European pluralist tradition, so too did "Marxism" penetrate the established institutions.

What the Eurocommunist parties have gained in the way of presence, however, must be evaluated within the larger context of their institutionalization—that is, their organizational merger with and absorption into the forms of bourgeois democracy. The PCI and PCF, in much the same fashion as the social-democratic parties of an earlier period, have moved steadily toward accommodation with the forces of monopoly capitalism. Of course it would be miraculous if, after so many years of parliamentarism, the parties had been able to avoid such stable institutional attachments—and indeed their political styles as well as their ideologies and programs more and more reflect this reality. Institutionalization thus dramatizes the underlying contradictions of structural reformism and calls attention to what Lenin called the "illusion of bourgeois democracy."

The basic problem is that the Eurocommunist struggle for democratization, whatever its expanded or "advanced" character, is ultimately limited in both theory and practice to the boundaries of bourgeois pluralism. Quite clearly this arena is open enough for genuine representation of interests, political contestation, and social reform—but how much? The question is this: Can fundamental change, expressed through popular anticapitalist movements, take place in such a public sphere? Is the parliamentarism of the PCI, PCF, and PCE compatible with efforts to dismantle the bureaucratic and repressive side of the bourgeois state apparatus, to create specifically new forms of community and workplace democracy? Having rejected Leninist centralism, the parties failed to arrive at any distinctly socialist conception of democracy or of the state; for to do so, even in theoretical terms, would be to make vulnerable their entrenched institutional position. Thus "democracy" amounts to the celebration (and extension) of liberal values and practices: universal suffrage, civil and political freedoms, the multiparty system, broadened mass and interest-group representation, and so forth. Except for some isolated attempts within the PCI and PCE,[39] party theorists have produced few critiques of bourgeois democracy (or of bureaucracy) and even fewer attempts to conceptualize new principles of collective participation.

Restricted more or less to representative structures, then, the project of democratization is expected to unfold within a formal political-institutional realm that encourages the most partial and fragmented sort of activity—a realm that is in many respects detached from conflicting social forces. The parliamentary setting hence gives support to an approach that Fernando Claudin has described as "fatalistic gradualism."[40] Because this setting is one that favors bargaining and exchange based upon interest-group politics—and because legislative decisions are so often blocked or trivialized by the extraparliamentary power of capital, the state bureaucracy, and the military—Marxist parties in bourgeois governments have historically faced insurmountable obstacles to the carrying out of any radical programs. (The failure of the Unidad Popular coalition in Chile is but one dramatic example.) Claus Offe's observation is worth citing: "The pluralistic system of organized interests excludes from the process concerned with consensus formation all articulations of demands that are *general* in nature and not associated with any status groups."[41]

Both the logic of pluralism and the historical experience of structural reformist parties therefore suggest that parliamentarism, whatever its various advantages, tends to impede class-based movements and programs that raise the issue of systemic change. The result is a compromised, diffuse, and minimalist politics. Even those Eurocommunist programmatic objectives that call for a degree of state control over monopoly interests—not to mention the possible overturning of the monopolies—will thus be difficult to pursue within a one-sided electoral strategy. Rationalization might still be realizable, but probably only through broad interclass formations and on a less ambitious scale than the parties now foresee.

If bourgeois democracy as a formal system of rules and mediations works against rapid or large-scale change, those forces standing outside the parliamentary arena are even more formidable. The Eurocommunist parties have no real strategy or tactics for confronting the massive power of multinational capital, the state administration, or the military. This deficiency is all the more crucial because, in a period of expanding international monopoly capital, authoritarian tendencies within each of these spheres (and especially the state) have overtaken parliaments and party systems, thereby reducing their participatory functions. Poulantzas has suggested that the bureaucratized state "represents the new 'democratic' form of the bourgeois republic in the current phase of capitalism."[42] As capital becomes more concentrated, as the pressures toward both economic and political rationalization increase, the state correspondingly loses much of its "popular" character.

The implication of this for Eurocommunism is simply that the participatory side of the bourgeois state is in decline. Any attempt to exercise democratic control over monopoly policy, the executive bureaucracy, the military, or the judicial system from inside parliament is almost certain to fail. The mechanisms that would permit such intervention are simply absent. Moreover, opposition parties will have even less access to these sectors unless they are willing to give up their autonomy in exchange for leverage within various state ministries and agencies. The PCI, for example, has become swept up in the symbiotic relationship involving the executive and parliament, with all of the patronage, clientelism, and logrolling that this produces; its strong role in the legislative committees has solidified one such linkage. It is not surprising that parties like the PCI and PCF, with their long history of adaptation to bourgeois parliaments, have been effectively absorbed into the administrative side of the state apparatus—a process that further electoral gains or even the emergence of a left-dominated government is not likely to reverse.[43] One conclusion to be drawn here is that, although parliament is the overriding focus of Eurocommunist strategy, the shrinking of that political terrain relative to other power structures compels the parties to seek out the bureaucratic sector. And of course this is perfectly congruent with their rationalizing impulses.

These dilemmas will be even more sharply posed should a leftist government come to power. The parties would be in a position of having to fulfill their promise of broad social reforms fairly rapidly, probably in a context of parliamentary immobilism and powerful bureaucratic interests hostile to change. The problem would then be how to initiate a process of transformation that is certain to threaten established interests, without at the same time precipitating disruptive and possibly violent conflict. Given this bind, structural reformist parties will probably opt for a stratagem of gradually colonizing the state bureaucracy from above through patronage, clientelism, and so forth; with sufficient time, a political milieu and organizational capacity oriented to change could presumably be established. But the price would almost surely be new levels of institutionalization, as in their efforts to "take over the summit" the parties would sooner or later assimilate the political norms of the bourgeois state—a pattern that already typifies PCI local governance. These pressures would be reinforced by the demands for efficiency and legitimation that would be imposed on any struggling leftist government. Under such circumstances, the trend toward corporatist and bureaucratic politics would be difficult to resist.

Decision-making functions of parliaments have atrophied and left opposition parties have become largely integrated into the orbit of state administration in late capitalism, but the party system itself has not correspondingly declined. Its role has simply changed. The organic relationship between mass parties and the state that accompanies institutionalization signals the erosion of the party system as an agency of popular mobilization at the very moment that the bureaucratic leverage of parties may increase. In Western Europe, this appears to be as true of the Eurocommunist parties as of the various labor and social-democratic parties. Some observers have argued that, as the mobilization tasks of leftist electoral parties disappear, the parties' main impact upon mass constituencies is to legitimate bourgeois authority relations by instilling a popular commitment to orderly, routinized, and controlled political activity.[44] Of course some mobilization generally occurs — party organizational strength would no doubt collapse without it — but such efforts are usually dictated by electoral calculations. Thus direct forms of struggle that threaten the existing political-institutional sphere are vigorously opposed, for they conflict at every turn with the logic of institutionalization.

The contemporary Italian situation is a case in point. In 1945 the PCI (along with the Socialists) emerged from the Resistance as a mass mobilization party. Its postwar institutionalization, however, has transformed it into the cornerstone of a party system that above all promotes stability beneath the surface fluctuations of persistent governmental crises and cabinet changes. Like other Italian parties, the PCI for decades has socialized its constituencies into remarkably stable and predictable patterns of identification.[45] Although electoral outcomes have exerted relatively little impact on policies, the process of sustaining attachments to the political system as a whole, along with the clientelistic relationships that have developed between party and mass base, has served to reproduce bourgeois hegemony. Yet the results were still partial, as the party system has itself experienced a series of crises and near decompositions, particularly since the late 1960s. In a period of upheavals and radical offensives, the parties (including the PCI) found themselves counterposed to popular movements that were directed against the state. As Sergio Bologna observed, "the party system no longer 'receives' thrusts from the base, it controls and represses them."[46] Faced with new challenges from below, notably in the appearance of local struggles seeking new forms of political organization, the major parties tend to converge in defense of the political system. In Italy, the most recent phase of convergence began during the mid-1970s, in response to the "emergent" movements and terrorism, and grew as the PCI stressed its *compromesso* line in the 1979 elections.

The transformation of modern party systems into mechanisms of cohesion and stability, accompanied by the nearly complete assimilation

of organized left opposition, therefore has two significant political implications for Eurocommunism: It reinforces alienated politics on the
mass level, and it strengthens the tendency toward consensus at the level
of party leaderships. Strategists in the PCI, PCF, and PCE are keenly
aware of this predicament, but none seems prepared to seriously question
the very assumptions of structural reformism that have given rise to it.

For the PCI, the obsession with becoming a *partito di governo* by electoral means has led to the detachment of power objectives from social
life — an instrumentalism that, as I have suggested, undercut the visionary and egalitarian side of Marxism. To an increasing degree, the
masses who are "represented" within parliament are kept distant from
the sphere of power conflicts and bureaucratic maneuvers. What
develops is an alienated politics in which democratic illusions conceal the
underlying authoritarian nature of the bourgeois state. This is typified by
the PCI's style of electoralism, which Maria A. Macciocchi has described
on the basis of her own campaign as a Communist parliamentary can-
didate in Naples. Her critique explored the PCI's inability, within the
electoral arena, to conduct ideological struggle and establish durable ties
with its constituents. Preoccupied with winning votes, party candidates
were forced to stick with an approach that emphasized minimal reforms
(e.g., better sanitation) and abstract generalities (e.g., peace) while
avoiding themes of popular struggle. Macciocchi wrote that the campaign largely degenerated into a "spectacle" that involved "oratorical
contests" between leaders who indulged the passivity of their supporters.
The PCI, which in this case nervously avoided references to Marxism or
even socialism, differed little from other Italian parties in its overall
political style — an ideological shallowness that Macciocchi attributed in
part to the legacy of frontism.[47]

Insofar as the PCI invested more of its resources in electoral politics,
the vitality of its mass organizational life therefore suffered. Despite its
huge membership, efforts to sustain ideological commitment at the base
level have succeeded only periodically since the early 1950s. In the late
1960s, with the challenge of the new left at its peak, political activity in
most of the PCI sections (the basic structural unit) had become lethargic,
especially in periods between the brief electoral campaigns.[48] Because the
PCI is so firmly situated within the legislative and administrative organs
of the Italian state, its grassroots involvement is much too limited for it
to effectively attack bourgeois social and authority relations. The PCI
presence in civil society is actually as extensive as ever, but it has assumed
a political-representational instead of a social-mobilizational character.[49] Electoral work carried out by PCI functionaries is tied primarily to
winning votes and is rarely based on the expectation of transforming social

life in the community; nor is there any real sense of linking immediate demands to general socialist objectives.

Within the party system, the process of convergence that I have analyzed recalls the traditional Italian phenomenon of *trasformismo* — the practice of domesticating class polarization through various forms of elite collaboration. Throughout the postwar years, and more visibly since the mid-1970s, the political distance between DC and PCI leaderships has shrunk considerably. An important reason is the PCI's growing parliamentary strength, which permits increasingly equal competition with the DC and makes PCI aspirations to govern realistic. It was in this context that Berlinguer introduced the *compromesso* tactics, which, even if they did not immediately lead to a new governing coalition, reflected opportunities afforded by a new phase of Italian political development.

The art of *trasformismo* has its origins in the regime of Agostino Depretis, a Liberal premier (1876–1887) whose pragmatic Realpolitik and shrewd machinations smoothed over left-right antagonisms and integrated the bulk of Depretis's own popular following into the dominant political structures. What Depretis hoped to establish was a stable, pluralistic framework for settling differences and molding a unity of interests; in the process he built a coalition that preserved the nascent bourgeois order at a time of severe turbulence. *Trasformismo* evolved into an even more sophisticated technique during the rule of Giovanni Giolitti (1903–1914), who manipulated it to absorb the rising Socialist party into the framework of liberal politics. Years of compromise with Giolitti sapped Socialist militancy, undermined grassroots mobilization, and ultimately destroyed the party's revolutionary identity. Antonio Labriola's prediction turned out to be correct: By giving the Socialists a share of institutional power, *trasformismo* was bound to convert them into just another bourgeois reformist party.[50]

The new *trasformismo* has been evolving for many years, even though it has yet to reach full political expression. It is the outgrowth of the PCI's patient and effective application of the *via italiana* in parliament, the trade unions, and local government. Strategically, the historic compromise turn of the 1970s can be seen as the logical extension of these successes. A variant of *compromesso* politics has actually been implemented for some time at the local level, where the PCI, in alliance with the Socialists and occasionally even the DC itself, controls hundreds of communal, municipal, and provincial governments. The PCI's electoral leap of 1975 and 1976 solidified this position, giving it unprecedented strength in the Chamber of Deputies (with 229 seats) and Senate (with 116 seats). All of this coincided with the DC's own crisis of hegemony, its severe factionalism, and its growing inability to rule as a *monocolore* force. However, the trend toward elite convergence was interrupted in 1979, when the PCI's election setback prompted it to drop the *compromesso* tactics and move back into "opposition."

Yet the new *trasformismo* appears to differ from the old, which was more mechanical and therefore also fragile and rather short-lived. Giolitti's consensus was built through a system of patronage and manipulation that involved a shaky harmonization of conflicting interests; the Socialists were only superficially integrated into the bourgeois political system. The present version goes much deeper than the vagaries of parliamentary politics. It is the outgrowth of a lengthy, organic process that is generating a confluence of interests among the reformist, "modernizing" wing of the bourgeoisie (the large monopoly sector), the politically weakened Socialists, and the Eurocommunist PCI, which views its own drive toward rationalization as the culmination of the *via italiana*.[51] Leadership styles, and even substantive policy orientations, are merging beneath the fluctuations of electoral outcomes — most visibly between the left faction of the DC and the right faction of the PCI. Should political stalemate persist in Italy, with neither the DC nor the PCI capable of constructing a durable majority, further convergence seems inevitable, although the PCI would be likely to suffer mass disaffection in the process. But for the Communists there is probably no turning back in the long run: *Trasformismo* offers a way out of years of frustrating opposition and, ultimately, can furnish the springboard to real political governance.[52]

In the case of the PCI, at least, the historical connection between electoralism and political assimilation had become by the early 1980s difficult to refute. This argument is not meant to imply that pluralist structures can be dismissed as strictly mechanisms of capitalist domination; their history is too complex, especially in countries like Italy and Spain where mass intervention against fascism revived them and where they remain important spheres of contestation. The point is that parliamentary democracy as a complex system of formal rules and procedures tends to block radical change. When strategies are oriented almost exclusively toward the bourgeois political-institutional sphere, as with Eurocommunism, that is where the bulk of organizational resources inevitably go. In time, institutionalization reinforces this commitment and confines the scope of popular mobilization.

A Party of a New Type

For all of its emphasis on parliament and the party system, decentralization, and mass participation, the Eurocommunist alternative never really counters the statism that has permeated the Marxist tradition — a statism, however, that in this instance is closer to the social-democratic variant than the Leninist or bureaucratic-centralist model it has outgrown. What is evolving in the Mediterranean is a pluralist statism rooted in a strategy built around the existing state apparatus (including its bureaucratic side) as the primary framework of political struggle. Once purged of bourgeois hegemony, the state apparatus becomes the main locus of the transition to socialism. It is also reflected in the parties' own centralized and authoritarian forms of organization, in their local clientelistic operations, and in their remoteness from popular movements.

In the end, the Eurocommunist project of democratization comes down to a gradual reconstitution of the state, where the legitimate political instruments are in effect turned around at the summit and imbued with new social priorities and new ideological content without disturbing the bureaucratic edifice. It would be unfair to criticize Eurocommunism, as some have done, for simply wanting to take over the leading positions of the state administration;[53] its objective is to restructure the bourgeois state. A more pervasive critique of structural reformism is its virtual muteness concerning new forms of political life (e.g., workplace and neighborhood councils, local assemblies, community institutions) that could lay the foundations of a nonauthoritarian state. The result is that, although the scope of mass involvement would presumably broaden within an "advanced" pluralist democracy, statism would intercept this transformation before the question of socialist democracy could even be posed. This is hardly surprising, as any radical transformation of bourgeois society would require a gradual disintegration of the existing state—a basic rupture of bureaucratic authority relations—whereas the Eurocommunist model stresses *internal* democratization.

This creates a double dilemma for parties like the PCI, PCF, and PCE. On the one hand, they are dedicated to constructing new bastions of institutional power with the aims of (1) initiating social reforms and (2) provoking a crisis of bourgeois hegemony. But such designs have generally turned out to be contradictory, because reforms enacted by parliament tend to stabilize rather than subvert the capitalist system. More significantly, although Marxist parties and the social forces they represent can by means of electoral successes gain positions within the bourgeois state, *they cannot reverse its fundamental direction from within;* the most they can hope to achieve is a reordering of priorities and, if power is consolidated over any length of time, a shift toward rationalized state capitalism. On the other hand, the parties naturally fear that expansion of grassroots movements will disrupt their organizational stability, undermine their parliamentarism, and weaken the infrastructure necessary for rationalization. It need not be emphasized that state planning, labor discipline, and routinized decision making all demand a great degree of centralized authority.[54] And this logic reproduces the social division of labor, which can be overturned only through the intervention of popular struggles directed *against* the bureaucratic state.

Of course the statism of Eurocommunist parties in many ways corresponds to those forms of political domination already present in late capitalism. At the same time, should the parties come to power they will no doubt set about reshaping the bourgeois state to meet new accumulation and legitimation requirements. More than ever, the state would be burdened with the task of combining political, economic, and ideological functions.[55]

The political role of a structural reformist government would be to modernize the state bureaucracy (by introducing meritocratic structures) in order to solidify "command" and "control" requirements vital to the Eurocommunist programs. Of course the parties' capacity to establish such administrative power, and to realize even short-term goals, would depend upon their strength relative to that of their partners in any coalition. But without a preponderance of control, such as the PCI has been able to exercise in many local governments, the Communists would be impotent in the face of urgent immediate pressures: planning, crisis management, structural integration of their constituencies. In economic terms, the state would lay the groundwork for rationalization by improving and maintaining the general conditions for reproducing capital. Functioning as a "collective capitalist," it would strive to mobilize and synthesize a diverse range of particular bourgeois interests where none acting alone could contribute to the overall systemic needs for accumulation. In this context, the state would appear as neither the pure instrument nor the absolute embodiment of capital; the relationship would be dialectical.[56] Hence, in contrast with the Soviet model, structural reformism would encourage an uneasy merging of the general and the particular, the public and the private, plan and market.[57] Ideologically, Eurocommunist attachment to the national state coincides with major efforts by the parties, especially since the early 1970s, to legitimate themselves within their respective political communities. Simple identification with the established governing apparatus, and with the patriotic symbols and cultural traditions that it has historically embodied, may be enough to reverse widespread anti-Communism and bring "Marxist" or "socialist" values into mainstream popular consciousness. Indeed, the evidence already reveals that, at least in the case of the PCI, such a legitimation process has occurred during the past decade.[58] (Of course this trajectory has been reinforced by the PCI's own moderation and by the secularization of Italian society as a whole.) Moreover, the state furnishes the natural terrain for consolidating a technocratic hegemony that Eurocommunism needs to recruit elements of the new middle strata that are so central to its alliance politics.[59]

If the historical forces and political conditions pushing the Eurocommunist parties toward statism appear irreversible, the leaderships insist that such tendencies can be negated by a strategy that emphasizes mass participation, decentralization, and local autonomy. This was the meaning Togliatti assigned to "party of a new type" after World War II. As we have seen, the Mediterranean parties have been anxious to finally leave behind the residues of Stalinist authoritarianism; with the partial exception of the PCF, their critique of Soviet bureaucratic centralism has been uncompromising. Attempts to move beyond the centralist flaws of both social democracy and Leninism have often been sincere if halting, and they have met with some successes—most notably the PCE's extensive (but ambivalent) presence within certain Spanish popular movements (the neighborhood struggles, the workers' commissions).

To date, however, only the PCI has really been able to establish a strong, nationwide power base in local and regional governments. In 1944 and 1945, the Communists rode the mass mobilization of the Resistance into governing control (or a share of it) over more than a third of the local jurisdictions—communes, provinces, cities—in northern and central Italy. In many of these areas, especially during the immediate postwar years, the PCI created direct and intimate linkages with the mass constituencies of workers, peasants, women, and others.[60] With the central government dominated by a reactionary DC, the PCI at the grassroots was often a force behind social reform, efficient and honest government, and even economic growth, the Bolognese administration always standing as an exemplary model. The PCI was able to magnify this presence, in both organizational and electoral terms, well into the 1970s.[61] At the end of the 1970s it was in a position to decisively shape public policy in almost every major Italian city.

But the promises of decentralization based on the *via bolognese* inspiration have faded during the past decade. It turns out that Communist local strategy is vulnerable to the same pressures that obstruct the *via italiana* at the national level. Efforts to shift the base of power toward local, smaller-scale governing units might increase popular access to decision making, but it does not necessarily alter the structure of authority or give encouragement to grassroots struggles. Provincial, municipal, and even communal governments can be statist, or at least conduits of a centralized state. The PCI has actually made very little progress in transforming those areas over which it has exercised local political hegemony (for however lengthy a period) because the logic of its structural reformism generates the same contradictions.

The immediate obstacles to democratization in local politics stem primarily from constraints imposed by the economic crisis. Severe fiscal pressures, leading in some cases to bankruptcy, have hit many Italian cities; there is little money to support new social programs, and many existing public services have been cut back. Under these circumstances, even left-controlled local administrations must be frugal and cost-efficient. Barriers to fiscal autonomy, created both by the Constitution and by the power recently usurped by state technocrats and planners, further complicate matters. In power, PCI politicians and administrators have therefore been obsessed with instrumental priorities: fiscal responsibility, harmonious relations with the central government, political stability. The result is that in cities like Naples and Genoa, where PCI-Socialist coalitions came to power with a commitment to reverse at least the worst manifestations of the crisis, few reforms have been carried out.[62] And meanwhile the PCI, as a local *partito di governo,* is forced to accept a share of the responsibility for deteriorating social conditions.

Beneath such anticipated roadblocks, however, there is a secular pattern of organizational development very much shaped by the larger process of institutionalization. In many areas local PCI politics takes on the character of a patronage machine. The PCI's institutionalization at the grass roots is most advanced where Communist administrations have a long and continuous history—for example in the Red Belt regions of central Italy. Here the party, responding to the imperatives of governmental efficiency and stability, has developed a variety of symbiotic ties with the dominant interests (industrial firms, banks, the church). In order to sustain these relationships, the PCI local organizations no longer put their resources into popular mobilization and indeed actively discourage forms of direct action that the leadership views as "disruptive" or "adventuristic." More than that, since the late 1960s the PCI has consciously striven to distance itself from grassroots movements, the new left, and other forces that make up the radical opposition. The bitter mutual antagonism that has grown out of this dynamic over the years helps to reinforce the PCI's statism.[63]

This phenomenon cannot be ascribed to the bad motivations of particular leaders; it can be better understood as the natural outcome of institutionalization. By the 1970s the Eurocommunist attachment to the bourgeois state apparatus was so deeply rooted—in both national and local, participatory and administrative spheres—that the parties were driven to protect existing institutions against encroachments and challenges from outside.

The most turbulent waves of revolutionary upheaval in postwar Western Europe—the antifascist struggles between 1943 and 1946, the peak years of the new left between 1967 and 1971—gave birth to strong dual-power movements (notably in Italy and France) in workplaces, communities, schools, and the military. The attitude of the Communist parties toward these movements has varied from ambivalence to contempt. In the end, the parties' legitimation needs, which derive from their commitment to electoralism and rationalization, have never been reconciled with the imperatives of local democratic mobilization around workers' self-management, neighborhood control, and feminism. Even where a merger between party and local forms did evolve (as with the PCI's presence in the Consigli di Gestione, or management councils, that grew out of the Committees of National Liberation during the Resistance), it quickly dissolved once the party leadership turned its energies toward electoral and trade-union politics. The local forms either disintegrated or were eventually absorbed by bureaucratic structures (the state, parties, unions). Since the late 1960s, when the May Events in France triggered a crisis within the Western European Communist parties, the PCF and PCI have mounted offensives against forces within what was once called the "extraparliamentary left."[64] These attacks were accompanied by a familiar list of epithets: the Maoists, Trotskyists, and others within the "revolutionary" orbit were denounced as infantile leftists, "Stalinists, and even provocateurs, while the popular movements (feminists, youth, students, unemployed, and so on) were dismissed as spontaneist or utopian. And elements of both groups were often branded as terrorists.[65]

The persistence of an active radical left in Italy throughout the 1970s created special dilemmas for the PCI. Though hardly a strategically unified or cohesive force, it took up issues that the PCI historically ignored or approached uncritically: self-management and bureaucracy; women, the family, and sexuality; the environment and nuclear power; the problem of youth and marginalization. Moreover, the radical left was the source of a constant and embarrassing critique of the PCI's role in Italian society. Thus, it was common in radical left circles to view the PCI as a "co-manager" of monopoly capitalism. And although the limited mass base and organizational strength of the radical left meant that it could not challenge the PCI for left hegemony, its intellectual and political impact was much greater than its numbers would indicate. And it did establish some institutional presence; for example, in 1979 the radical left won 5.6 percent of the vote and elected twenty-four deputies (the combined total of Proletarian Democracy and the Radical party), more than double its 1976 results. It is too soon to determine whether this signifies a trend. Yet it seems clear that the PCI's support among the marginalized strata of youth, women, and the unemployed is slowly declining.[66]

The Italian radical left built its presence mainly around the explosive urban movements that proliferated during the 1967-1975 period. Frustrated by the stabilizing influence of the PCI and CGIL, these movements consciously broke with conventional Marxist forms and strategies; although inspired by the spontaneous euphoria of the new left, they looked to more broad-based, durable forms of organization. Thus the urban struggles incorporated diverse strains of activism: rent reductions, building occupations, tenants' committees, women's groups, neighborhood councils like the *comitati di quartiere,* and so forth.[67] Within this panorama of activity, the radical left hoped to overcome the traditional split between the workplace and community by focusing simultaneously on the factories, neighborhoods, and schools. But it made only limited advances. Lacking unity, it never developed into a comprehensive political movement capable of defining a national strategy and program, so that, by 1975-1976, its momentum had visibly halted.

What has been the PCI response to this challenge? For years its verbal assaults were accompanied by a contemptuous indifference. Since the early 1970s, however, the party leadership has employed two methods: cooptation and repression. The cooptative approach has been directed mainly toward the feminist, youth, and student movements. Some issues relevant to these movements are taken up and even put into legislation, meetings and conferences are sponsored,[68] leading activists are often courted and recruited, new language is adopted in party statements – all with the goal of integrating this political energy into the party's own electoral priorities. The PCI tries to distinguish between the leaders, organizational forms, theories, and above all tactics of these movements (which it rejects) and their objectives (which it says are legitimate). Likewise, the PCI has sought, with mixed results, to assimilate autonomous neighborhood councils in cities like Bologna into its own municipal administrative network. Repressive methods, on the other hand, have been applied more selectively. Although it is true that local PCI organizations generally do everything possible to contain or discredit mass action that is not sanctioned by the party leadership, such efforts usually stop short of direct repression.[69] At times, however, the PCI has gone further, utilizing its governmental machinery to physically attack leftist and popular groups. The most dramatic episode occurred in

Bologna in March 1977, when city authorities brutally dispersed a large demonstration of feminists, students, and other groups directed against an antiabortion Catholic group and also closed down the leftist radio station.[70]

Such episodes, along with the PCI's general antagonism toward movements outside its own orbit, has produced widespread dissension within the party organization, especially from the ranks of young workers, students, and intellectuals. Tension over the historic compromise tactics mounted during the period 1976–1979, provoking a large number of resignations (a peak of 78,000 in 1979) and calls for a basic reorientation of PCI strategy.[71] But the contradictions of structural reformism were too fundamental and the logic of PCI institutionalization too deep-rooted for any such internal shift to be engineered, even assuming that the leadership could be motivated to attempt it. Given PCI preoccupation with mobilizing the technocratic middle strata into its electoral bloc, any alliance that would incorporate the goals and styles of the emergent groups was unthinkable; the political methods were too contrasting, the approaches to bureaucracy, technology, and culture too conflicting. Consider that the PCI took stands diametrically opposed to ones taken by the radical left: acceptance of the EEC, NATO, and the multinationals, a general prolandlord attitude, support for austerity, acceptance of nuclear power, and a basic law-and-order stance. The main premise of the PCI's approach to the popular movements, moreover, is that the conditions of marginalism that give rise to these struggles are the product of a retarded, uneven capitalism and will disappear once "new modes of economic development" are realized.[72] Ironically, not a disappearing but a growing marginalism is what the PCI program of rationalization is bound to create.

There is no way of fully analyzing PCI strategy without looking at the problem of left-wing terrorism, which since the mid-1970s has both illuminated and reinforced the dilemmas of statism. In contrast to West Germany, where the Baader-Meinhof group expressed the desperate isolation of a handful of urban guerrillas, in Italy terrorism developed into a relatively large-scale phenomenon with roots in the radical left and an organizational capacity to seriously disrupt political life. Insofar as it has become an element in the crisis-polarization cycle that has often typified Italian mass politics, the new terrorism has resisted all attempts to repress or exorcise it. And of course the PCI, with a commitment to peaceful and institutional forms of struggle and a fear of being tarnished by the provocative and violent actions of those who claim to be Marxists, has completely dissociated itself from the insurrectionary left.

Italian left-wing terrorism has taken three forms, all interconnected: the Red Brigades, small isolated guerrilla formations like the Armed Proletarian Nuclei, and the sporadic, often spontaneous violent outbursts by workers, students, and others.[73] There are differences in strategic outlook and preparation, but left-wing terrorist groups share one guiding objective: to operate as a catalyst, through direct armed action, of an intensified class struggle that would lead to civil insurrection and, ultimately, to a revolutionary conquest of power. Their hope is to explode the contradictions of the "multinational corporate state" through exemplary struggles, opening the door to expansion of an anti-state popular insurgency. As a corollary to this "strategy of tension," the terrorist groups hope to reveal the true colors of the PCI as a "bulwark of the status quo." If they have so far fallen short of their general aim, they have nonetheless partly succeeded in pushing the PCI even further rightward. And whatever theories and strategic principles motivate their actions, the fact is that the spread of terrorist groups has driven the DC and PCI closer together; in other words, it has contributed to the dynamic of *trasformismo*. At the same time, repeated waves of kidnappings, shootings, and street violence have created a mood of fear and confusion within the general population (and within the left). The dramatic abduction and subsequent murder of former premier Aldo Moro by the Red Brigades in the spring of 1978 had precisely such a dual impact.

Italian terrorism initially appealed most to those who had abandoned the radical left out of disillusionment over its failure to more rapidly advance revolutionary goals. Many felt that unity and leadership were lacking; others thought that there was too much timidity on the issue of armed struggle; still others may have been looking for more dramatic and immediate successes. By the mid-1970s, soaring unemployment and the growing marginalization of youth contributed to the sense of frustration and alienation underlying the terrorist impulse. Finally, there was the institutionalization of the PCI itself, which produced a certain closure in the political system that denied access to the most disenfranchised groups. The result was a vicious cycle involving economic crisis, the PCI's statism, and political violence.

The PCI leadership responded to the terrorist challenge, however, with an analysis that was both shallow and moralistic, combined with an authoritarian politics. Ignoring the social and political conditions that had driven many young Italians toward extremist violence, the PCI attacked Red Brigade cadres as "criminals," "fascist thugs," and "reckless conspirators" regularly in the party press and in official statements[74]; it likewise attacked elements of the radical left, such as Workers'

Autonomy, for their "sympathy" with terrorist goals—despite pains taken by left groups to distinguish their strategies from those of the *Brigatisti*. In rather un-Marxian fashion, the PCI has approached terrorism as an act of individual malevolence, as simply another form of violent criminal behavior, rather than as an expression (however distorted) of social despair.

So Italian Communism, predictably enough, emerged during the late 1970s as an integral if sometimes reluctant agent of state repression, of what some referred to as the "Germanization" of Italy. The PCI presented itself as the main defender of law and order, the indispensable champion of the political system. To support this claim it worked closely with the DC in parliament to help enact first, the *legge reale* (an extension of the fascist legal code that permits sweeping police and court powers) and, later, new antiterrorist legislation that drastically curtails civil liberties in "emergency" situations and sanctions a military response to controlling social disruption. It also called for massive increases in law-enforcement expenditures, with the idea of modernizing, reforming, and extending the national police apparatus. Finally, the PCI vigorously supported and at times even initiated governmental surveillance and arrests of leftist intellectuals and activists—in connection with the Moro episode, for example.[75] Hence terrorism, which was initially interpreted as a threat to the PCI, has supplied the party leadership with a convenient pretext for both further attaching itself to the bourgeois state and justifying political and legal assaults against the entire radical left. In this way terrorism feeds into the dialectical antagonism between statism and popular movements. (Ironically, efforts by groups like the Red Brigades to make the state more vulnerable to attack have achieved just the opposite. Instead of the PCI being thrown into disarray, it is the left that has been most harmed by random violence.[76]) Yet, however much repressive measures against terrorism might be justified, the larger effect has been to accelerate the PCI's statist development. From the standpoint of democratization, therefore, terrorism dramatizes even more sharply the impasse of structural reformism.

What Kind of Democracy?

The PCI's deep predicament, although in certain respects unique to the Italian situation, nonetheless reveals the general and seemingly fatal deficiencies of Eurocommunist theory and strategy. If the pessimistic outlook for a PCI-engineered democratization can be attributed on one level to the pitfalls of institutionalization, in a larger sense it can be understood as the necessary consequence of structural reformism.

Despite recent breaks with past orthodoxy, Eurocommunist parties have actually inspired little movement toward innovative conceptions of democracy. More or less confined to the sphere of the bourgeois state, they find it more and more difficult to sustain a broad democratic vision, let alone carry out mass mobilization. It is conceivable that the entry of Eurocommunists into the governments of Italy, France, and Spain, following the example of their social-democratic forerunners, might improve working-class living standards. But such entry would also produce a new system of power in which the state would penetrate even more of civil society than it now does in late capitalism. Where the state expands its domination over the social order, even within an "advanced" pluralist democracy, the transformation of everyday life (including the struggle for new forms of state authority) is undermined. The Eurocommunist strategy of democratization is so centered in the political-institutional realm that it sooner or later engulfs and distorts vital elements of the transition: ideological hegemony, social bloc, self-government.[77] The content of this process more aptly fits the transition from liberal capitalism to organized state capitalism, where leftist political formations achieve some measure of hegemony. Although more rationalized and (possibly) socially egalitarian, it would still be a system where class oppression, statism, bureaucracy, and commodity production are sustained and even extended.

The probable future role of Eurocommunist parties as either institutionalized oppositions or new legitimating instruments of domination suggests further that their very theory of democratization is formulated within the confines of the pluralist tradition. Above all, this theory downplays or ignores the role of popular forms that could subvert the logic of statism and prefigure a new kind of state rooted in collective, nonhierarchical authority relations. It presents no vision beyond the parliamentary system. All spheres of participation remain indirect, mediated, representative—that is, they embody an essentially bourgeois relationship between political institutions and mass activity. In presenting the choice as one between the dictatorship of the proletariat and parliamentary democracy, between Leninism and structural reformism, Eurocommunism has thus sidestepped the issue of *socialist* democracy, which requires, among other things, a strategy for breaking down centralized decision-making structures within government, the economy, and the communities. The result is that the real bureaucratic impediments to democratization have been more or less evaded.[78]

The outer limits of democratization are also set by bureaucratic processes internal to the parties and their supporting organizations. Aversion to the themes of self-management and social struggle is conditioned as much by the survivals of democratic centralism as by strategic priorities and institutional commitments. The question here is, Can a party or movement that is internally centralized and hierarchical be a force behind democracy in society as a whole? Interestingly enough, Eurocommunist statements endorsing a non-Leninist road to socialism say little about departing from the authoritarian premises of democratic centralism. And the parties remain largely closed to real internal debates and factional conflict, their leaderships still capable of exerting overwhelming control over the base. While a certain degree of open discourse has been established, especially in the PCI, it rarely touches upon issues of immediate policy or tactics. Nonetheless, the days of monolithic party unity are probably numbered, as rumblings among the rank and file and intellectuals in opposition to Leninist norms (notably in the PCF and PCE) have been increasingly explosive and open. A major factor in the erosion of such norms is that they clash with the imperatives of electoral politics and above all with the needs of pluralistic legitimation.

The Eurocommunist version of the democratic road ultimately fails to point toward a radical transformation of social and political life not because it is committed to preserving pluralist democracy, but because it views the transition as a process that runs almost exclusively through the bourgeois state machinery. If the complex task of building a new ensemble of relations is obscured by Leninism, with its classic scenario of frontal maneuvers against the state, it is also distorted by Eurocommunism, with its nearly singular preoccupation with internal modification of structures. It is this strategic focus—not electoral politics per se—that underlies institutionalization and statism. And given the Eurocommunist project of rationalization in the Mediterranean context, this approach no doubt possesses a certain logic. From a democratic socialist perspective, however, the primary question is not whether to retain or destroy representative institutions but how to enlarge the struggle for democracy and social transformation to include the development of autonomous centers of dual power. As Poulantzas has argued, only a synthesis of the two levels—a combining of the "transformation of representative democracy with the development of forms of direct rank-and-file democracy or the movement for self-management"—can counter the statism and depoliticization that follow from either extreme.[79]

5

A Return to Social Democracy?

The international Communist movement spawned by the Bolshevik Revolution first appeared in Western Europe as a response to the collapse of social democracy. To Communist leaders of the post–World War I period, social democracy in both its Bernsteinian and Kautskyist varieties had become theoretically and politically bankrupt and would have to be combatted because of its destructive impact upon working-class politics. Immobilized by a fatalistic and chauvinistic Marxism, the social democrats (with the German party leading the way) uniformly failed to take advantage of the breakthrough opportunities presented in Europe during the years 1914–1923. This loss of revolutionary capacity (or will) was seen, moreover, as the product of a narrow parliamentarism and trade unionism that had trapped the Second International within the rules of bourgeois politics and thus closed off a genuine socialist alternative: popular insurrection, united front, dictatorship of the proletariat. From the viewpoint of classical Leninism, the very notion of winning proletarian victories at the polls—of legislating socialism into existence—was considered utopian in the general context of capitalist power. The success of the Russian Revolution had conclusively demonstrated the superiority of vanguardist over parliamentary methods.

Subsequent historical events were to prove the early Communist assessment of social demoracy prophetic enough. Beginning with the Swedish electoral victory in 1931, social democrats have come to power for varying lengths of time in at least a dozen European countries, but nowhere has there been even a modest effort to overturn capitalism. In all cases, the bourgeois system of production—market relations, private property, profit incentives, the class structure—has remained solidly intact. I would go even further and argue that the historical role of social democracy in northern Europe has been to manage, on a foundation of increased working-class participation, a planned and regulated bureaucratic capitalism. Despite in some cases decades of Keynesian crisis-containment measures, welfare programs, and progressive social policies, the dream of an egalitarian society is still as far away as ever. In the words of one observer: "After 35 years of socialist rule in Sweden, income differentials between working-class and middle-class occupational groups are no narrower than in Western societies ruled by bourgeois governments."[1] That is, even the most ambitious and far-reaching reform projects initiated by social democracy have failed to produce more than a slight dent in the armor of bourgeois economic and social hierarchies. And this failure could no longer be glibly attributed to "revisionism," leadership "betrayal" of the masses, or elite "embourgeoisement," particularly as the parties in question commanded widespread popular support. The reality is that, whether in power or in opposition, the social-democratic tradition that is indebted to the structural reformist theories of Bernstein and Kautsky had by the late 1950s finally renounced any Marxist pretensions whatsoever (a turn most clearly reflected in the SPD's Bad Godesburg Program of 1959). With very few exceptions, social-democratic parties have made their peace with capitalist society even on theoretical grounds.

The logic of this historical evolution raises some intriguing questions for Eurocommunism. For parties like the PCI, PCF, and PCE, as we have seen, Leninism has been for all practical purposes jettisoned as a strategic model. From the standpoint of the analysis presented in the foregoing chapters, therefore, a crucial question must ultimately be posed: Are the contemporary Eurocommunist parties in essence social-democratic, or are they at least in the initial stages of becoming so? Is the modern viewpoint of the democratic road really a third path to socialism, or is it merely a recycling of the classical Bernstein-Kautsky synthesis of the Weimar period? To date, most writers on this topic have shied away from historical parallels. Where comparisons have been established, however, they have usually rested upon certain textual deviations from Marx or Lenin rather than an analysis of party development in its totality. But the weight of the evidence here seems rather conclusive: In strategic and programmatic terms, Eurocommunism represents a return to social democracy.[2] At the same time, despite a striking similarity in political orientation, it is much less obvious that the future evolution of Eurocommunist parties will in fact duplicate the social-democratic pattern. The historical conditions are different enough to rule out such facile assumptions.

Eurocommunist leaders, of course, have strongly rejected the argument that their own brand of structural reformism has much in common with that of classical social democracy. They insist that, whatever the two traditions share, the differences are more fundamental; and they still abhor any association with the theories of Bernstein and Kautsky, any identification with the politics of the Second International.

Togliatti, the chief architect of contemporary structural reformism, consistently emphasized the uniqueness of Italian Communism. He objected not so much to the particular methods and tactics of the social democrats, which after all were not too different from those employed by the PCI, but rather to their abandonment of socialism as the final goal. He argued that although in many countries social democracy had been able to retain its hold over large sections of the working class, its historical mission was to administer capitalism more effectively, not to transform it.[3] Later PCI theorists have reiterated this theme: the Communists, unlike the social democrats, remain committed to the dialectical methodology of Marxism, to the leading role of the working class, *the socialist* transformation. The social democrats, lacking any real Marxist identity, long ago degenerated into opportunistic mediators between labor and capital.[4] To dramatize these contrasts, the PCI often calls attention to its Leninist heritage – democratic centralism, "proletarian internationalism," the leading role of the USSR – which has for decades constituted a barrier between the two dominant Marxist tendencies. Although this barrier is today increasingly symbolic rather than real, its influence on the political actors involved cannot be discounted.

Yet even this symbolic difference is rapidly disappearing. Insofar as Eurocommunism has already served to demythologize Leninism and the Soviet model within the Western European Communist parties and has thereby strengthened the role of distinctly national or indigenous forces in party development, it has cleared the way for precisely this sort of ideological realignment. In the case of parties like the PCI and PCE – and to a slightly lesser extent the PCF – it is immediate political calculations rather than old doctrinal attachments that have come to shape strategic priorities.

And beneath the various Marxist symbols and theoretical formulations, these strategic priorities are in effect designed not to overthrow but to rationalize the economic and political structures of bourgeois society. Eurocommunist claims to the contrary, the parties' actual observable pattern of institutional attachments, programmatic commitments, and everyday political practice reveals a manifestly social-democratic orientation that, if successful, would function to stabilize a crisis-ridden capitalism. Hence the PCI, as we have seen, looks to manage, plan, regulate, and "meritocratize" the existing Italian economy; it accepts, less and less critically, the agencies of international capital, such as NATO, the EEC, and the multinational corporations; it endorses market relations and commodity production in principle; it stands as a beacon of electoral and parliamentary respectability—indeed, as a bulwark of political and legal order; it is the vehicle of a corporatist-interest-group politics in the labor movement and in local government; it tries to either repress social movements or assimilate them into its own electoral apparatus; and so forth. The PCI does all this ostensibly to salvage the capitalist economy, to "get Italy out of the crisis" so that a transition to socialism can be initiated—a project that in the long run is bound to be contradictory, as I shall argue in this chapter.

Two Converging Traditions

The strategic points of convergence between conventional social democracy and modern Eurocommunism are becoming more and more visible. In fully exploring both traditions, it is of course impossible to ignore the serious differences that exist within and between the large number of parties: the division between left and right tendencies, the contrasting positions on specific policy issues, the diverse ways that general theoretical and strategic principles are translated into unique national contexts. Such differences, however, are secondary to the more overriding conception of socialist transformation—the theory of transition—that the traditions have come to share. On the question of internal factions, it is important to remember that the concrete political direction of the party leadership is usually defined by right (or center) tendencies rather than by the left. As Henri Weber has noted in the case of the PCI, ". . . the politics of the Italian CP are the politics of Amendola using the language of Ingrao. Berlinguer's job is to do the translation."[5]

The Eurocommunist theory of transition is above all compatible with the Bernsteinian notion that socialism must develop out of the very enlargement of bourgeois social and political forms. Its prospects rest upon a growing public sector, entrenched liberal traditions, the rise in educational levels and political consciousness of the working class, and the progressive role of the new middle strata. Structural crisis is viewed as an inevitable feature of capitalist development, but systemic collapse is essentially ruled out. The assumption is that any catastrophic upheaval, any real social disturbance would jeopardize working-class gains and possibly open the door to fascism—a stance that, as Mandel has pointed out, ultimately requires a politics of compromise, order, and manipulation.[6] Eurocommunism anticipates a gradual, unilinear conquest of power that in effect would minimize the scope of direct popular mobilization against capital. This rejection of orthodox Marxist crisis theory is congruent with the political evolutionism of both Bernstein and the late Kautsky, that is, with social democracy in its formative post–World War I phase, when the early differences between Bernstein and Kautsky narrowed in the aftermath of the Bolshevik Revolution. Broad strategic parallels of this sort were probably first detected by Claudin, who referred to "the covert return of the European Communist Parties to Kautskyism."[7] And covert this association has remained, as no Eurocommunist leader or theorist appears willing to openly concede the obvious parallels, no doubt because the Bernstein-Kautsky synthesis is historically tainted with failure.

Yet their unwillingness to explicitly acknowledge this social-democratic lineage in no way renders the Eurocommunists immune to its debilitating logic. In the absence of explosive crises leading to mass up-heavals and frontal attacks against capitalist power, it is hard to imag-ine the kinds of popular intervention necessary to overthrow bourgeois domination. The transition from capitalism to socialism necessarily in-volves, at some point, a qualitative break with the old forms of social heirarchy—a break that is nowhere indicated in structural reformist theory. Such a break, of course, would be incompatible with the statist premises of Eurocommunism. European political history suggests that it is crisis and class polarization, not stability or the pluralist balancing of interests, that generate new opportunities, create space for popular strug-gles, and break down the old institutionalized patterns sufficiently to allow for the expression of radical opposition. In this respect, Luxem-burg's critique of Bernstein is still valid—namely, that far from being more "realistic," the idea of a stable, nonconfrontational path to socialism is actually quite utopian.[8]

This rejection of a crisis scenario is linked to the Eurocommunist turn toward a modified Keynesianism, which likewise has parallels with Bern-stein's approach. For years social-democratic parties have employed an array of Keynesian policies in their efforts, however successful, to ad-minister and control the crisis tendencies of monopoly capitalism.[9] The Eurocommunists have strayed very little from this path, except that their social programs would (circumstances permitting) be more extensive. Keynesianism assumes that the state can function—by means of economic planning, fiscal and monetary controls, welfare expenditures, regulation, and the like—to contain the cyclical fluctuations of capitalism within tolerable limits. To the extent that the central govern-ment can supplement and mitigate the role of market forces, it could fur-nish the missing ingredient of systemic economic rationality that would enable it to "manage" such problems as inflation, unemployment, and fiscal deficits within the framework of existing property and class rela-tions. For any Keynesian solution to work, however, two general conditions would have to be met: steady economic expansion and relative quiescence of working-class and popular struggles. These conditions have in fact prevailed in most northern European countries since World War II; the result has been social-democratically engineered "welfare states" built upon a foundation of institutionalized class conflict.[10]

What then of the situation in southern Europe in the 1980s? Can the Eurocommunist parties duplicate this Keynesian feat of utilizing the bourgeois state for long-term system-sustaining purposes? The prospects are not very good. For the new phase of crisis, in contrast with the cyclical flows that typified postwar capitalism through the mid-1970s, appears to be deeper—more structural and global—and thus much less amenable to governmental intervention. Inflation, unemployment, the energy drain, and the fiscal crisis of the state are all intractable problems manifested in a declining stimulus to capital accumulation on an international scale. Slackening economic growth rates, not to mention the dependent and weakened position of countries like Italy and Spain, will surely persist even with structural reformist governments in power. Thus to the extent that the Eurocommunist model depends upon accelerated economic and technological development, large increases in public spending, and the capacity of the state to manipulate market (and social) forces, it will encounter new obstacles as the contradictions in the Mediterranean systems intensify.[11] It is therefore conceivable that the crisis might become unmanageable, especially with developed countries like West Germany and the United States immobilized by their own challenges.

Yet even if Keynesian state manipulation could somehow work to rationalize the economy, even if a social-democratic solution were possible in the Mediterranean, it would take place within the parameters set by capital. Not socialist transformation, but capitalist stabilization would be the probable outcome. Once in power, the Eurocommunist parties would have to bow to the requirements of capital accumulation or risk governmental collapse as a result of corporate sabotage. Programs and policies would have to be compatible with the imperatives of exchange value: profitability, material incentives, market criteria. Efforts to even initiate a transition to socialism, to carry out anticapitalist mobilization of any sort would put the parties in a contradictory situation of being forced to consolidate the existing economy while striving to overturn it. A further problem arises: Because the state itself is so thoroughly embedded in the capitalist system of production, any attempt to utilize the state as a technical instrument against that system is not likely to be very fruitful. Crisis management is one thing, systemic rupture another. The fact is that public intervention is essential for capital accumulation and is generally considered legitimate by "modernizing" elements of the corporate bourgeoisie.[12] Beneath the rhetoric of "social ownership," therefore, both social democracy and Eurocommunism have made their peace with this neo-Keynesian conception of the state.

The third parallel between social democracy and Eurocommunism involves their common attachment to the rationalizing side of Marxism—in particular, their strong faith in science and technology as a lever of progress and emancipation. One of the great promises of northern European social democracy was to boost levels of economic productivity so that the living standards of workers could be dramatically improved. This objective it was able to partially achieve during the postwar period, mainly through a strengthened accumulation process and a restructuring of large-scale industry that depended upon new kinds of labor power, revamped (and technocratized) educational systems, research and development, and so on. It also created streamlined transportation and communication networks, meritocratic public bureaucracies, a technologically advanced medical structure, and more effective military weaponry. Eurocommunism, as we have seen, upholds more or less the same goals.

Impressive as many social-democratic accomplishments were, their transformative impact was structurally limited because they were carried out within the framework of capital. Tied to an instrumentalized ideology, social-democratic parties embraced science and technology as a largely "neutral" tool of change that, in permitting expanded human control over nature, would (once put to use by the right leaders) lay the groundwork for socialist transformation. What resulted in northern Europe, however, was a more streamlined capitalism that served to even further bureaucratize the economy, the political system, and everyday life; create new levels of environmental destruction; and build nuclear power systems as a means of solving the energy crisis. Technological modernization thus meant, in most cases, a competitive and expansive capitalism that produces not only greater material comfort but also greater social and environmental devastation. The problem is that both social democracy and Eurocommunism ignore the democratizing conditions indispensable for imbuing scientific-technological progress with an emancipatory content. So long as structural reformism does not implant the technical dimension in a newly evolving system of production and social relations, so long as it does not marshal technology against the structure of bourgeois domination, such one-sided development cannot facilitate the transition to socialism. More than that: Without a struggle to democratize and socialize knowledge, modernization simply reproduces the various hierarchies in new and often more oppressive ways.[13]

The fourth area of convergence lies in the very definition of the democratic road itself, which in both cases is seen as passing through the bourgeois political-institutional sphere. Bernsteinian social democracy, and later the Bernstein-Kautsky synthesis, looked to the acquisition of a solid political majority within parliament as the basis of a socialist conquest of power; the insurrectionary model was discarded in part because it was seen as undemocratic. Guided by a rationalist optimism, the European parties anticipated a gradual shift in economic and political power favoring an emergent proletariat (and its allies), making possible extensive social reforms and, in the long run, the organization of society along progressively egalitarian lines. Such a transition was expected to occur within the representative state, that is, within parliamentary structures and the party system (as well as the trade unions and cooperatives), to be realized only after securing a popular consensus. The classical Marxist idea of the withering away of the state was regarded as utopian and so too, at a later point, the Leninist dictatorship of the proletariat was dismissed as excessively authoritarian. Social democracy projected no historical break with previous forms of bourgeois state power.

After nearly fifty years of development, social democracy has established a broad and durable presence within the bourgeois state in many Western European countries, and it has carried out some far-reaching reforms. Nowhere, however, has it made much progress in democratizing the state or in breaking down the class structure. On the contrary, it has functioned to reinforce the social division of labor, to legitimate the relations of domination in those systems where it has achieved hegemony. The attempt to impart new "content" (socialism) to old "forms" (the bourgeois state) has proven illusory.

The outcome for Eurocommunism will probably be little different, assuming it is able to duplicate the power conquests of social democracy. For despite its similarly impressive electoral gains and the appeal it has for large sectors of the working class, Eurocommunism is disarmed by a one-sided conception of the transition. It has given expression to a false dichotomy between the political-institutional and the social, the parliamentary and the extraparliamentary, the "internal" and the "external," the consensual and the coercive dimensions of change. Put another way, the Eurocommunist parties have not formulated a comprehensive vision and strategy of democratization that would link the necessary dual imperatives of revolutionary process: electoral politics and social struggle, parliament and councils, ideological transformation and popular insurrection, "war of position" and "war of movement." By stressing the first element of each pair to the almost total exclusion of the second, structural reformism collapses the dialectic of socialist tranformation into an instrumentalized process that cannot struggle free of bourgeois hegemony. The result is a certain impotence in confronting non-parliamentary forces—for example, the state, corporations, and the multinationals—reflected in the absence of any transitional program for dismantling such institutions. As we have seen, Eurocommunism lacks a schema for combatting both class and bureaucratic forms of domination; it seems clearly willing to accept a *modus vivendi* with (planned and regulated) capitalist enterprises and with permanent professional bureaucracies in national and local government.

Here the illusion of parliamentary democracy returns to haunt the Eurocommunists: Democratization is arrested within the political infrastructure of bourgeois society, far short of the ideal projected by the theory. References to socialist democracy are not grounded in a qualitatively new state that could embody the structural components of democratized social and authority relations. Statism compels the parties to sidestep the question of popular participation and decision making *in all spheres of society,* to ignore the requirements of collective, local involvement in resource allocation, to retreat from the goal of active and generalized self-management. To pose this question is to raise the radical theme of conciliar democracy expressed through local organs of popular control: workers' and neighborhood councils, community assemblies, women's organizations, and so forth.[14] Emergent local structures constitute a potential counterweight to the bureaucratic state and are thus an indispensable element in the transition. Conciliar democracy represents the dissolution of the administrative-repressive state machinery and its gradual replacement by nonbureaucratic forms through which the democratic transformation of parliament, parties, labor organization, and local and national administrations can take place.[15] It further means the extension of workers' control throughout all sectors of the economy. Without this commitment, the various Eurocommunist utterances in favor of *autogestion,* decentralization, and democratic planning are reduced to hollow platitudes.[16]

The underlying fallacy here is that electoral processes and parliamentary forms can be somehow reshaped independent of the totality of social and political relationships. The nature of power in late capitalism is simply too complex and diffuse, too bound up with the pervasive system of ideological hegemony, for this to be possible. The system of domination goes far beyond formal political institutions, encompassing those realms of public life—the factory, neighborhoods, churches, schools, family, and so on—that cannot be transformed through legislative activity alone. As Gramsci stressed, no socialist movement could hope to succeed without articulating a qualitatively different politics within the framework of a new "integrated culture." In overlooking this totality, structural reformism has fallen prey to a narrow instrumentalism with all of its deradicalizing implications. In this respect the Eurocommunists, following the example of the social democrats, could only wind up obliterating the crucial distinction between bourgeois democracy and socialist democracy.

The final parallel is an extension of the previous one: In both instances, a primary emphasis on electoral-parliamentary politics has served to downplay the class struggle, mass mobilization, and the transformation of everyday life. As efforts to conquer the state took precedence over struggles within civil society, politics has inevitably become detached from (or superimposed upon) the larger social context. A major flaw of social democracy has been its repeated inability to establish a bridge between concrete parliamentary and trade-union-based reform on the one hand and the historical objective of socialism on the other.

In Western Europe, social-democratic strategy has rested on four implicit premises: construction of a broad multiclass alliance, a primarily electoral definition of politics, an interest-group approach to the labor movement, and the avoidance of direct confrontations with the ruling class. These premises have remained essentially constant during the postwar years, varying but little with changing conditions. From the outset, they reflected a concept of socialism that minimizes the early Marxist commitment to direct popular involvement. Still, social democracy has managed to accomplish through electoral victories what no insurrectionary or vanguardist party has ever been able to duplicate—a broad base of popular support, leading in several cases to a share of governmental power. Reform legislation made possible by a long period of economic prosperity has enabled the parties to solidify and even expand their electoral base, especially in countries where Communist competition was weak. Not only reformist gains, but the deep popular reaction against fascism (and Stalinism) after the war reinforced working-class attachment to social democracy, instilling in the consciousness of an entire generation the identification of "freedom" and "democracy" with pluralist institutions and processes. At the same time, what has finally emerged within the present-day Socialist International is an assortment of moderate, diffuse "catch-all" parties with roots in many different constituencies, with only periodic and indirect contact with the grass roots and with no real Marxist identity. Such parties (exemplified by Scandinavian social democracy, the British Labour Party, the SPD) have developed according to "representative" rather than conventionally Marxist "mobilization" functions.[17]

The Eurocommunist parties have not yet become so thoroughly deradicalized. But their strategic assumptions, judging from the analysis presented in the previous chapters, are almost certain to generate the same results over time, barring a sudden and improbable upheaval within the parties. Clearly, the PCI has advanced furthest along this road: It has already revived with few reservations the classical social-democratic separation between politics and economics, politics and social life. For the PCI, this has given rise to a pattern of development that stresses institutional adaptation over popular mobilization, trade-union corporatism over anticapitalist offensives, frontism and bureaucratic calculation over grassroots struggles. Whether in the sphere of electoral-parliamentary activity (the party) or collective bargaining (the unions), the result is a growing detachment from the daily experience of the general population. The ultimate irony is that, institutionalized within the bourgeois state, the PCI now commonly finds itself in a position of repressing, in the name of its own "Marxist" heritage, the spontaneous and militant thrust of Italian popular movements.

Going into the 1980s, then, the southern European Communist parties carry forward not the substance but the mythology of socialist revolution,[18] not an optimistic third path but a return to the original path of Bernsteinian social democracy. Fully absorbed into the bourgeois political system, these parties are experiencing the gradual but incessant erosion of their historically distinct Marxist character. Behind ideological appeals to "socialism" and the "workers' movement" lies a powerful integrative and modernizing process; Marxism in this sense becomes less and less an ideology of transformation, more and more the legitimation of new forms of bureaucratic planning and control. The "Communist" label too has all but lost its meaning, as even some party leaders have already conceded openly, especially as the parties themselves have grown more distant from their origins in Bolshevism, the Soviet model, and the international Communist movement. Aside from some Leninist organizational trappings, they are not too distinguishable from social-democratic parties—certainly not in their stated goals, programs, strategies, and mass constituencies.[19] Disengaged from its revolutionary past, Eurocommunism can more easily fill the political space previously occupied by social democracy in northern Europe, assuming that future conditions will permit it—space the parties could utilize to stabilize weak and crisis-ridden capitalist systems through their programs of rationalization. Here, as in earlier phases of European development, "Marxism" supplies an ideological rationale for actually extending the authoritarian tendencies already present in late capitalism.[20]

Eurocommunism, Crisis, and Transition

The failure of Leninism in the West has been matched by the failure of structural reformism; the choice between insurrectionary and parliamentary strategies has proven to be illusory. Disclaimers to the contrary, the stage has been set for the complete social democratization of the Western European Communist parties. As the analysis in this volume has shown, the issue here is not a matter of simple revisionism, incorrect party lines, or leadership betrayal; it involves nothing short of a fundamental transformation of the parties, which must be understood as the outgrowth of a gradual and complex interaction between subjective and objective factors, between strategic designs and historical processes in the postwar period. Nor is it a matter of political contingency—the momentary adaptation to unique pressures—as the pattern I have described appears rather general and uniform, even beyond the boundaries of the Mediterranean. From the German Social Democratic party at the turn of the century to contemporary Eurocommunism, Marxist parties of structural reform have invariably moved toward accommodation with the capitalist system.

This rather pervasive logic of deradicalization cannot be attributed to changes at the level of working-class composition, as the "end of ideology" theorists have suggested; although certain moderating pressures from below cannot be discounted, the main explanation lies in the spheres of leadership, organization, and strategy. For one thing, during the past two decades there has been a marked radicalization of both workers and sectors of the middle strata in Italy, Spain, and France. Second, the evidence reveals no significant lessening of economic and social inequality in such countries and, moreover, no tendency among "affluent" workers to switch political loyalties as their income rises. A more fruitful explanation begins with Michels's classic analysis of the pre–World War I SPD.[21] The process that Michels defined as *embourgeoisement* had its origins in bureaucratic degeneration at the top. Characterized by the party's organizational adaptation to the German state, it was shaped by more than two decades of successful parliamentary strategy. Committed at first to the revolutionary overthrow of capitalism and to democratic participation within the party, SPD leaders rapidly developed their own interests, privileges, and culture apart from the masses they set out to "represent." A new leadership identity came into conflict with the SPD's stated goals, leading to deflection of the party's original socialist (and democratic) ideology. The institutionalization of the PCI that I analyzed in Chapter 4, although more complicated in certain respects, roughly corresponds to this pattern. Yet the deradicalizing thrust is activated by a dialectic that runs much deeper than organizational adaptation—in this case, it ultimately stems from the particular (rationalizing) strategic and programmatic framework of Eurocommunism. We are confronted here not with an inexorable bureaucratic logic, but with the historical reality of institutionalization that is encouraged by certain theoretical perspectives, strategic choices, and ideological commitments. For the PCI, and for Eurocommunism, the critical points of departure were the Popular Front politics of the 1930s and Togliatti's elaboration of structural reformism in the early postwar years.

In the end, the much-celebrated third road turns out to be a fiction built upon the euphoria that accompanied impressive Communist electoral gains in Italy during the 1970s. The anticipated new Marxist synthesis was nothing more than a replay of the old Bernstein-Kautsky model that crystallized during the Weimar period. Appeals to Gramsci, even to Austro-Marxism,[22] have been merely attempts to render the present version of structural reformism ideologically more palatable by symbolically divorcing it from a social-democratic tradition that has found its historical expression in a rationalized state capitalism.

The reality is that Eurocommunism has never even theoretically outlined a third alternative; it poses the ultimate choice as one between insurrection and parliamentarism, with only nuances in the latter.[23] This simple distinction obscures the very possibility of conceptualizing a third road that goes beyond past roadblocks and incorporates radical assumptions—one that envisages the transition to a self-managed socialism that is clearly at odds with the instrumentalist premises of both Leninism and structural reformism. Such a comprehensive model of democratic transformation would be grounded in a basically nonstatist logic. Thus, in balancing institutional struggles with movements for workers' control and community self-management, a new strategy would redefine and broaden the arena of popular contestation. In this schema social democratization would be counterposed to and incompatible with a much deeper process of radical democratization. The latter would not only preserve but transcend bourgeois politics, insofar as it would also unfold on the terrain of social and cultural relations—that is, within a process that could challenge bourgeois hegemony. To accomplish this, a viable third road would have to subvert the premises of capital accumulation, private property relations, and bureaucratic domination more fully than has ever been suggested by Eurocommunist theorists. Only from this standpoint can an emancipatory approach to economic and technological development have any chance of success.[24]

In European history, as we have seen, the radical alternative to

Leninism and social democracy achieved its most mature political expression through the great working-class and popular upheavals that swept Russia, Germany, and Italy during 1914–1923; the Spanish insurgency of the 1930s; the Hungarian uprising of 1956; the events of May 1968 in France; and the broad emergent movements in Portugal, Spain, and Italy in the 1970s. Influenced by Marxism yet antagonistic to many aspects of the Marxist tradition, the radical left strategy has roots in the anarcho-syndicalist and council movements, the new left, feminism, and the contemporary popular struggles of workers, women, youth, unemployed, and environmental activists that have sprung up in the Mediterranean and elsewhere.[25] To the extent that this current is likely to flourish in the midst of crisis and stagnation in bourgeois society, such radicalism can be expected to reappear on an even larger scale as the present structural crisis of global capitalism intensifies.

This raises one final question: Given the likelihood of sustained crisis in the 1980s, will the Eurocommunist parties ever be capable of carrying out a social-democratic integration in southern Europe? For the immediate future, realization of an effective structural reformist program in any of these countries would appear very unlikely. In the first place, the balance of political forces is still highly unfavorable. The PCE remains a marginal force in Spain, while the PCF has long been trapped in an electoral impasse; only the PCI has built the necessary momentum to make a serious bid for national power. If the parties hope to achieve real political hegemony, they must further extend their electoral legitimacy in order to destroy the remaining ideological barriers to growth, which in turn means that they must strengthen their organizational presence, parliamentary representation, and clientele networks far beyond what now exists. To accomplish this, however, is also to further encourage the logic of institutionalization. And such advances would require a sustained phase of relative economic and political stability not only for the Mediterranean, but for European and global capitalism as a whole.

The long-term prospects for a Eurocommunist-inspired social democratization appear equally bleak. As I have argued, a major premise of structural reformism—that of a more or less stable, non-disruptive, even depoliticized transition—will be undermined if the crisis intensifies. Moreover, the historic accomplishments of social democracy have depended upon lengthy periods of economic growth and prosperity, but this too, for similar reasons, is unlikely to be duplicated.[26] The space for social-democratic intervention, whatever the designs of party leaders, is therefore actually shrinking; and the room for structural reformist maneuver will probably narrow even further as pressures from international capital on the one side and radicalized sectors of the general population on the other converge on the parties. In power, the Eurocommunists would have to manage economies weakened by a continuing energy and resource crisis as well as by flights of capital under conditions of corporate fear and hostility. The dependency of countries like Italy and Spain would grow, leading to accelerated economic decline (worsening of the balance of payments, inflation, unemployment) that would surely stimulate additional drops in investment along with renewed demands for austerity. The twin political outcomes would probably be increased chaos within ruling circles along with rising mass politicization as the bourgeoisie moved desperately to recapture its fragile domination. Under these circumstances, the Eurocommunists would find it almost impossible to rule, let alone initiate socialist programs; the most they could hope for would be a limited (and always precarious) containment of the crisis. And whatever the policies chosen by a structural reformist government, there would be no escape from a double-bind situation: Rapid implementation of reforms would risk a Chilean-style capitalist counteroffensive; moderation would allow the parties to be outflanked on the left and (barring a drastic and improbable shift in strategy) undermined as a credible socialist force.

The point of this book, however, has been not so much to indulge in such political speculation as to furnish the basis of a critical theoretical and strategic assessment of Mediterranean Communism. And through this critique I have tried to demonstrate that however successful Eurocommunism might be on its own terms, its very logic fits the requirements not of socialist transformation — leaving aside the intentions, hopes, and self-concepts of party leaders — but rather those of a rationalized state capitalism. The Marxist ideal of a classless and stateless future, of an egalitarian and democratic community is thus finally reduced to an ideological rationale for the renewed bourgeois drive toward a modernized, secular, and administered system of commodity production. Yet new sources of conflict and renewal, many of them as yet unforeseen, will inevitably appear on this reconstituted terrain. Structural reform parties in power will therefore face a legitimation crisis of their own, as statist and instrumentalized "solutions" to the problems of a decaying capitalism will in the end only replace the traditional approaches with even narrower and more administered forms, giving rise to new contradictions and very possibly to rejuvenated movements of opposition.

EPILOGUE

Gramsci and Eurocommunism

Perhaps no twentieth-century theorist has contributed more to the revitalization of Marxism in the advanced capitalist countries than Antonio Gramsci, whose fragmentary but original and compelling work has since the 1960s reached a large audience of left intellectuals and activists far beyond its Italian birthplace. In some circles, Gramsci has emerged as *the* architect of a new strategy for socialist transformation in industrialized societies. Whatever the validity of this claim, and despite the very amorphous and often disorganized character of his writings, Gramsci's own commitment seemed clear: From beginning to end, from his early journalistic essays through the factory council articles in *Ordine Nuovo* to the Communist party writings and the *Prison Notebooks,* he stressed the actuality of revolutionary struggle. Gramsci's thought was above all directed toward creating new organizational forms and social institutions that would embody the totality of socialist production, authority relations, and culture, whether in the councils as the "nucleus of the new state" or in the mass party, the "modern prince," of popular insurgency. He was preoccupied, sometimes to the point of obsession, with the problem of revolutionary identity in the Italian working-class movement.

Yet the fate of Gramscian Marxism has not always been consonant with its origins; the very amorphousness of Gramsci's intellectual style has encouraged a remarkably diverse range of interpretations of his theory, including some that appear at odds with both the substance and guiding motivation of his prolific work. The recent appropriation of Gramsci by the leading Eurocommunist strategists in the Italian, French, and Spanish parties constitutes one example of such a conflicting and distorted interpretation. Hence, by a strange twist of historical irony, one of the founders of the PCI, who, like Lenin, was inspired by the urge to break with the paralysis of traditional social democracy and form a more viable revolutionary instrument, reappears as the legitimating "founding father" of a modern structural reformism that may provide the rationale for a new version of social democratization in Western Europe. Seizing on Gramsci's theoretical legacy, his immense appeal among European intellectuals, his "open," "creative," and "Western" Marxism, along with his status in the international Communist movement (in part the result of his long incarceration in Mussolini's prisons), Eurocommunism has sought to depict him as the true inventor of the democratic road—that is, of a gradualist and peaceful strategy rooted in electoral politics and leading, presumably, to an extensive internal democratization of the bourgeois state apparatus. Within this perspective, Gramsci is viewed as the original theorist of a tradition that extends through Togliatti and present-day Eurocommunist innovators like Berlinguer and Carrillo.

This appropriation of Gramsci, however, rests upon a serious mystification of the active historical and theoretical record. Gramsci's early role in the founding of the Italian Communist party, and in the formation of its political strategy, has been grossly distorted. More significantly, the full range of Gramscian revolutionary concepts—for example, ideological hegemony, social bloc, war of position, and democratic transformation—has been taken over by the Eurocommunist leaders, integrated into an essentially minimalist, social-democratic framework, and robbed of its meaning as a guide to revolutionary praxis. This process has gone far beyond the normal redefinition of themes and concepts that is always a part of the theoretical renewal necessary to meet new social conditions. The instrumentalized fate of Gramsci at the hands of the Eurocommunists more closely parallels the fate of Marx within the development of Soviet politics. In each case, revolutionary theory and vision served to legitimate a political practice that ultimately subverted the very source of legitimacy.

From Gramsci to Berlinguer

Although the label "Eurocommunism" goes back only as far as 1975, and the initial proclamations came only with the Berlinguer-Carrillo-Marchais statement in March 1977, the theory underlying it has much earlier origins. As we have seen, these origins can be traced to the years 1944-1947, when Togliatti initiated the *svolta di Salerno* and outlined broad elements of a structural reformism that would shape PCI politics (the *via italiana*) after 1956. Thus, insofar as recent Eurocommunist departures contain any real novelty, it is precisely in their codification of rather longstanding world views, strategies, and practices; it lies in their openly systematic elaboration of Togliattian Marxism rather than in any fundamentally new vision of the transition to socialism. Moreover, to the extent that this version of the democratic road owes any theoretical debt to the Marxist classics, it is not to the heroic founding figure personified by Gramsci but to Bernstein's prewar "evolutionary socialism" and to the Bernstein-Kautsky synthesis of the 1920s. But the PCI leadership of the 1970s, anxious to disavow the imagery of social democracy, embraced Gramsci while distancing itself (at least ideologically) from any tendency associated with the Second International.

The legacy of Gramsci in the postwar evolution of European Communism has its origins in the PCI's crisis of identity during the late 1950s and early 1960s. Despite Togliatti's moderate "new course" of the late 1940s, PCI strategy had followed a certain tense dualism: electoralism and rejection of insurrectionary politics in practice, Leninism in official ideological pronouncements. Togliatti's famous critique of Stalinism triggered the first real break with this dualism, for it led to further and rather pointed attacks on the Soviet model and Leninism itself as a valid strategy for the advanced countries. At this point, with dissent and confusion spreading throughout PCI ranks, the party leadership turned to Gramsci as a presumed link between the Bolshevik tradition and structural reformism.[1] Throughout the 1960s and into the 1970s, the PCI, under the leadership of Luigi Longo, patiently constructed a "Gramscian" identity, in certain respects quite distinct from Leninism, that served to justify the party's strategic adaptation to the bourgeois political system.

One result of this strategic development, and of the theoretical revision that accompanied it, was an increasingly "Gramscian" PCI. Berlinguer, since his ascent to the position of party secretary-general, ceaselessly stressed the PCI's Gramscian origins and political strategy—a self-concept that seems most appropriate to Italian traditions and to the peculiar conditions of Western European capitalism. During the PCI's celebration of the fortieth anniversary of Gramsci's death in 1977, he was repeatedly praised as the real inventor of the *via italiana* and of a genuinely pluralistic socialism. Party leaders, especially in their visits to foreign countries, advertise PCI strategy as a continuous development from Gramsci to Togliatti to Berlinguer. This theme emerged from the presentation of Sergio Segre and Lucio Lombardo-Radice (both Central Committee intellectuals) at a conference on Eurocommunism held in the United States in late 1978.[2]

PCI efforts to imprint Gramsci's stamp on the Eurocommunist model have generally stressed all the leading motifs of Gramscian Marxism: hegemony, social bloc, war of position, organic intellectuals, and so forth. For Pietro Ingrao, Gramsci is understood as much more than a great intellectual who also happened to be one of the PCI's founders and a tragic victim of fascist repression. He is seen as the originator of the "war of position" strategy that emphasizes ideological preparation and social struggle as a prelude to the conquest of power, that counters Lenin's "seizure of the Winter Palace" approach with a gradual buildup toward proletarian-socialist hegemony within the political infrastructure of bourgeois society.[3] For Paolo Bufalini, the PCI has been steadily advancing toward hegemony through its participation in local and national government, made possible by the successful (electoral) mobilization of a "new historical bloc" — the very approach outlined by Gramsci. Indeed, "never has Gramsci been so relevant today, never have his thought and teachings been so alive." More specifically, "the road to the formation of our party's strategy — the national democratic road to socialism — was opened by Gramsci. . . . [He] laid the groundwork and began the elaboration of this strategy with the contribution of many other militants . . . with the contribution of Togliatti."[4] According to Bufalini, Gramsci's concept of "proletarian hegemony" (closely tied to the democratic road and to the idea of a pluralistic state) was the real point of departure for the contemporary *via italiana.* Togliatti's refinement of this strategy came in two stages, during 1944–1946 and 1956–1957, each representing a further advance along the path of "progressive democracy."[5]

The theoretical equation of Gramsci and Eurocommunism, as reflected in the work of Carrillo and others, is not limited to PCI interpretations within the Italian context. The positive image of Gramsci also looms large in the Spanish, French, Japanese, and Australian parties, to name only the most prominent. The appearance of Carrillo's *Eurocommunism and the State,* probably more than any other work, served to solidify and legitimate this imputed relationship. Fundamental to Carrillo's understanding of structural reformism is the struggle for democratization of the existing state apparatus — the gradual overturning of capitalist domination through, and not against, bourgeois political structures — made possible by the worsening crisis of ideological hegemony in the West, especially in the Mediterranean. Thus, "The problem which we must tackle is, in substance, the struggle to win positions, dominating as far as possible, for revolutionary ideas in what are today the ideological apparatuses of society, those on which the authority and moral and material force of the capitalist state are based."[6] Carrillo found in the Eurocommunist vision "the idea of a new political formation [which] is linked with that of the hegemony of the bloc of forces and culture in society." The result is a confederation of political parties and social organizations that would carry out the democratic road strategy on a consensual basis.[7]

The tendency to see in Gramsci the main inspiration of Eurocommunist strategy is shared by diverse theorists and observers, from "left" Eurocommunists like Fernando Claudin to Italian writers like Franco Ferrarroti to American commentators like Max Gordon. In Claudin's view, the democratic road flows logically out of the "war of position" strategy, which is grounded in Gramsci's original analysis of the state in European capitalism. He suggested that "from 1934 onwards Togliatti readopted the Gramscian analysis, modified by gradualism and tacticism characteristic of his own vision." This laid the basis for working-class ascent to hegemony within the confines of capitalism and representative democracy.[8] In a similar vein, Ferrarroti commented, "It is no wonder that Gramsci's theories have become so popular with the Eurocommunists. His concept of social hegemony insofar as it is possible to oppose this to Lenin's concept of proletarian dictatorship is an invaluable contribution."[9] Gordon stressed the importance of Gramsci's influence on the PCI's break with "Bolshevik orthodoxy" and the Soviet model of political organization, for what Gramsci bequeathed was a "legacy hostile to the substitution of dogma for analysis of reality in the application of the classics of revolutionary socialism."[10] Here, as elsewhere, the Gramscian connection is presented in quite general and impressionistic terms, embellished with frequent references to concepts like hegemony, bloc, and democracy but lacking any real assessment of the original theory itself.

Gramscian Strategy and the State

Had Gramsci not been such a heroic figure in the development of Italian Communism, it is unlikely that his theoretical legacy would have been so enthusiastically harnessed to the politics of Eurocommunism. For, as I shall emphasize, Gramsci's thought was in fact consistently and even harshly antagonistic to the themes, strategies, and objectives that characterize structural reformism: electoralism, economistic trade unionism, antimonopoly alliances, political evolutionism, internal transformation of the bourgeois state. From the early years (including the *Biennio Rosso,* or "Red Two Years," and council phase) through the formation of the PCI (1921–1926) and to the final period of incarceration and the *Prison Notebooks,* Gramsci, whatever his special emphasis of the moment, insisted that the transition to socialism requires a sweeping overthrow of bourgeois political institutions, meaning a qualitative rupture with the entire capitalist "ensemble of relations" and the construction of a new popular system of authority. Although history might impose changing obstacles and provide new alliance possibilities, necessitating a reformulation of tactics, this strategic objective always remained in focus. For Gramsci, the main task at hand, through phases of both crisis and stability, was development of an autonomous proletarian culture and network of institutions.

In his early writings (from roughly 1915 to 1920), Gramsci has already developed a powerful critique of the way in which electoral-parliamentary activity and trade unionism had come to dominate the politics of the Socialist party, which consequently lost its capacity to carry out anticapitalist struggles. The difficulty was that the party system, unions, and parliament had evolved mainly in the sphere of bourgeois democracy and that, although such structures constituted an arena of limited, tactical mass struggles, they could never become genuinely transformative instruments for advancing revolutionary goals. However "neutral" they might appear, they imposed an instrumentalist logic that functioned to legitimate capitalist interests. From Gramsci's perspective (at that time the left wing of the Socialist party), the abysmal failure of the party and unions was reflected in the (internal) decline of popular commitment and spirit.[11]

Gramsci characterized the pre-1920 Socialist party as an immobile "conglomeration of parties"; incapable of taking political initiative, it shifted its colors in order to satisfy the requirements of vote-getting and institutional bargaining. Never a principled abstentionist, he argued that socialist involvement in electoral politics makes sense only insofar as it forces the bourgeoisie to reveal its "fraudulent commitment to democracy," provokes an authoritarian response, and thereby opens the door to crisis and mass upheaval.[12] The goal is to expose the contradictions of parliament by "stripping the democratic mask away from the ambivalent face of the bourgeois dictatorship and revealing it in all its horrible and repugnant ugliness." Gramsci referred to the "parliamentary circus" — a bogus public sphere that deludes the masses into believing that real change can be achieved only through electoral and reformist action — outside of and against which revolutionary politics must in the final instance be directed.[13]

Likewise, "trade union action, within its own sphere and using its own methods, stands revealed as being utterly incapable of leading the proletariat to its emancipation. . . ."[14] From a standpoint typical of his *Ordine Nuovo* essays, Gramsci argued: "Trade unionism stands revealed as nothing other than a form of capitalist society, not a potential successor to that society. It organizes workers not as producers, but as wage-earners, i.e., as creatures of the capitalist, private property regime, selling their commodity labor." In the end, the unions reproduce narrow self-interest, commodification, and individualism rather than revolutionary solidarity.[15] Moreover, in the case of both parties and trade unions, their increasingly bureaucratic structures produced an alienated politics remote from the everyday life of the masses.

This critique involved not only an attack on the specific Italian institutions and processes that Gramsci closely observed in his own practice, but a more comprehensive rejection of bourgeois democracy as a primary realm of political contestation. These forms were part of the bourgeois totality that had to be transcended. Thus:

> . . . the revolutionary process can only be identified with a spontaneous movement of the working masses brought about by the clash of contradictions inherent in the social system characterized by the regime of capitalist property. Caught in the pincers of capitalist conflicts and threatened by condemnation without appeal to the loss of civil and intellectual rights, the masses break with the forms of bourgeois democracy and leave behind them the legality of the bourgeois constitution.[16]

Gramsci added that the socialist movement is compelled to "ceaselessly spread the conviction that the current problems of industrial and agricultural economy can be resolved only outside parliamant, against parliament, by the workers' state."[17] With each advance of the movement, the old structures lose their credibility (and legitimacy), increasingly taking on the character of "empty shells."

Gramsci contended that a fallacy of all previous Marxist strategies had been "the acceptance of historical reality produced by capitalist initiative," which meant preoccupation with the existing state as something to be either seized or transformed. Hence a new approach to politics and authority was needed: "We are persuaded, after the experience of the Russian, Hungarian, and German revolutions, that the socialist state cannot emerge within the institutions of the capitalist state, but is a fundamentally new creation in relation to them, if not in relation to the history of the proletariat."[18] Not the conquest of power, but a process of revolutionary development rooted in everyday proletarian life and culminating in new forms, was the basic premise of Gramsci's *Ordine Nuovo* theory.

Given the strategic bankruptcy of bourgeois institutions, Gramsci looked for inspiration to the syndicalist tradition. He wrote that ". . . the solution to the pressing problems of the current period can be found only in a strictly proletarian center of power"—namely, the factory councils (which had already appeared in Turin and elsewhere) and popular assemblies, or "soviets," which were expected to mushroom Russian-style as the movement progressed.[19] The councils and soviets, as organs of direct, grassroots democracy, would be the nucleus of an unfolding revolutionary state that, counterposed to the centralized bourgeois state apparatus, could give expression to the historic emancipatory principles of workers' control and self-government. As autonomous structures created by the workers themselves at the point of production, they would broaden the scope of democracy and channel popular revolt against the established political mechanisms.[20] The local organs, moreover, would expand the very definition of the political, creating more space for subjective involvement in the revolutionary process: "The existence of the councils gives the workers direct responsibility for production, leads them to improve their work, institutes a conscious and voluntary discipline, and creates the psychology of the producer, the creator of history."[21]

With the paralysis of the Socialist party in the post–World War I crisis, and following the collapse of the council movement in 1920, Gramsci and the Ordine Nuovo group became leading forces in modeling the new Communist party. The formative politics of the PCI—and of Gramsci as well—was shaped by the Bolshevik Revolution, the Comintern, and by what was understood as Leninism. To a great extent, however, Gramsci stood outside the early centralist and sectarian tendencies of the dominant faction led by Amadeo Bordiga. While agreeing with Bordiga's critique of social democracy (especially on the issues of parliamentarism and economics) and with the concept of a disciplined revolutionary party, Gramsci subscribed to a Leninism that was less vanguardist insofar as it continued to stress the role of "national-popular" formations, such as councils and the newly formed workers' and peasants' committees. And although Gramsci's own strategic approach became more centralist during 1921–1926 than in the preceding years, he remained as uncompromisingly hostile to bourgeois political institutions—and as attached to the idea of a new proletarian state—as ever. Thus, although local democratic structures do not receive as much attention in the PCI writings, the search for a "prefigurative" synthesis of party and councils is still evident. Finally, although the rise of fascism sharply influenced PCI priorities during this period (especially after 1924, when leadership shifted to the Ordine Nuovo faction), Gramsci himself never abandoned the primacy of socialist objectives. What "united front" tactics meant for Gramsci, in contrast to the Popular Front approach later supported by Togliatti, was a process of mass mobilization combining both the antifascist and anticapitalist phases of struggle in one, directed not only against the Mussolini regime but against all forms of bourgeois domination.

The real significance of the early PCI presence in Italian society, as Gramsci saw it, was its embodiment of a clear revolutionary identity. Through the Communist Party the working class was able, for the first time, to break decisively with bourgeois traditions and with the "bureaucratic-parliamentary state"; the PCI opened up the possibility of independent socialist forms within a "new state system."[22] The party's historic goal, even if it was not always effectively pursued in the early years, was to create the basis of socialist democracy out of the ashes of bourgeois democracy, to assist in the "explosion of new democratic institutions that would counterpose themselves to parliament and replace it."[23] Gramsci argued, in a fashion typical of this period, that "it is a necessary precondition for revolution that the complete dissolution of parliamentary democracy should occur in Italy."[24] Breaking with bourgeois traditions also meant a critical (though by no means unambiguous) approach to the unions, which Gramsci viewed as a "source of bourgeois ideology and capitalist discipline." Here he disagreed with the PCI's initial tendency to completely remove itself from trade-union struggles in the name of "purity." Gramsci pushed a strategy of building revolutionary groups within the factories, around the councils and committees, that could split the internal commissions (grievance bodies) away from the union heirarchy and "enlarge the sphere of activity."[25]

From time to time, even with the consolidation of fascist power, Gramsci returned to the earlier themes of workers' control and revolutionary democracy. In an essay on party strategy written in April 1924, Gramsci affirmed the relevance of the Ordine Nuovo experience, despite its failures: Revolution was still on the agenda, no matter how loudly the Socialists called for an essentially defensive posture to combat fascism. The PCI's line was "opposed as much to constitutional opposition as it was to fascism — even if the constitutional opposition upholds a programme of freedom and order which would be preferable to fascism's one of violence and arbitrary power."[26] In Gramsci's estimation, the strength of fascism was illusory; it had created nothing more than a false national integration, leaving the regime vulnerable to new crises and renewed cycles of mass mobilization. Anticipating a massive democratic upsurge against Mussolini's rule, Gramsci hardly considered a scenario based upon long-term political stability. Again, his vision was shaped by the "actuality of the revolution" — perpetual crisis leading to popular insurgency.[27] His injunction to "overthrow not only Mussolini but Turati" (a socialist leader) must be viewed in this context.

In the "Lyons' Theses" — a strategic and programmatic document written for the PCI's Third Congress in January 1926 — Gramsci's main objective was to translate Marxism and Leninism into the language of Italian history and politics. The guiding principle was the broadening or "democratizing" of Leninist strategy to fit the more complex conditions of European capitalism. The revolutionary party was still indispensable, but the actual conquest of power would have to be grounded far more in popular movements and ideological consensus than had been the case in Russia. From this premise, Gramsci argued that an effective Italian politics of socialist transformation would have to move beyond the limits of both ultra-leftist centralism (which placed its hopes in a rapid insurrectionary seizure of power and in rigid organizational formulas) and social-democratic reformism (which looked to nothing more than an internal restructuring of the bourgeois state).[28] While the "Lyons' Theses" is sometimes cited as the PCI's initial departure along the democratic road (possibly because Togliatti had a hand in writing it), such an interpretation rests upon confusion between Gramsci's emphasis on collective participation as an element of socialist democracy and the strategic commitment to bourgeois democratic institutions. On this issue Gramsci did not waver: The fundamental task of the PCI was "to organize and unify the industrial and rural proletariat for the revolution" and to mobilize "all the forces necessary for the victory of the revolution and the foundation of the workers' state," placing "before the proletariat and its allies the problem of insurrection against the bourgeois state. . . ."[29] Even the most partial struggles would have to be linked to socialist objectives; even antifascist maneuvers would be directed toward "new forms of organization."[30]

These themes were carried forward and theoretically elaborated in the *Prison Notebooks*. Removed for the first time from daily political involvement, Gramsci embraced a Marxism in this period that took on a more pronounced Jacobin or Leninist character. Despite his obsession with antifascist struggle (or perhaps because of it), Gramsci devoted even greater attention to the problems of revolutionary identity and political autonomy, of the transformative role of the party, of the directive function of intellectuals. At the same time, he revised his assessment of fascism: Not only was the regime itself more stable than he had predicted, its diffuse reactionary ideology also corresponded to certain widespread elements already present in the Italian mass consciousness. Thus, although Gramsci continued to stress the "actuality of revolution"—the objective conditions for the transition to socialism presumably being just as ripe as ever—he adopted a larger historical perspective. The "forced integration" of fascism made immediate popular insurrection less likely. This produced Gramsci's well-known turn toward the "subjective" dimension in the *Prison Notebooks,* where the concerns of philosophical renewal, mass consciousness, ideological hegemony, and the role of intellectuals gave new depth and complexity to his theory of the party and of the transition.

In his conception of the party as "modern prince," Gramsci looked to Machiavelli and Lenin for inspiration: Both were theorists of the "primacy of politics." Gramsci referred to Machiavelli as the "first Jacobin" who sought to combine the passion of a global, transformative vision (never confined to "effective reality") with the power of political action as the only viable means of constructing a new social order.[31] What Lenin meant was of course less metaphorical and more historically specific—a vanguard party strong and cohesive enough to counter the economism and parochialism of popular struggles, to attack the very logic of bourgeois politics. The Leninist party was designed to restore socialist identity through organizational unity and discipline; build a cadre network for mobilizing the masses; seize power and establish a new revolutionary state—the dictatorship of the proletariat; and provide leadership for carrying out postrevolutionary construction. To the extent that this was one of Gramsci's fundamental premises in the *Prison Notebooks,* it reflected an implicit critique (though by no means a total rejection) of the council period. Gramsci now concluded that an external mediating force (politics) would be necessary to raise social struggles to the level of systemic contestation, rendering total and qualitative the discrete movements of revolt and transforming partial demands into revolutionary ones that could challenge the basis of class society. Lenin's attack on economism was therefore correct, as "here we are dealing with a subaltern group which is prevented by this theory from ever becoming dominant, or from developing beyond the economic-corporate stage and rising to the phase of ethical-political hegemony in civil society, and domination of the state."[32]

It was his concept of hegemony, at the same time, that enabled Gramsci to advance beyond Lenin's one-sided vanguardism. This was the vital source of Gramsci's dual perspective (the *doppia prospettiva*), which restored the dialectic to the equations politics/civil society, organization/ideology, and force/consent and which laid the foundations of his strategic contrast between the "conjunctural" and "organic" elements of the transition. This dualism, in turn, corresponded to his famous categories "war of movement" and "war of position," which are roughly equivalent to the phases of insurrection and the struggle for ideological hegemony. From Gramsci's viewpoint, therefore, the success of popular movements would depend on the extent to which they become "counterhegemonic". They would have to undermine bourgeois domination throughout civil society—in social and authority relations, production and work, culture and education—before effective "frontal assaults" on state power could be mounted. The breaking down of old institutions was seen by Gramsci as a single phase in the long-term modification of social forces that occurs "beneath the surface" of formal laws and institutions.[33] Counterhegemonic politics would thus be conducted primarily outside the bourgeois political sphere by means of mobilizing a social bloc or "revolutionary historical bloc" against the existing state apparatus.

Gramsci understood "bloc" to be a historical synthesis of popular movements, defined by their sense of common political motion rather than by sociological categories. The "bloc" concept suggested the building of broad social alliances that transcend a narrow class basis and coalesce around an immediate psychological stimulus—for example, around nationalism, economic crisis, anticlericalism, or regionalism. Such appeals, though often not explicitly socialist, can serve as radicalizing catalysts at certain historical junctures, linking up diverse strata within a counterhegemonic movement. Gramsci's concept of bloc thus signified more than party alliances, elite coalitions, or loose configurations of political groups established for the purpose of winning new positions within the bourgeois state. On the contrary, it was viewed as reflecting a process of mass mobilization compatible with Gramsci's overall strategic aim of developing a new "ensemble of relations."

Gramsci's *doppia prospettiva* projected a strategy for overcoming the bureaucratic-centralist impediments of Leninism. Whereas the Leninist preoccupation with "conjunctural" politics, or "war of movement," may have fit the Russian context where "the state was everything and civil society nothing," a new strategy was required in the West to take account of the great "ideological entrenchment" of the bourgeoisie, within a "civil society [that] has become a very complex structure and one which is resistant to the catastrophic incursions of the immediate economic element."[34] Presumably, therefore, Gramsci's "war of position" was designed to take into account the expanding role of ideological and cultural forces in advanced capitalism. In contrast with Lenin's relatively uncritical acceptance of modernizing goals for Russia, moreover, Gramsci's approach retreated from the tempting fetishism of science and technology, which he predicted would have a strong depoliticizing impact.[35]

Insofar as the "Jacobinism" of the prison writings incorporated Gramsci's earlier commitment to popular struggles and workers' control, he ended up—in whatever haphazard fashion—with a more dialectical concept of the transition than Lenin, one rooted in a complex, organic relationship between the "global" and local element, between party and councils, between the process of destroying the old state and that of generating a new one in its place. Gramsci not only shared Lenin's insistence upon a total break with bourgeois institutions. His dualistic model went much further than the statist premises of Bolshevik strategy, by linking politics with daily life, the struggle for social and cultural renewal, and, above all, the task of creating a democratic socialist state.[36]

Enter Togliatti

Although any effort to pinpoint the theoretical and strategic origins of Eurocommunism is bound to be rather arbitrary, a good case can be made for the period beginning in the mid-1930s. For it was at this time that the PCI, under Comintern guidance and the leadership of Togliatti, first took up Popular Front tactics. Indeed it was Togliatti who, along with Dimitrov, helped author this policy at the Seventh Comintern Congress in 1935. In a complete turnaround from the "left" confrontational politics of the "third period," the frontist approach looked to a broad alliance of antifascist forces, with the Communist parties tactically committed to electoral-parliamentary activity, as a means of defending liberal democracy and bolstering the international role of the Soviet Union at a time when Mussolini and Hitler had already consolidated power. "Frontism" thus came to be identified with the defensive struggle against reaction, not a revolutionary struggle against capitalism and for socialism. Throughout the late 1930s, Togliatti (exiled in Moscow) strongly endorsed frontist politics in a series of articles published in the party journal *Stato Operaio;* and with the PCI leadership either underground or in exile, the party seemed prepared to accept the Comintern-Togliatti line.[37] In July 1941, the PCI proclaimed that its objectives were to overthrow the fascist regime, reestablish constitutional freedoms, form a popular government, and arrest the fascist heirarchs. This reflected a dramatic shift from the PCI's Fourth Congress at Düsseldorf in 1930, at which Togliatti had called for an insurrection of the Italian people against fascism, the destruction of fascism *and* capitalism by insurrectionary methods, and the establishment of soviets and a dictatorship of the proletariat.[38]

An important Comintern figure for eighteen years, Togliatti internalized the outlook of the Soviet leadership—its perception of world politics, its sense of priorities, its strategic and tactical orientation. His attachment to the CPSU was unqualified. Togliatti's influence encouraged the development among PCI leaders of frontist attitudes that carried over into the Resistance and postwar years. Hence the real consequences of the Popular Front would not be felt until the mid-1940s and later, when short-range tactics (for the overthrow of fascism) were transformed into an institutionalized long-term strategy that became known as the democratic (or "peaceful") road to socialism. By 1944–1945, the war and the partisan mobilization appeared to have generated new revolutionary opportunities: The power structure was in shambles, councils and other local organs had spread throughout northern and central Italy, and the PCI had grown rapidly into a thriving "national-popular" party. But such opportunities were never actually pursued. Togliatti, on his return from Moscow in 1944, steered the party toward a frontist and defensive "new course" strategy. The PCI spurned insurrection, turned away from local democratic forms, induced the partisans to surrender their arms, and moved toward collaboration with bourgeois parties around the immediate goals of "reconstruction," enacting a Republican constitution, and building a government of "national unity." The PCI entered every Italian cabinet between April 1944 and May 1947, hoping to institutionally solidify its attempt to create a popular antifascist coalition.

The PCI's close relationship with the Soviet Union during those years was reinforced by the Soviet role in defeating Germany and by the common struggle against fascism. Yet Stalin's aims were far removed from those of "proletarian internationalism"; they were primarily to secure a sphere of control in Eastern Europe and to maintain global stability so that the USSR could rebuild its own society. A revolution in Italy (or elsewhere in Europe) would disrupt these prospects by forcing a Soviet conflict with the Allies. Hence a frontist policy that defined fascism rather than capitalism as the target of struggle and emphasized moderate, electoral tactics was functional for Soviet interests but devastating for socialist movements in Western Europe. It may well be that such tactics also corresponded perfectly to the Soviet premise of "capitalist stabilization" and the decline of the proletariat as a revolutionary agency in the advanced capitalist countries.[39] Whatever the case, the PCI (and the USSR) did operate as an instrument of postwar stabilization.

Togliatti's genius—in terms of both his party leadership and theoretical guidance—lay in his shrewd application of Resistance themes and Gramscian concepts, within a frontist orientation, to the challenges and pressures of the postwar situation. For example, Togliatti quickly appropriated Gramsci's ideas of national-popular struggle, social bloc, and ideological hegemony, but translated them into a framework of electoral mobilization, elite alliances, and structural reform of the bourgeois state. The Gramscian vision of a revolutionary transformation aimed at subverting the totality of bourgeois society was jettisoned. The "party of a new type" envisaged by Togliatti was a mass-based national formation, but one that would help create an "expanded democracy" within the political institutions of the reborn Italian Republic. Togliatti's famous editorials in *Rinascita* during the late 1940s and early 1950s ceaselessly hammered away at this departure from pre-1935 PCI strategy, all the while legitimating it through explicitly Gramscian (and even Leninist) imagery. Of course the Comintern's Popular Front politics originated as a strictly tactical maneuver, and this was surely the definition given to it by the PCI during and immediately after the Resistance. In retrospect, however, frontism can be understood as the genesis of the *via italiana,* as an institutionalized tactics that evolved into the contemporary structural reformist strategy.

Only after 1956, however, with the Soviet de-Stalinization campaign and Togliatti's affirmation of a polycentric world Communism, could the PCI launch the *via italiana* in earnest. Togliatti now began to spell out theoretically the premises of a strategy charted within and through the bourgeois democratic state. Instead of being overthrown from below and replaced by a new proletarian state, the power apparatus would be internally democratized as part of a lengthy transitional process. This perspective dismissed the traditional Marxist and Leninist warning against utilizing the bourgeois state as the primary mechanism for advancing socialism. Togliatti noted the "complexity" and the increasingly popular character of modern parliamentary systems and concluded that the state could be transformed from an instrument of capitalist domination into a sphere of open competition within which a working-class (and socialist) presence could be extended. In PCI parlance, the idea of a "secular, nonideological" state would supplant the outmoded Marxist concept of an "instrumental" state.[40] Thus, with each new social reform, with each new institutional position conquered, the PCI, in alliance with other "democratic" antimonopoly forces, could set in motion a shift of power away from the large corporations and favoring the working class. It could, in the language of Gramscian strategy, hope to achieve hegemony within a reconstituted state that was no longer controlled by a single monolithic ruling class. As the boundary separating state and civil society in "neocapitalism" was relatively more diffuse than that in early capitalism, bourgeois political institutions were seen as more vulnerable to incursions of all sorts.[41]

These were the strategic assumptions, linked to an evolutionary, peaceful, and more or less stable transition, that paved the way to the Eurocommunism of Berlinguer, Carrillo, and Marchais a decade after Togliatti's death. While introducing no real theoretical originality, Eurocommunism, like the *via italiana* that preceeded it, does carry forward a refinement of traditional social-democratic and frontist currents. It reflects therefore not the extension of Gramsci's theory—for Gramsci the democratic road was nothing but a massive deception—but its misappropriation for clearly nonrevolutionary objectives. The reintroduction of Gramscian concepts barely conceals an underlying strategic content that actually recalls Bernstein rather than Gramsci, as I argued in Chapter 5. For the PCI, the theoretical and historical determinants of the present strategy go back to 1944, or even to 1935, but certainly no earlier.[42]

Structural Reformism or Socialism?

We thus arrive at a Eurocommunist construction of a semiofficial and instrumentalized Gramsci that, though appealing to contemporary proponents of the democratic road, bears little resemblance to Gramsci's original theory. Basic Gramscian concepts — war of position, ideological hegemony, social bloc, democratization — have been systematically misused by Eurocommunist strategists, beginning with Togliatti. Ideas have been translated into a political framework that has emptied them of their earlier meaning. Although this phenomenon is hardly new within the Marxist tradition, what makes the attempt to legitimate structural reformism through Gramscian symbols different is the extent to which it has been successful. After all, the language appears to be the same, and Gramsci was one of the founders (and martyrs) of Italian Communism. And of course Gramsci did articulate philosophical and cultural themes that have deep roots in Italian (and Western European) history[43] — themes that modern Communist parties are anxious to co-opt.

The PCI's fetishism of the "war of position" schema perhaps best demonstrates this misappropriation of Gramsci's theory. For Gramsci, as we have seen, the war of position was only one side of a complex dualistic strategy that also incorporated the war of maneuver. Whereas the former applied to the "organic" phase of ideological-cultural transformations within civil society, the latter involved the "conjunctural" dimension of a political-military struggle for institutional power. Gramsci's *doppia prospettiva* thus assimilates both the consensual and the coercive element of the transitional process:[44] the reconstitution of everyday life (including mass consciousness, social and authority relations, culture) and the overturning of bourgeois institutions within a context of crisis, class polarization, and popular upheavals. The Eurocommunists have completely jettisoned this second dimension — the war of maneuver — and have thereby abandoned the very possibility of rupture, or revolutionary break, that has always been central to Marxism.[45] If democratic road theorists allow for economic crisis, they do not expect it to lead to intensified class struggle and popular mobilization; and if they envisage a legitimation crisis, they do not see it as explosive enough to challenge the structural basis of the bourgeois state. As Henri Weber has suggested, the Eurocommunists have in effect denied that a revolutionary situation can occur in late capitalism.[46]

Beyond this, the war of position itself has been radically reconceptualized within Eurocommunism. Instead of broadening the terrain of contestation to encompass new spheres of social life within civil society, it has effectively narrowed conflict to the bourgeois political-institutional realm, in ways that I described in Chapter 4. The PCI, for example, has pursued the *via italiana* with the aim of broadening its parliamentary room to maneuver and (especially during the years of the historic compromise) with hopes of gaining a share of national governmental power. It has, in other words, sought to consolidate positions of strength within political structures that have at best a peripheral connection with the social struggles at the workplace or in the community. From Togliatti to Berlinguer, the PCI has accentuated the political over the social, efforts to penetrate and colonize the bourgeois state over attempts to establish a new kind of grassroots presence.[47] And this strategy, owing to the great electoral advances it produced, has achieved considerable success on its own terms. At the same time, however, the *via italiana* has failed to present an alternative beyond a rationalized state capitalism and has even stood as an obstacle to the development of the popular movements that have emerged in Italy since the mid-1960s. The contrast with Gramsci's vision of a counterhegemonic movement rooted in civil society could hardly be more striking.[48]

Gramsci's concepts of hegemony and social bloc have met the same fate. In its earlier Gramscian usage, hegemony referred to the ideological and cultural side of bourgeois domination, to the complex relationship between state and civil society that was long a crystallized feature of the advanced countries. As the cornerstone of Gramsci's Marxism, it corresponded not only to the consensual dimension of ruling-class power but (conversely) to an emergent proletarian-socialist "integrated culture" that would subvert such power—in other words, to the war of position. Breaking with the narrow instrumentalism of orthodox Marxism, Gramsci introduced the concept of hegemony not only to broaden the analysis of the state but to completely redefine the very meaning of socialist transformation: To be a viable revolutionary force, the new social bloc would have to elaborate its own insurgent world-view and build the nucleus of a new system of lived social relations. This is the essence of a counterhegemonic movement. Again, it is this emphasis on qualitative change that is strikingly missing from contemporary Eurocommunism. As we have seen, the struggle to transform civil society—embodied today in nascent popular movements around workers' control, community self-government, feminism and environmental and youth issues—has been repressed, deflected, and co-opted by parties like the PCI. Hegemony is thereby reduced to a rationale for a noncoercive, parliament-centered politics (compatible with the "peaceful transition"), to a minimalist strategy oriented toward winning positions of institutional strength within the structure of bourgeois democracy. Its dialectical content disappears from sight. The Eurocommunists thus wind up reversing the primacy of civil society over the state that was the centerpiece of Gramsci's theory.[49]

Similarly, the notion of social bloc was grounded in the possibility of an emergent counterhegemonic formation—a unique configuration of social forces that achieves its initial political expression within civil society at the grassroots level. In part this coincides with Gramsci's vision of a distinctly national (or national-popular) movement shaped by particular traditions and extending beyond a homogeneous proletarian base. The continuity from Gramsci to Eurocommunism on this point seems rather obvious until we consider the second premise. Social bloc from Gramsci's viewpoint was always tied to the idea (following Sorel) of an organic, ideologically cohesive insurgency from below rather than to that of institutionally based coalitions or alliances. Indeed, Gramsci no doubt formulated the concept of social bloc with precisely this distinction in mind, insofar as alliances were associated with partial, reformist movements that never posed the question of hegemony.[50] Togliatti's version of bloc, however, grew mainly out of his Popular Front experience. In the postwar years it evolved into an alliance strategy tied to electoral-parliamentary politics, party coalitions, and an antimonopoly constellation of forces that sought to incorporate sectors of the bourgeoisie itself. Thus, instead of a unified revolutionary subject we arrive at an atomized, fragmented conglomeration of voters. It is this mechanistic conception of social bloc that Eurocommunism has inherited.

Finally, we return to the Eurocommunists' leading claim that through the legacy of Gramsci (among others) they have been able to initiate the first truly democratic path to socialism—or at least that path which is most appropriate to the conditions of advanced capitalism. The reality, however, is that the Gramscian and structural reformist approaches to democratization have little in common. For Gramsci, whatever his ambiguities on the theory of the state, democracy always meant proletarian or socialist democracy built around popular struggles for workers' control and direct self-government. It necessitated a break with the bourgeois state, and with the distortions and mystifications of representative democracy intrinsic to parliament, culminating in the development of local forms that could give expression to a qualitatively new politics and structure of authority. Hence pluralism for Gramsci took on an entirely new connotation: It applied not to multiparty and interest-group competition limited to the bourgeois public sphere, but to an organic diversity expressed through popular forms and movements. Already in the 1920s, Gramsci had assumed that parliaments would soon become outmoded with advancing monopoly capitalism, enfeebled by the encroachments of mammoth corporations and the state bureaucracy.

The Eurocommunist project of democratization, with its origins in Togliatti's theory of structural reforms, seeks to extend and perfect bourgeois democracy along the lines elaborated in Chapters 2 and 3. In Bernsteinian fashion, it assumes that by winning economic and social reforms—in the process bringing previously disenfranchised strata into the parliamentary arena—socialist parties can gradually whittle away at the inequalities of power and privilege while expanding the terrain of democratic participation. This social-democratic schema has produced certain successes in the past, but its future outlook, depending as it does on a phase of prolonged stability, is rather dismal. A further problem is that whatever objectives it manages to achieve on its own terms, structural reformism is still confined to the boundaries of bourgeois democracy. Having rejected the Soviet (and Leninist) model, it has failed to articulate a concept of socialist democracy appropriate to new collective modes of political opposition. In avoiding the problem of how to generate new centers of political life, of how to create a nonbureaucratic relationship between socialist organization and mass activity, Eurocommunism has in the end ignored the real corporate and bureaucratic obstacles to democratization, with the fatal consequences that I analyzed in Chapter 4.[51]

If Eurocommunism has opened the door to an innovative Marxist strategy that invokes the mystique and political language of Gramsci, it owes very little to the living historical Gramsci. By the late 1970s, Eurocommunist theorists had come to the point of explicitly and emphatically denying the "actuality of revolution." Thus Jean Elleinstein, a PCF theorist, has argued that Bernstein's premise of an infinitely flexible capitalism was essentially correct after all. Eurocommunism abandons the very possibility of workers' control, social struggle, and popular revolt because it sees these dimensions of social transformation as dangerously "utopian" and "adventurist." It still formally clings to anticapitalist, egalitarian programs, but claims to such programs appear more and more remote insofar as they are detached from the strategies, methods, and vision necessary to achieve them. This divorce of goals from strategy inherent in a linear evolutionism that centers the transition within the bourgeois political system was the essence of traditional social democracy—and a major source of its ultimate impasse. Not Gramsci, then, but Bernstein emerges as the first creative theoretical genius behind the Eurocommunist dream of a democratic road to socialism.

Notes

Chapter One

1. Pete Hamill, "A New Communism Haunts the Kremlin," *Village Voice,* March 29, 1976.

2. The terms *parliamentary democracy* and *bourgeois democracy* will be used interchangeably throughout this volume; they correspond to the particular institutions, norms, and practices typical of the forms of representation, party systems, and electoral processes in most advanced capitalist countries today. In contrast, *socialist democracy* refers to a more comprehensively democratized system in which networks of popular control develop outside of, and in congruence with, parliamentary structures, reaching into every sphere of civil society and allowing for the relative autonomy of local movements.

3. Those few studies that have analyzed classical Marxist movements and parties from the viewpoint of democracy were, significantly, written mostly by non-Marxists. These include Robert Michels, *Political Parties* (New York: Collier, 1962); Peter Gay, *The Dilemma of Democratic Socialism* (New York: Schocken Books, 1961); and Guenther Roth, *The Social Democrats in Imperial Germany* (Totowa, N.J.: Bedminster Press, 1963). One important Marxist exception is Arthur Rosenberg's classic *Socialism and Democracy* (Boston: Beacon Press, 1965).

Only since the mid-1970s has there been an explosion of Marxist literature on the relationship between democracy and revolutionary strategy, much of it inspired by the rise of Eurocommunism. See, for example, Fernando Claudin, *Eurocommunism and Socialism* (London: New Left Books, 1978); Santiago Carrillo, *Eurocommunism and the State* (London: Lawrence and Wishart, 1977); Nicos Poulantzas, *State, Power, Socialism* (London: New Left Books, 1979); Ralph Miliband, *Marxism and Politics* (London: Oxford University Press, 1977); Goran Therborn, *What Does the Ruling Class Do When It Rules?* (London: New Left Books, 1978); Erik Olin Wright, *Class, Crisis, and the State* (London: New Left Books, 1979); Geoff Hodgson, *Socialism and Parliamentary Democracy* (London: Spokesman, 1977); and the various contributors to *Il marxismo e lo stato* [Marxism and the state] (Roma: Mondoperaio, 1976).

4. On the underdeveloped nature of political theory within Marxism, see Miliband, *Marxism and Politics,* Ch. 1; Perry Anderson, *Considerations on Western*

Marxism (London: New Left Books, 1976), p. 103; "Interview with Lucio Colletti," *New Left Review,* no. 86 (July-August 1974), pp. 13-29; Henri Weber, "Eurocommunism, Socialism and Democracy," *New Left Review,* no. 110 (July-August 1978), pp. 3-14; and Carl Boggs, "Revolutionary Process, Political Strategy, and the Dilemma of Political Power," *Theory and Society,* Vol. 4, no. 3 (Fall 1977), pp. 359-393.

5. See Miliband, *Marxism and Politics,* p. 7.

6. Stephen Bronner, "The Socialist Project: In Memory of Rudi Dutschke," *Social Research,* Vol. 47, no. 1 (1980), p. 11.

7. On this point see Anderson, *Considerations on Western Marxism,* Ch. 5.

8. Indeed, fragments of at least three distinct political strategies can be detected in the writings of Marx and Engels—although none is integrated into any refined theory of the state. Stanley Moore, in *Three Tactics: The Background in Marx* (New York: Monthly Review Press, 1961), distinguished between "reformism" (Bernstein), "majority revolution" (Kautsky), and "minority revolution" (Lenin).

9. See the excellent treatment of this point by Massimo Salvadori, *Karl Kautsky and the Socialist Revolution, 1880-1938* (New York: Schocken Books, 1979), introduction.

10. Ibid., p. 140. Although Kautsky understood this process as one rooted in the dialectic of wage labor versus capital, he did argue for temporary alliances with progressive nonproletarian forces and parties in the struggle against Wilhelminian state domination. See Ibid., pp. 150-152, and Gary P. Steenson, *Karl Kautsky, 1854-1938: Marxism in the Classical Years* (Pittsburgh: University of Pittsburgh Press, 1978), pp. 112-114.

11. A good overall view of Kautsky's strategy, which demonstrates the absence of any cataclysmic crisis theory, is presented in Salvadori, *Karl Kautsky and the Socialist Revolution,* pp. 59-73.

12. Here the objectivism of Kautsky's Marxism is most apparent: Capitalist development bears the seeds of its own transcendence. On Kautsky's faith in science and "historical necessity," see ibid., p. 33.

13. Kautsky's *Dictatorship of the Proletariat* (Ann Arbor: University of Michigan Press, 1961), written to show the necessary connection between socialism and democracy, clearly reveals this bias.

14. See Salvadori, *Karl Kautsky and the Socialist Revolution,* p. 14.

15. Eduard Bernstein, *Evolutionary Socialism* (New York: Schocken Books, 1961), pp. 154, 163.

16. Lucio Colletti, in *From Rousseau to Lenin* (London: New Left Books, 1969), p. 54, makes this point very effectively.

17. For an extensive discussion of Bernstein's theory of the state, see Gay, *Dilemma of Democratic Socialism,* Chs. 8 and 12.

18. John H. Kautsky, "Karl Kautsky and Eurocommunism," *Studies in Comparative Communism,* Vol. 14, no. 1 (spring 1981), pp. 13-14. This abandonment of the last vestiges of Marxist "orthodoxy" (the dialectic, crisis theory, the notion of rupture) on the part of Karl Kautsky and others needs to be seen as part of the general rightward trend in European social democracy during the 1920s.

Hence John Kautsky's explanation of this shift, which focuses on the comparatively more democratic character of the Weimar state, needs to be supplemented by looking at the reaction of the Second International to the events in Russia and to the Comintern's role in European politics.

19. V. I. Lenin, "State and Revolution," in James E. Connor, ed., *Lenin on Politics and Revolution* (Indianapolis: Pegasus, 1968), p. 186. Addressing the Kautskyist and Menshevik concept of the state, Lenin went on to add: "In the opinion of the petty-bourgeois politicians, however, order means the reconciliation of classes, and not the oppression of one class by another; to alleviate the conflict means reconciling classes and depriving the oppressed classes of definite means and methods of struggle to overthrow the oppressors." Ibid., p. 186.

20. For a lengthy discussion of Lenin's fascination with bourgeois technique (including Taylorism), see Fred and Lou Jean Fleron, "Administrative Theory as Repressive Political Theory: The Communist Experience," *Telos,* no. 12 (Summer 1972), pp. 63-92.

21. This argument is further developed in Boggs, "Revolutionary Process, Political Strategy, and the Dilemma of Political Power," pp. 364-371. See also Robert V. Daniels, *The Conscience of the Revolution* (New York: Simon & Schuster, 1960), Chs. 3-6.

22. Wright, *Class, Crisis, and the State,* pp. 194-204, also argues that Lenin — whatever his democratic vision — failed to confront the problem of organizational accountability, so consumed was he with the *class* basis of the state.

23. Like both Kautsky and Bernstein, Lenin saw the transition to socialism as a process anchored in large-scale organization. Even in *State and Revolution* he argued that popular control was no longer possible under conditions of production in advanced industrial society, that "complex technical units," such as factories, railways, and banks, could not operate without "ordered cooperation" and subordination (p. 212).

24. Rosa Luxemburg, "Organizational Questions of Russian Social Democracy," in Dick Howard, ed., *Selected Political Writings of Rosa Luxemburg* (New York: Monthly Review Press, 1971), pp. 283-306.

25. Rosa Luxemburg, "Social Reform or Revolution," in Howard, *Selected Political Writings of Rosa Luxemburg,* pp. 113-123. On Luxemburg's approach to parliamentarism and the bourgeois state, see Gay, *Dilemma of Democratic Socialism,* pp. 261-272; J. P. Nettle, *Rosa Luxemburg* (London: Oxford University Press, 1969), Ch. 6; and Andrew Arato, "The Second International: A Reexamination," *Telos,* no. 18 (Winter 1973-1974), pp. 2-52.

26. Luxemburg, "Organizational Questions of Russian Social Democracy."

27. Anton Pannekoek, "German Social Democracy," in Serge Bricianer, *Pannekoek and the Workers' Councils* (St. Louis: Telos Press, 1978), p. 57.

28. Pannekoek argued, along the lines of Michels, that social democracy

takes the form of a gigantic and powerful organization, almost a state within a state, with its own officials, finances, press, spiritual universe, and specific ideology (Marxism). By its general character, it is adapted to the pre-imperialist peaceful phase. The thousands of officials, secretaries, agitators, parliamentarians, theoreticians, and publicists — who already form a distinct caste, a group with very distinct interests — rule the organization on both the material and spiritual levels; and express its general character. . . . Their tranquil work, in conferences and committees, in offices and editorial rooms, is threatened by the storms of the imperialist era.

Anton Pannekoek, "The World War and the Workers' Movement," in Bricianer, *Pannekoek and the Workers' Councils,* p. 140.

29. Pannekoek, "German Social Democracy," pp. 61, 65–67.

30. Pannekoek, "The World War and the Workers' Movement," p. 140.

31. Pannekoek, "Tactical Differences within the Workers' Movement," in Bricianer, *Pannekoek and the Workers' Councils,* pp. 96–97. It should be noted that Pannekoek's tactical approach to parliamentary struggles was more complex. He argued that although it could never be the "locus of class war itself," electoral politics could enlighten the workers about their class situation and therefore should not be rejected outright by revolutionaries. The simplistic picture of council communism as "abstentionist" — a stereotype long cherished by Leninists and social democrats alike — is totally fallacious.

32. Anton Pannekoek, "World Revolution and Communist Tactics," in D. A. Smart, *Pannekoek and Gorter's Marxism* (London: Pluto Press, 1978), p. 116.

33. Anton Pannekoek, "Principles of Organization," in Bricianer, *Pannekoek and the Workers' Council,* p. 276.

34. This is the central theme of several essays, written at various points in Pannekoek's life, assembled in the volume *Lenin as Philosopher* (London: Merlin Press, 1975).

35. For an analysis of the political failures of traditional council movements (in Russia and Italy as well as Germany), see Carl Boggs, "Marxism, Prefigurative Communism, and the Problem of Workers' Control," *Radical America,* Vol. 11, no. 6 (November 1977), and Vol. 12, no. 1 (February 1978).

36. This denial of politics by the council theorists extended beyond their critique of parliamentarism to a rejection of the party form as such. This was the substance of Lenin's attack on "Horner" (Pannekoek) and other radical leftists in *Left-Wing Communism* (New York: International Publishers, 1940): "What the opposition has come to is the repudiation of the party principle and of party discipline. And this is tantamount to completely disarming the proletariat for the benefit of the bourgeoisie" (p. 28).

37. This is one of Colletti's main critiques of Bernstein's theory. See *From Rousseau to Lenin,* p. 106.

38. For an analysis of this phenomenon in Soviet-type systems, see Rudolf Bahro, *The Alternative in Eastern Europe* (London: New Left Books, 1978), pp. 30–37.

39. Richard Gombin, *The Radical Tradition* (London: Methuen, 1978), Ch. 2. Similar arguments are presented by Alvin W. Gouldner in "Prologue to a Theory of Revolutionary Intellectuals," *Telos,* no. 26 (Winter 1975-1976), pp. 3–36.

40. It is doubly ironic that the first concrete expression of this new tendency

came in Chile, where the Unidad Popular coalition (Communists and Socialists) held constitutional power from 1970 to 1973. Not only was this "Eurocommunism" distinctly non-European, it also met with tragic failure.

41. Although it might be proper to speak of Eurocommunism as a Mediterranean phenomenon, rooted primarily in the experience of the Spanish, French, and Italian Communist parties, the theoretical aspects of the transition to socialism raised in this volume have general implications that already extend to the evolution of other parties—for example, the Finnish, Japanese, and Australian.

42. A good case can be made for the thesis that the European Communist parties, with only brief exceptions (e.g., during the Resistance struggles of the 1940s), were never really Leninist apart from their ideological pronouncements. The very idea of an insurrectionary, vanguardist seizure of power in the advanced capitalist countries does not seem to have been taken seriously by any of the parties, especially in the postwar period.

43. This point needs to be qualified. In fact, of the Eurocommunist parties only the PCE has managed to establish a positive (if nonetheless tense) relationship with the emergent popular movements in Spain. See Temma Kaplan, "Democracy and the Mass Politics of the PCE," in Carl Boggs and David Plotke, eds., *The Politics of Eurocommunism* (Boston: South End Press, 1980), pp. 103–129.

44. The "participatory" sphere of state activity includes parliament, elections, the party system, local representative assemblies, and various aspects of interest-group (e.g., trade-union) politics; the "administrative" sphere refers to the national and local public bureaucracies, the military, the police, and court systems.

Chapter Two

1. This declaration appeared in *l'Unita,* March 4, 1977, and was reprinted in *Italian Communists,* no. 1 (January-March 1977), pp. 123–124.

2. For a good summation of this process, see Neil McInnes, *The Communist Parties of Western Europe* (London: Oxford University Press, 1975), Ch. 4.

3. See George Ross, "The PCF and the End of the Bolshevik Dream," in Boggs and Plotke, *Politics of Eurocommunism,* pp. 26–33.

4. Lucio Magri, "Italian Communism in the Sixties," *New Left Review,* no. 66 (March-April 1971), pp. 40–42.

5. In the 1975 local elections for regional, provincial, and municipal offices, the PCI received 32.4 percent of the vote—an impressive gain over the 27.5 percent won in 1972. More strikingly, it polled 34.4 percent of the vote in the 1976 national election, an unprecedented increase of 7.2 percent over 1972. Since 1976, however, the PCI's electoral status has declined. Its share of the vote in the 1979 national election was reduced to 30.7 percent. Still, it remains the most electorally successful Communist party in the world. For a breakdown and analysis of the PCI's postwar electoral growth, see Giacomo Sani, "Italy: The Changing Role of the PCI," in David E. Albright, ed., *Communism and Political Systems in Western Europe* (Boulder, Colo.: Westview Press, 1979), pp. 44–51.

6. See, for example, *Dialogue on Spain* (London: Lawrence and Wishart, 1976), based on interviews by Regis Debray and Max Gallo, and *Eurocommunism and the State* (London: Lawrence & Wishart, 1977).

7. *Dialogue on Spain,* p. 15.

8. The first major Soviet outburst was directed against Carrillo's *Eurocommunism and the State,* in the Moscow periodical *New Times* (July 1977), which accused the PCE leader of betraying "proletarian internationalism" and "denigrating real socialism" in those countries that have succeeded in creating a new society. For an account of this, see Ernest Mandel, *From Stalinism to Eurocommunism* (London: New Left Books, 1978), Ch. 6.

9. See Mandel, *From Stalinism to Eurocommunism,* Ch. 3. For a discussion of events and perspectives leading up to this conference, see Robert Levgold, "The Soviet Union and Western European Communism," in Rudolf L. Tökes, *Eurocommunism and Detente* (New York: New York University Press, 1978).

10. Togliatti's strategically most important essays of this period have been assembled by Luciano Gruppi in the volume *Il compromesso storico* [The historic compromise] (Roma: Editori Riuniti, 1977).

11. On the frontist origins of postwar PCI strategy, see Giuseppe Mammarella, *Il partito comunista italiano* [The Italian Communist party] (Florence: Vallecchi, 1976); Magri, "Italian Communism in the Sixties"; and Alastair Davidson, "The Italian Communist Party and Elections," in Louis Maisel, ed., *Changing Campaign Techniques: Elections and Values in Contemporary Democracies* (London: Sage Publications, 1976).

12. The first openly critical discussions of Leninism within the PCI date back to 1956, following the CPSU's Twentieth Congress. See Valentino Gerratana, "La teoria marxista dello stato a la via italiano al socialismo" [The Marxist theory of the state and the Italian road to socialism], *Rinascita,* August-September 1956. Gerratana argued that, under conditions of neocapitalism (given the "complexity" of political structures that did not exist in Russia), the classical Leninist thesis that the bourgeois state is dominated through coercion by a single class was no longer valid. For Italy, therefore, the concept of the dictatorship of the proletariat was an abstraction that could never guide an effective political strategy.

13. Two of the best examples of Togliatti's thinking during this period are "A proposito di socialismo e democrazia" [On the question of socialism and democracy], *Rinascita,* April 1961; and "La svolta a sinistra" [The turn to the left], from the proceedings of the 10th Congress, December 1962, in Palmiro Togliatti, *La via italiana al socialismo* [The Italian road to socialism] (Roma: Editori Riuniti, 1964).

14. This was the message of Togliatti's Yalta Memorandum (or "testament"), written in the Soviet Union just before he died. See "Promemoria sulle questione del movimento operaio internazionale e della sua unita" [Memorandum on the questions of the international workers' movement and its unity], *L'Unita,* September 4, 1964.

15. The PCI's appropriation, and distortion, of Gramsci's thought will be discussed at length in the epilogue.

16. The discussions that led to the PCI's incorporation of "Gramscian"

strategy crystallized at the Tenth Congress in 1962. See "Report on the Debate of the Central Committee of the Italian Communist Party on the Twenty-Second Congress of the CPSU," *New Left Review,* nos. 13-14 (April-June 1962).

17. This was the essence of Berlinguer's three important *Rinascita* articles that appeared in the fall of 1973. These are reprinted along with a collection of other speeches and documents in Antonio Tato, *La "questione comunista"* [The "Communist question"] (Roma: Editori Riuniti, 1975), vol. 2.

18. Enrico Berlinguer, "Report to the 15th National Congress of the PCI," *The Italian Communists,* no. 1 (January-June 1979), p. 8.

19. This post-Thirteenth Congress theoretical gestation took place mainly in the pages of *Rinascita,* where party leaders contributed to a long series of articles, many of which were assembled by various authors and published as anthologies. The most comprehensive of these volumes (which also includes some earlier material) is Gruppi's *Il compromesso storico.* Others include Tato's *La "questione comunista,"* Gruppi's *Togliatti e la via italiana al socialismo* [Togliatti and the Italian road to socialism] (Roma: Editori Riuniti, 1975), and, from a "left" perspective, Pietro Ingrao, *Masse e potere* [The masses and power] (Roma: Editori Riuniti, 1977). A brief but illuminating sketch of the historical experiences underlying the PCI's democratic road is Giorgio Napolitano, *Intervista sul PCI* (Bari: Laterza, 1976)—an interview by E. J. Hobsbawn that has been published in English as *The Italian Road to Socialism* (Westport, Conn.: Lawrence Hill, 1977).

20. Carrillo, *Dialogue on Spain,* p. 198. In a 1976 interview, Carrillo was even more explicit on this point:

> We are ready to get out if we lose elections—just like any other party. When I speak of democracy I mean Western Democracy. I consider universal suffrage to be the criterion. I said this in front of Brezhnev. We don't want power by force. I am a Spaniard, not a Russian. I certainly don't want to be another Franco but it would be impossible for me to be a Lenin. I believe in the ultimate goal of convergence of ideologies. The West must become more socialist but the East must become more democratic.

New York Times, August 6, 1976.

21. The vote to dispense with Leninism at the PCE's Ninth Congress was 968 to 248; however, intense debate over this and related issues continued afterward, inspired in part by the bitterness of many delegates over what they felt were Carrillo's manipulative tactics. In the long run, according to some observers, the move toward "de-Leninization" was primarily a response to new democratizing impulses from the PCE's base. See José Rodriguez-Ibáñez, "Spanish Communism in Transition," in Boggs and Plotke, *Politics of Eurocommunism,* pp. 90-93.

22. See Georges Marchais, "Liberty and Socialism" and "In Order to Take Democracy Forward to Socialism, Two Problems are Decisive," in Etienne Balibar, *On The Dictatorship of the Proletariat* (London: Unwin Brothers, 1977), especially pp. 161-164 and 184-186. Balibar's defense of traditional Leninism is spelled out in the same volume, in "On the Dictatorship of the Proletariat." For

an excellent assessment of this debate in terms of its impact on PCF development, see Louis Althusser, "What Must Change in the Party," *New Left Review,* no. 109 (May-June 1978), pp. 19-45.

23. Even the PCF's official departure from Leninism at the Twenty-Second Congress, which was preceded by virtually no internal party debate, angered many delegates who felt the party had abandoned its role as a class-based revolutionary organization. For a sampling of the post-congress debate, see Balibar "On the Dictatorship of the Proletariat."

24. This line of thinking is particularly visible in the Soviet attack on Carrillo's theoretical work. See the editorial, "Contrary to the Interests of Peace and Socialism in Europe," *New Times,* June 1977.

25. Soviet discomfort with Eurocommunism can also be explained by other factors—for example, by its fear of "Atlanticism" (the idea of a regional European block of Communist parties)—but the emphasis here is on party strategy. A good overview of the CPSU approach is furnished by Levgold, "Soviet Union and Western European Communism."

26. Togliatti, *La via italiana al socialismo,* pp. 181-182.

27. Pietro Ingrao, "Democrazia borghese o stalinismo? No: democrazia di massa" [Bourgeois democracy or Stalinism? No: Democracy of the masses], *Rinascita,* February 6, 1976. An excellent recent elaboration of this is Ingrao's introduction to *Masse e potere.* See also Luciano Gruppi, "Partecipazione al governo, alternanza, compromesso storico" [Government participation, shifts of power, historic compromise], in *Almanacco PCI '79* (Roma: Fratelli Spada, 1979). For the PCE, see Carrillo, *Eurocommunism and the State,* pp. 89-91.

28. Guy Besse, "Reply to Balibar," in Balibar, *Dictatorship of the Proletariat,* p. 177.

29. Gruppi, "Partecipazione al governo," p. 64.

30. Ibid.

31. Carlo Cardia, "Una proposta nuova nel 'dialogo' con il mondo cattolico" [A new approach to the "dialogue" with the Catholic world], in *Almanacco PCI '79,* p. 58. See also the joint statement of the three parties on their commitment to pluralist democracy (note 1 of this chapter).

32. *Eurocommunism and the State,* pp. 101-102. Carrillo defined the "new political formation" as a "confederation of political parties and other forces" that would expand on the basis of growing socialist consensus. Ibid., p. 102.

33. Ingrao, *Masse e potere,* p. 43.

34. Strong forces within the PCI, led by Giorgio Amendola, moved to discard this vanguardist ideology in the 1960s but were repulsed at the Twelfth Congress in 1969. At one point Amendola argued for junking the label "Communist" and adopting in its place "Party of the Working Class."

35. Fernando Claudin's critique of Eurocommunism on this score is valid for the PCF but much less accurate in the more ambiguous and complex cases of the PCE and PCI. See *Eurocommunism and Socialism,* pp. 131-132.

36. An excellent analysis of PCI alliance politics is Stephen Hellman's "The PCI Alliance Strategy," in Donald L. M. Blackmer and Sidney Tarrow, eds., *Communism in France and Italy* (Princeton, N.J.: Princeton University Press, 1975), especially pp. 383-389.

37. According to Ingrao, the "crisis of institutions" in Italy has three dimensions: (1) the backwardness and inefficiency of the state bureaucracy; (2) the weakness of parliament vis-à-vis the executive; and (3) the immobilism of the political parties. *Masse e potere,* pp. 259-260.

38. Max Jaggi, Roger Muller, and Sil Schmid, *Red Bologna* (London: Writers and Readers, 1977), pp. 34-42. In Bologna there are eighteen neighborhood councils with nearly 300 councillors – a more developed local network than exists in any other Italian city.

39. See the interview with Bologna mayor Renato Zangheri in ibid., pp. 199-200. Zangheri stated: "Our aim is reform of state industry but not its expansion. In a country like Italy, there are hundreds of small enterprises and industrial firms. The whole Bolognese and Emilian economy consists of such small enterprises. To do away with them would mean a death-blow for production and productivity. We believe, therefore, that it is more a question of allotting these firms a new role inside a democratically-planned economy."

40. Enrico Berlinguer, "Report to the 14th National Congress of the PCI" (March 18-23, 1975), *Italian Communists,* no. 2 (March-May 1975), pp. 102-103. Stated Berlinguer: "We have said and we repeat that we do not raise the question of withdrawal from the Atlantic Alliance, but we have also said and repeat that while remaining in this Alliance, we can and must work in favor of detente, which necessarily implies not pitting ourselves against either the United States of America or the Soviet Union" (p. 102).

41. Santiago Carrillo, *Triunfo,* July 3, 1976, p. 7, and *Il Manifesto,* November 1, 1975, p. 2, both quoted in Eusebio M. Mujal-Leon, "The Domestic and International Evolution of the Spanish Communist Party," in Tökes, *Eurocommunism and Detente,* pp. 243, 245.

42. See William E. Griffith, "The Diplomacy of Eurocommunism," in Tökes, *Eurocommunism and Detente,* p. 411-412.

43. The PCF officially rejects the goals of European integration, but since its support of the Joint Program (with the Socialists) in 1972 it has agreed in practice to "participate in the further extension of the EEC and its institutions." See Heinz Timmerman, "Democratic Socialists, Eurocommunists, and the West," in William E. Griffith, *The European Left: Italy, France, and Spain* (Toronto: D.C. Heath, 1979), pp. 180-184.

44. One of the first public statements of this sort came, predictably, from Giorgio Amendola, who argued that the EEC would be more effective in fighting the crisis of capitalism than any single country. "It is for this reason that we Italian Communists are fighting for a democratic transformation of the EEC, to give it democratic legitimacy through direct elections on the basis of universal suffrage and to provide it with the necessary powers to solve the new problems that the individual states, in their sovereign independence, cannot solve: the monstrous power of the multinational companies, international capital movements, energy, transportation." See "Working Class Initiative to Build European Cooperation," *Italian Communists,* no. 3 (June-August 1975), p. 62. Also, Gian Carlo Pajetta, "Il movimento comunista e la sinistra europa" [The communist movement and the European left], *Rinascita,* May 30, 1975, and Napolitano, *Italian Road to Socialism,* pp. 57-59.

45. The emphasis on ideological hegemony—and the looming but often distorted shadow of Gramsci—is clearly evident throughout Napolitano's *Intervista sul PCI* and in Carrillo's *Eurocommunism and the State,* Ch. 3. See also Ingrao's *Masse e potere,* pp. 240–253.

46. Ingrao, *Masse e potere,* pp. 42–47, 250–253, and 259–261. For a more general theoretical discussion of the state that is compatible with this perspective, see Poulantzas, *State, Power, Socialism,* pp. 12–35, 154–157.

47. Ingrao, *Masse e potere,* pp. 240–241.

48. Ibid., pp. 250–253. This takes up a familiar Togliattian theme—the gradual modification of structures—and carries it one step further by arguing that the party itself should never be the exclusive agency of hegemony. Of all PCI theorists, Ingrao has probably the most elaborate views on the transition.

49. Carrillo, *Eurocommunism and the State,* pp. 27–28. Carrillo stressed that as the bourgeois state expands in scope and functions it becomes a major locus of social contradictions in late capitalism. However, he never really developed this point.

50. In this respect it is misleading to argue, as the editors of *Monthly Review* have done, that Eurocommunist strategy is nothing but a recycling of Kautskian social democracy because it shares the same parliamentarist illusions. See "The Age of Reform," *Monthly Review,* Vol. 28, no. 2 (June 1976), pp. 1–17.

51. Carrillo, *Eurocommunism and the State,* p. 28. It is necessary to distinguish here between *chronic,* ongoing crises that are endemic to capitalism—basic contradictions—and *catastrophic* crises of the sort that might lead to systemic collapse. The Eurocommunists recognize the first—indeed they base their strategy on it—but they insist that global capitalism (in the absence of war) is strong enough to contain the latter. The theoretical outlook of orthodox Marxism was that normal crises, manifest in the falling rate of profit, immiserization of the proletariat, and conflict between the forces and social relations of production would gradually build toward cataclysmic crisis and immobilize the capitalist system.

52. Henri Weber, "Eurocommunism, Socialism, and Democracy," *New Left Review,* no. 110 (July-August 1978), p. 13.

53. In general, Eurocommunist leaders and theorists do not want their concept of the democratic road, which they regard as *sui generis,* confused with the Popular Front approach of the 1930s. However, those who have been identified with the "right" tendency in these parties—for example, Giorgio Amendola of the PCI—have not expressed embarrassment at this association. Jean Elleinstein of the PCF has strongly praised the Popular Front, which he saw as hindered in its development everywhere by Stalinism. Thus, "The international situation spoilt any hope of pursuing this [the frontist] path, whose importance for contemporary history should not be underestimated." *The Stalin Phenomenon* (London: Lawrence & Wishart, 1976), pp. 204–205.

54. To this list might be added the influence of the *later* (i.e., Weimar period) Kautsky. As we have seen, a good case can be made that the strategies of Bernstein and Kautsky for all practical purposes merged in the wake of the Bolshevik Revolution and the establishment of more mature bourgeois democratic institu-

tions in Germany. As John Kautsky argued, moreover, this new strategy bears a striking resemblance to Eurocommunism. He noted that

> recent PCI strategy is not the one advanced by Kautsky in imperial Germany when, because of the lack of democracy, he strongly disagreed with Bernstein's faith in the possibility of an imperceptible, gradual growth into socialism. However, it is the Weimar Kautsky that I think is similar to Eurocommunism for, with the establishment of Weimar democracy, this difference between Kautsky and Bernstein had disappeared, and the Historical Compromise is hence as Kautskian as it is Bernsteinian.

See "Karl Kautsky and Eurocommunism," pp. 9–10.

55. On this point, see Claudin, *Eurocommunism and Socialism,* pp. 102–104, and Lucio Colletti, "The Three Faces of the Italian Communist Party," *Telos,* no. 42 (Winter 1979-1980), pp. 117–120.

Chapter Three

1. It is not my intention here to make a case for any singular logic of rationalization, much less for any irreversible trend toward state capitalism in Western Europe. In the first place, to establish general patterns or *tendencies* is different from assuming predetermined outcomes where politics all but vanishes. But an even more general disclaimer needs to be made: Economic development, or "modernization," can obviously take a variety of forms. For example, one can distinguish a socialist mode of transformation from those I have mentioned here—capitalist, social-democratic (or state capitalist), and bureaucratic-centralist. The socialist approach contrasts with the latter three in that it attacks the social division of labor by struggling to extend nonbureaucratic authority and social relations throughout every sphere of society. Economic development is thus combined with a broad process of democratization; emphasis is directed toward popular activity, workers' control, and social struggle. John Gurley differentiated between two similar models in his "Maoist and Capitalist Economic Development," *Monthly Review,* Vol. 22, no. 9 (February 1971), pp. 15–35. The significant question posed in this chapter is whether, and to what extent, Eurocommunism has elaborated a socialist alternative to previous forms of rationalization.

2. The "modernizing" obsession of Leninism, and its impact on Soviet development, are analyzed by Fred and Lou Jean Fleron in "Administrative Theory as Repressive Political Theory: The Communist Experience." This is not to argue that *every* Marxist current has been oblivious to this critique or has failed to articulate elements of an antiauthoritarian, antistatist theory. One notable exception, as I pointed out in the introduction, was the European radical left (including council communism)—but it never outgrew its marginal status within the left. Recent theoretical tendencies within Marxism have shared such a critique, but they have never been translated into organized political movements.

3. For a critique of Marxist (and especially Communist) approaches to science

and technology from a variety of perspectives, see the contributions to Fred Fleron, ed., *Technology and Communist Culture* (New York: Praeger Publishers, 1977).

4. Paul Mattick, *Marx and Keynes* (Boston: Porter and Sargent, 1969), p. 322. For an extensive discussion of this phenomenon, see Alex Dupuy and Barry Truchil, "Problems in the Theory of State Capitalism," *Theory and Society,* Vol. 8, no. 1 (June-December 1979), pp. 1–38.

5. See Poulantzas, *State, Power, Socialism,* pp. 181–183, and Dupuy and Truchil, "Problems in the Theory of State Capitalism," pp. 30–32.

6. Larry Hirschhorn, "The Political Economy of Social Service Rationalization," *Contemporary Crises* Vol. 2 (1978), especially pp. 66–69. See also Morris Janowitz, *Social Control of the Welfare State* (New York: Elsevier, 1976).

7. Andre Gorz, "Technology, Technicians, and the Class Struggle," in Andre Gorz, ed., *The Social Division of Labor* (Atlantic Highlands, N.J.: Humanities Press, 1976).

8. This is the thesis of Barbara Ehrenreich and John Ehrenreich's "The Professional-Managerial Class," in Pat Walker, ed., *Between Labor and Capital* (Boston: South End Press, 1979), pp. 5–45. In departing from the "new working class" theories of Gorz, Serge Mallet, and Alain Touraine, the Ehrenreichs come closer to agreeing with Poulantzas's concept of the intellectuals in advanced capitalism as the "new petty bourgeoisie."

9. The concept of "contradictory class locations" as applied to the intellectuals is developed by Erik Olin Wright, "Intellectuals and the Class Structure of Capitalist Society," in Walker, *Between Labor and Capital,* pp. 191–211. Wright argued that "intellectuals typically occupy a contradictory class location between the working class and the petty bourgeoisie at the economic level, but between the working class and the bourgeoisie at the ideological level" (p. 204).

10. Herbert Marcuse, *One-Dimensional Man* (Boston: Beacon Press, 1964), and Jurgen Habermas, *Legitimation Crisis* (Boston: Beacon Press, 1973), pp. 37, 75–78.

11. Harry Braverman, *Labor and Monopoly Capital* (New York: Monthly Review Press, 1976).

12. Stuart Ewen, *Captains of Consciousness* (New York: McGraw-Hill, 1976).

13. Marcuse, *One-Dimensional Man,* Chs. 2 and 9.

14. Habermas, in *Legitimation Crisis,* argued that a narrowly administered technocratic rationality typical of advanced capitalism cannot supply the normative foundations of legitimacy necessary to sustain bourgeois institutions for a lengthy period of time. See pp. 92–93.

15. See Alvin W. Gouldner, "The New Class Project—II," *Theory and Society,* Vol. 6, no. 3 (Fall 1978), pp. 375–378.

16. George Ross, "Marxism and the New Middle Classes," *Theory and Society,* Vol. 5, no. 2 (March 1978), pp. 163–190.

17. John Low-Beer, *Protest and Participation: The New Working Class in Italy* (New York: Cambridge University Press, 1978), Ch. 4. On the general struggles against rationalization in Western Europe, see Angelo Picchierri, "Diffusion

and Crisis of Scientific Management in European Industry," in Salvador Giner and Margaret Scotford Archer, *Contemporary Europe* (London: Routledge and Kegan Paul, 1978), pp. 55–73.

18. Antonio Gramsci, "Fordism and Americanism," in Quintin Hoare and Geoffrey Nowell-Smith, eds., *Selections from the Prison Notebooks of Antonio Gramsci* (London: Lawrence & Wishart, 1971), p. 279.

19. Ibid., p. 312.

20. From Gruppi, *Il compromesso storico,* p. 241.

21. The systemic necessity of social investments (and social wages) for capitalist accumulation *and* legitimation, within the overall drive toward rationalization, is analyzed by Hirschhorn, "Political Economy of Social Service Rationalization." For a comparative focus on the *ideological* side of this phenomenon, see William Leiss, "Technology and Instrumental Rationality in Capitalism and Socialism," in Fleron, *Technology and Communist Culture,* pp. 171–203.

22. The statist component of rationalization is not the function of a particular internal or autonomous logic of technique, as theorists like Jacques Ellul have argued. It is rather one aspect of the capitalist imperatives of accumulation, legitimation, and domination—technique itself being only one part of this totality. For Ellul's perspective, see *The Technological Society* (New York: Vintage, 1964), pp. 133–134, 194, 207–209, 280–288. An antidote to this outlook, and one that avoids the other extreme of reducing the problem of rationalization to its class dimension, is Henry Jacoby, *The Bureaucratization of the World* (Berkeley: University of California Press, 1973), pp. 61–110, 147–168.

23. Samir Amin stressed this point in "Toward a Structural Crisis of World Capitalism," *Socialist Revolution,* no. 23 (April 1975), pp. 33–37. Amin noted that "the failure of social-democratic integration makes southern Europe a weak link in the present crisis. Its class alliances limit the competitiveness of its capital with respect to the northern countries, and an attempt to make the working class bear the burden of crisis risks creating an explosive situation in those countries with a revolutionary tradition" (p. 35).

24. It is important to stress here that *popular* radicalization is not necessarily accompanied by similar leftward changes within the leadership of the Communist parties. On the contrary, the pressures toward "austerity" and economic caution that grow out of crisis and dependency may actually encourage moderation within these parties and the trade unions.

25. Fred Block, "Eurocommunism and the Stalemate of European Capitalism," in Boggs and Plotke, *Politics of Eurocommunism,* pp. 260–265.

26. The term "imperfect bipartism"—a reference to what is essentially a two-party system in which one of the parties remains hegemonic—is taken from Giorgio Galli's *Il bipartismo imperfetto* (Bologna: Il Mulino, 1967).

27. See Ronald Fraser, "Spain on the Brink," *New Left Review,* no. 96 (March-April 1976), pp. 3–33; and Kaplan, "Democracy and the Mass Politics of the PCE."

28. The impact of the May Events in redefining French politics—and in opening the PCF to new currents—is examined by Andrew Feenberg, "From the May

Events to Eurocommunism," *Socialist Review,* no. 37 (January-February 1978), pp. 73-107.

29. On the problem of uneven development in Italy, see Livio Maitan, *Dinamica delle classi sociali in Italia* [Dynamics of social classes in Italy] (Roma: Savelli, 1975); Antonio Negri, *Crisi dello stato-piano* [Crisis of the planned state] (Milano: Feltrinelli, 1974); and Eugenio Peggio, *La crisi economica italiana* [The Italian economic crisis] (Milano: Rizzoli, 1976). Peggio is a leading PCI intellectual and member of the party's economic study bureau.

30. Henri Weber, "In the Beginning was Gramsci," in *Autonomia: Post-Political Writings* (New York: Semiotext Intervention Series, 1980), p 85.

31. P. A. Allum, *Italy: Republic Without Government?* (London: Weidenfeld and Nicolson, 1973), Ch. 5.

32. Peggio, *La crisi economici italiana.*

33. In many regions of the south even the Communist party apparatus adapted to and became integrated into this traditional social system, with severe ideological consequences. See Sidney Tarrow, *Peasant Communism in Southern Italy* (New Haven: Yale University Press, 1967).

34. Kevin Allen and Andrew Stevenson, *An Introduction to the Italian Economy* (London: Martin Robertson, 1974), pp. 250-255.

35. See Allum, *Italy: Republic Without Government?,* Ch. 6. This counters the view held by Sartori and others that the problem of "ingovernability" is really a matter of stifling control exercised by the various party organizations over Italian political life — a phenomenon known as *partitocrazia.* See Giovanni Sartori, "European Political Parties: The Case of Polarized Pluralism," in Joseph LaPalombara and Myron Weiner, eds., *Political Parties and Political Development* (Princeton, N.J.: Princeton University Press, 1966), pp. 137-176.

36. Napolitano, *Italian Road to Socialism,* pp. 56-57.

37. Ibid., p. 49. This theme permeates PCI literature and statements, whatever the disagreements among party leaders regarding the precise role of the state in the transition (e.g., concerning the relationship between central government and local structures, the nature of state economic planning, and the problem of decentralization).

38. Ingrao, *Masse e potere,* p. 376.

39. Ibid., p. 40, and Napolitano, *Italian Road to Socialism,* p. 51.

40. This point is regularly emphasized in Berlinguer's speeches and writings. See *La grande avanzata comunista* (Roma: Sarini, 1976), pp. 95-97. See also Ingrao, *Masse e potere,* p. 377; Lucio Libertini, "The Problem of the PCI," in Austin Ranney and Giovanni Sartori, *Eurocommunism: The Italian Case* (Washington, DC.: American Enterprise Institute for Public Research, 1978), pp. 157-159; and Renato Zangheri, interviewed in Jaggi et al., *Red Bologna,* p. 98. Zangheri's statement is typical of the recent PCI line: "The economic situation is very serious, and we do not intend to improve it by further nationalizations. In Italy, there is already a significant proportion of state ownership. Here the problem consists of running the already existing industries better" (p. 198).

41. Quoted in Norman Kogan, "The Italian Communist Party: The Modern Prince at the Crossroads," in Tökes, *Eurocommunism and Detente,* p. 98.

42. *New York Times,* October 10, 1977.

43. For the Bologna case, see Gianluigi Degli Esposti, *Bologna PCI* (Bologna: Il Mulino, 1966), Chs. 13 and 14.

44. "The Political Resolution of the XIV National Congress of the PCI," *Italian Communists,* no. 2 (March-May 1975), p. 133.

45. Achille Occhetto, "Austerita e sviluppo della democrazia" [Austerity and the development of democracy], *Rinascita,* June 17, 1977.

46. Berlinguer and other PCI leaders also distinguish their approach to planning from the social-democratic one, but on the basis of the criteria outlined here the contrast seems neglible. See Berlinguer, *La grande avanzata comunista,* pp. 21-24.

47. Ingrao, *Masse e potere,* pp. 37-39.

48. Enrico Berlinguer, *Austerita occasione per trasformare l'Italia* [Austerity as the basis for transforming Italy] (Roma: Editori Riuniti, 1977), p. 18.

49. Napolitano, *Intervista sul PCI,* pp. 98-99, and Occhetto, "Austerita."

50. Berlinguer, *Austerita,* pp. 47-52.

51. See Lama's statement in *La Repubblica,* January 24, 1980. In October 1979, during a period of intense political violence in Italy, Fiat fired sixty-one workers at one of its Turin plants for their presumed "association" with left-wing terrorist activities. Even though such charges were never proven, neither the CGIL nor the PCI defended the dismissed workers — to do so would have violated the tacit agreement between unions and management to preserve industrial order.

52. For a more extensive discussion of this measure, see Joanne Barkan, "Italy: Working-Class Defeat or Program for Transition?" *Monthly Review,* Vol. 29, no. 6 (November 1977), pp. 26-38.

53. Ingrao, *Masse e potere,* pp. 27-29. Also, Occhetto, "Austerita."

54. The general PCI strategy for agricultural development is elaborated in Gerardo Chiaromante and Giancarlo Pajetta, *I comunisti e i contadini* (Roma: Editori Riuniti, 1970).

55. See "Il PCI e le multinazionali," in Giacomo Luciani, *Il PCI e il capitalismo occidentale* (Milano: Lunganesi, 1977). There is also a brief discussion of this problem in Heinz Timmerman, "Democratic Socialists, Eurocommunists, and the West," in Griffith, *European Left,* pp. 180-185.

56. Lucio Libertini, "The Problem of the PCI," in Ranney and Sartori, *Eurocommunism: The Italian Case,* p. 159.

57. Ian Gough, *The Political Economy of the Welfare State* (Atlantic Highlands, N.J.: Humanities Press, 1979).

58. Antonio Carlo, "The Italian Crisis and the Role of the Left," *Telos,* no. 42 (Winter 1979-1980), pp. 71-72.

59. On this point see Gorz, "Technology, Technicians, and the Class Struggle," and Low-Beer, *Protest and Participation,* Ch. 7.

60. This is not to be confused with a critique of the PCI's *alliance* strategy, which is something else. All Marxist movements — at least those that have been successful — have depended upon broad social alliances or coalitions of some sort. The difficulty with the PCI concept, however, is that it views alliances in strictly *electoral* terms and that it dispenses with the notion of class antagonism — not that

it has abandoned a singular commitment to the traditional proletariat.

61. Antonio Negri, "Theses on the Crisis," in *Working-Class Autonomy and Crisis* (London: Conference of Socialist Economics Books, 1979), pp. 40–43.

62. See Diana Johnstone, "Fiat: The Technological Revolution," *In These Times,* December 1979–January 8, 1980.

63. Low-Beer, *Protest and Participation,* pp. 25, 40, 186.

64. Sidney Tarrow refers to the PCI's "well-rationalized instrumentalism" in this context. See *Peasant Communism in Southern Italy,* pp. 267–268.

65. Such a ruling stratum would probably not constitute a unified "new class" of Marxist technocratic intellectuals whose historical mission is to dispossess the entrepreneurial bourgeoisie and construct a more or less monolithic party-state as the primary agency of capital accumulation. This generalization has been applied to the role of Marxist parties and regimes by Richard Gombin, following the work of Jan Machajski, Milovan Djilas, and others. See *Radical Tradition,* especially p. 66. Gombin's argument fits the Soviet case, but I have suggested that the bureaucratic-centralist model differs considerably from the state-capitalist one typical of Eurocommunism, as market relations and the private sphere of production are not abolished in the latter case.

66. This is a crucial factor separating capitalist from emancipatory modes of development. See Gurley, "Capitalist and Maoist Economic Development," pp. 19–25. For Gurley, whereas capitalist rationalization places techniques, machines, and things at the center of economic transformation, the revolutionary approach affirms that "economic development can best be promoted by breaking down specialization, by dismantling bureaucracies, and by undermining the other centralizing and divisive tendencies that give rise to experts, technicians, authorities, and bureaucrats remote from or manipulating 'the masses'" (p. 19).

Chapter Four

1. Lucio Magri, "Italian Communism in the Sixties," *New Left Review,* no. 66 (March-April 1971), pp. 37–52.

2. The tendency to view politics as the reflection of class forces is visible even in such unorthodox theorists as Poulantzas. See his *State, Power, Socialism,* especially pp. 125–142.

3. Ibid., p. 129.

4. This generalization applies to other Mediterranean countries without strong Eurocommunist-type parties, such as Portugal and Greece, but not really to France, where the process of rationalization is clearly much more advanced and where the state already furnishes a bureaucratic planning infrastructure. See Stephen Cohen, *Modern Capitalist Planning: The French Model* (Cambridge, Mass.: Harvard University Press, 1969).

5. Habermas, *Legitimation Crisis,* pp. 43–46. Also, Renate Mayntz, "Legitimacy and the Directive Capacity of the Political System," in Leon Lindberg et al., eds., *Stress and Contradiction in Modern Capitalism* (Lexington, Mass.: D.C. Heath, 1975).

6. This argument parallels the thesis, developed by Habermas, Claus Offe,

James O'Connor, Alan Wolfe, and others, that advanced capitalist systems must inevitably confront the basic contradiction between consensual or "democratic" legitimating requirements and the needs of capital accumulation. According to these theorists, the failure to reconcile such competing demands produces a natural tendency toward legitimation crisis. See, for example, Habermas, *Legitimation Crisis,* pp. 41–75; Wolfe, *The Limits of Legitimacy* (New York: Free Press, 1977), Chs. 8–10; and James O'Connor, "The Democratic Movement in the United States," *Kapitalistate,* no. 7 (1978), pp. 7–23. My concern here is less with "democracy," at least that which is equated with *representative* democracy, than with the impact of *traditional* belief systems.

7. At present, of the Eurocommunist parties only the PCI has begun to experience this conflict in concrete political terms – in part because its governmental presence is more extensive, in part because it is the only party to legitimate itself among broad groups (notably the middle strata) outside the industrial proletariat. The PCI's commitment to rationalization, which is stronger than that of either the PCF or PCE, suggests an additional factor.

8. Poulantzas noted that this *transcendent* component of ideological hegemony is peculiarly essential to organized capitalist states, as the forms of domination (e.g., bureaucracy) tend to be more direct and naked. See his *Political Power and Social Classes* (London: New Left Books, 1973), p. 218. See also Herbert Marcuse's *One-Dimensional Man* (Boston: Beacon Press, 1964) for a general discussion of technological rationality consistent with this approach.

9. The classical and still unsurpassed analysis of this phenomenon, which seems even more valid today, is Herbert Marcuse's *Soviet Marxism* (New York: Vintage, 1957), especially Chs. 1–5.

10. The concept of the "public sphere," following the work of Habermas and of Oskar Negt and Alexander Kluge, refers to the totality of political (and cultural) space available for the development of oppositional communities and movements and is not reducible to discrete sets of institutions, the state, or the public *sector.* See Habermas, "The Public Sphere," *New German Critique,* Vol. 1, no. 3 (Fall 1974), pp. 49–65, and *Legitimation Crisis,* pp. 36–37, 70. Negt and Kluge's thesis is contained in *Oeffentlichkeit und Erfahrung* (Frankfurt am Main, 1973) and is outlined by Eberhard Knodler-Bunte, "The Proletarian Public Sphere and Political Organization," *New German Critique,* no. 4 (Winter 1975), pp. 51–75.

11. My argument appies only to the orbit of the Eurocommunist parties, not to the sphere of oppositional politics in general. In this respect it stops short of Marcuse's more sweeping formulation, which holds that technological rationality restricts politics to questions of technique, empties the democratic process of all radical content, and renders oppositional tendencies impotent. See *One-Dimensional Man,* pp. 156–165.

12. Svetozar Stojanovic, *Between Ideals and Reality* (New York: Oxford University Press, 1973), Ch. 3. My emphasis differs from that of Stojanovic, however, in that he associated the rise of statism within the Marxist tradition with the Stalinist phase of development in the Soviet Union.

13. Such an outcome, though by no means certain, would at least temporarily

"solve" the legitimation crisis under Eurocommunist governance, as the "technical" needs of accumulation and the "consensual" requirement of legitimacy would at least be synchronized. But persisting class contradictions would sooner or later surface in new ways, precipitating a return to crisis both within and outside the orbit of Eurocommunist parties.

14. In this respect Max Weber's theory of legitimacy rooted in an understanding of modern "rational-legal" bureaucratic states is more helpful than Gramsci's concept of hegemony based upon preindustrial "survivals" typical of the transitional period between early and late capitalism. Hence most of Gramsci's attention was focused on the role of Catholicism, liberalism, and certain unique cultural traditions in Italy and elsewhere; one exception was his essay "Americanism and Fordism" (in the *Prison Notebooks*), although even this brief effort does not analyze the state apparatus directly. Of course Gramsci did assign the state a positive, transformative role (the Jacobin "modern prince") in *socialist* development — a theme that did not exactly preoccupy Weber.

15. Growth in the percentage of middle-strata membership within the PCI has been dramatic: From 1950 to 1974, the increase was from 8.9 percent to 22.5 percent (a figure that includes professionals, teachers, white-collar workers, and merchants). An even more illuminating statistic is the increase in the proportion of PCI members from middle-strata origins who held federation committee positions — from 50.4 percent in 1950 to 65 percent in 1975. See Joanne Barkan, "Italian Communism at the Crossroads," in Boggs and Plotke, *Politics of Eurocommunism,* pp. 60–61.

16. This historical and theoretical background of the PCI's alliance politics is outlined by Hellman, "The PCI's Alliance Strategy and the Case of the Middle Classes." See also Jon Halliday, "Structural Reform in Italy — Theory and Practice," *New Left Review,* no. 50 (July-August 1968), pp. 30–53.

17. Feenberg, "From May Events to Eurocommunism," pp. 88–91. Feenberg commented that the

> old pessimistic analyses of a C. Wright Mills are outdated and unilateral. The middle strata are not necessarily committed to a "politics of the rearguard," nor to technocratic ambitions either. Most basically, the modern middle strata are not afraid of losing a capital they do not in any case possess, and so in the context of the Southern political system large sectors of them can enter into a principled alliance with workers for socialism.

He added:

> During May many teachers, scientists, journalists, and other cultural workers openly and enthusiastically supported the most radical goals of the movement: the overthrow of the state and the institution of a council communist regime (p. 88).

For a more general discussion of the middle strata in the French context, see Ross, "Marxism and the New Middle Classes." On the PCF's strategic conception of the middle strata, see Keitha Sapsin Fine, *Theory and Practice in the French*

Communist Party: State Monopoly Capitalism and Class Struggle (London: George Allen and Unwin, forthcoming).

18. The PCE received less than 10 percent of the vote in the June 1977 elections. Carrillo's strategy is to construct a broad political bloc around a democratic platform that could crystallize leftist opposition and transform it from an antifascist into an anticapitalist formation. Yet the alliance Carrillo has in mind is, for good tactical reasons, quite amorphous and all-inclusive; this means that the Spanish middle strata have not been *theoretically* assigned any specific or leading role in socialist transformation.

19. Tactical alliances with elements of the bourgeoisie must be differentiated from strategic formulations like those incorporating the new middle strata. Thus, Carrillo argued for a convergence between the PCE and dynamic sectors of the bourgeoisie that see in fascism an "obstacle to the development of modern capitalism in Spain. . . . It is this that is bringing about an objective convergence between the revolutionary forces and this sector of Spanish capitalism. . . . It is a question, then, of a momentary convergence, and it is clear that after this stage we are going to diverge." *Dialogue on Spain,* p. 169.

20. This normative rationale is of course "Marxism." Here a point made earlier bears repeating: Whereas technological rationality might furnish an instrumental ideology, the need for a more purposive system of values – especially within the party itself – does not disappear. It is the latter that instills sustained political commitment. See Alvin W. Gouldner, *The Dialectic of Ideology and Technology* (New York: Seabury Press, 1976), p. 241.

21. The essays by Gorz, "Technicians and Class Struggle," and Steve Marglin, "What Do Bosses Do?" in Gorz, *Social Division of Labor,* pp. 13–54, develop this point very effectively.

22. For example, Gian Franco Vene, *La borghesia comunista* (Milan: Sugarco Edizioni, 1976). Some of Vene's arguments echo Milovan Djilas's thesis in *The New Class.* He associated the PCI's rightward move with its electoral appeals to the new middle strata, including "left" elements of the church and Christian Democracy, and concluded that such "interclassism" has subverted the party's proletarian identity (pp. 189–199).

23. Of course this contradicts the traditional Marxist "instrumentalist" view according to which the state in capitalist society is the "executive committee of the bourgeoisie" – a view that in less vulgar formulation is accepted by most Marxists even today. It should be noted, however, that the concept of a ruling class grounded in the state (rather than a proprietary grouping) was explicit in Marx's theory of the Asiatic mode of production. For a discussion of this point, see Alvin W. Gouldner, *The Two Marxisms* (New York: Seabury Press, 1980), pp. 331–343.

24. The weakness of the Italian Socialists relative to the PCI helps to account for the latter's strong presence within the middle strata, as in postwar Western Europe the socialists have been the party most closely linked to this constituency. In France, where the political balance between Socialists and Communists is more even, and in Spain, where the PCE is overwhelmed by a much larger "catch-all" party, the Spanish Socialist party (PSoE), the dilemmas of building middle-strata support are more obvious. In these cases, alliance strategy can be expected to

assume a more decidedly frontist character if Eurocommunist strategy is to make inroads.

25. Hellman, "PCI's Alliance Strategy," p. 418.

26. See Low-Beer, *Protest and Participation,* Chs. 4 and 7. Interestingly enough, Low-Beer concluded on the basis of his investigation of class consciousness and political activity among technical workers in Milan that the traditional separation between mental and physical tasks is disappearing with the proletarianization of the former. This helps to explain the greater preoccupation with issues of self-management among this sector of the new middle strata. With higher levels of education and greater expectations from their jobs, these workers are quicker to chafe under bureaucratic norms and restrictions. To what extent scientific and technical workers ultimately align themselves with industrial workers therefore remains to be seen.

27. Nicos Poulantzas, "The New Petty Bourgeoisie," in Alan Hunt, ed., *Class and Class Structure* (London: Lawrence & Wishart, 1977), p. 123.

28. Looking at the PCF, Andrew Feenberg and George Ross presented quite opposed assessments of alliance politics. Feenberg saw in the new middle strata a radicalizing potential that to some extent the PCF has already absorbed through its capacity to build upon the currents of May 1968 and adapt to various new left themes such as *autogestion.* See "From the May Events to Eurocommunism." Ross, on the other hand, argued that the middle strata have at best only a moderate and vague commitment to socialism, which makes them an uncertain ally of the working class. Such an alliance produces the conditions of deradicalization, for it requires the PCF to downplay the appeals of socialism. Thus, "Since the non–working class sectors of this alliance cannot yet be expected to identify their long-range class interests with socialism, workers will probably have to restrain themselves in order to accommodate these less radical groups." "The PCF and the End of the Bolshevik Dream," in Boggs and Plotke, *Politics of Eurocommunism,* p. 43. See also "Marxism and the New Middle Classes," p. 180.

29. Amendola's charges are contained in *Rinascita,* November 19, 1979. He said that the working class could present itself as the future ruling force in Italy only if it learned to curb its "excessive" economic demands. His criticisms were so strident that even his comrades in the PCI directorate felt compelled to rebuke him. In fact, Amendola was only expressing openly and angrily what was at the core of the PCI's austerity politics.

30. As in other realms of Eurocommunist theory, the PCI was first to reconceptualize the party-union relationship as part of structural reformist strategy for advanced capitalism during the early 1960s. The theory, however, was not systematized until nearly a decade later. The rationale for this change can be found in Fernando Di Giulio, "La Politica, partiti, e il movimento sindicale" [Politics, parties, and the trade union movement], *Rinascita,* April 9, 1971; and "Unita sindicale e nuovo blocco di forze sociali e politiche" [Trade-union unity and the new bloc of social and political forces], *Critica Marxista,* Vol. 8, no. 6 (November-December 1970), p. 46–59.

31. Corporatism within the CGIL should be understood more as a tendency,

which *could* become institutionalized over time, than as an irreversible process. It is worth noting here that the Italian trade-union movement, having ridden the crest of working-class radicalism in the late 1960s, experienced a degree of rejuvenation and even democratization during much of the 1970s. Rank-and-file initiative, expressed through the rebirth of popular structures like factory councils and the *comitati di base* (committees of the base), forced the unions to take up a broad range of social issues—at times, however, in conflict with the official priorities of the PCI. But since the mid-1970s, with the intensified economic crisis, and following the party's turn toward the *compromesso* strategy, the local forms disappeared or were reabsorbed into a more conventional bureaucratic hierarchy as the corporatist direction became more pronounced. Of course capitalist management itself has also been instrumental in pushing for corporatism.

32. The PCI's perspective on this aspect of trade-union strategy, which influences but does not fully determine the CGIL position, is spelled out by Berlinguer in *Austerita occasione del sviluppo*. For the CGIL approach, see Luciano Lama's contribution to *Crisi economica e condizionamenti internazionali dell' Italia* [Economic crisis and international forces in Italy] (Roma: Editori Riuniti, 1977).

33. This theme permeates the literature of the Italian revolutionary left. See, for example, Mario Tronti, "The Strategy of Refusal" (pp. 28–35); Sergio Bologna, "The Tribe of Moles" (pp. 36–61); and Toni Negri, "Domination and Sabotage" (pp. 62–71), in *Autonomia: Post-Political Writings,* Vol. 3, no. 3 (1980). My concern here is primarily with a critique of the PCI rather than with the strategic alternatives devised by theorists and political groups to the left of the Communists.

34. One example here: The "left" CGIL theorist Bruno Trentin proposed in late 1979 the construction of an alliance between unionized workers and the unemployed, but this was rejected by both the PCI and CGIL leaderships.

35. This is not meant to imply that Eurocommunist strategy has *created* the dualism politics-economics; it simply reproduces what is already deeply embedded within bourgeois society. As Poulantzas has noted, the very specificity of modern capitalism—and the modern state—relies on the separation between politics and economics that is part of the larger social division of labor. See *State, Power, Socialism,* pp. 54–55.

36. Whether Eurocommunist attempts (even if successful for a time) to strengthen the existing political and economic system would *also* strengthen the position of the Communist parties once in power, or whether they would so undermine these parties' socialist identity as to precipitate a debilitating internal crisis, is a crucial question that at present can be answered only on the basis of conjecture. For brief arguments in favor of the latter prediction, see Elmar Altvater, "L'Egemonia borghese e l'alternativa del movimento operaio" [Bourgeois hegemony and the challenge of the working-class movement], *Problemi del socialismo,* no. 5, (1977), pp. 83–109; and Mandel, *From Stalinism to Eurocommunism,* Ch. 6.

37. Some trade unionists, including Bruno Trentin, have recently questioned

the wisdom of union "autonomy" and have urged a complete reassessment of the PCI's relationship to the working-class movement. Trentin has pointed to the need for a merging of politics and economics, with an emphasis on self-management, in this context. See "Only Conflictive Democracy Can Guarantee Liberty," in *Power and Opposition in Post-Revolutionary Societies* (London: InkLinks, 1979), pp. 203–206.

38. As a measure of the PCI's serious commitment to working within the Italian parliament, it has since the mid-1950s consistently pushed for an expansion of legislative powers under the Constitution. It has been more deeply involved in the operations of parliamentary committees than any other party, its deputies have the best attendance record in the lower house, and parliamentary activities demand the bulk of attention at party congresses. See Giorgio Galli and Alfonso Prandi, *Patterns of Political Participation in Italy* (New Haven: Yale University Press, 1970), pp. 263–271.

39. Ingrao, *Masse e potere* (pp. 385–386), argued that a dialectical relationship between "central" and "local" forms must be characteristic of the democratic road, but he hedged by deferring construction of the local organs to a future moment when socialist democracy can presumably be posed. More typical of PCI, and Eurocommunist, thinking is Napolitano, who in *Intervista sul PCI* (p. 104) stressed that parliament must be the "basic center of decision-making."

40. Claudin, *Eurocommunism and Socialism,* p. 74.

41. Claus Offe, "Political Authority and Class Structures," in Paul Connerton, ed., *Critical Sociology* (New York: Penguin Books, 1976), p. 404. Italics mine.

42. Poulantzas, *State, Power, Socialism,* p. 209.

43. Eurocommunist tactics do in fact anticipate a leftward shift among state employees in the event of a leftist government, allowing for a smooth and continuous transition to a new order of priorities, but this schema is rarely discussed in detail. In any event, such a change in the ideological balance of administrative personnel, though important, would not involve dismantling the bureaucratic hierarchy itself or the private interests that have colonized it. This is another way of saying that the parties have never extended their strategy of democratization into the executive sphere. On the limitations of the PCI's approach to the public sector, see Paolo Flores and Franco Moretti, "Paradoxes of the Italian Political Crisis," *New Left Review,* no. 96 (March-April 1976), pp. 52–54.

44. See, for example, "Political Parties and Capitalist Development," *Kapitalistate,* no. 6 (Fall 1977), pp. 7–38; Wolfe, *Limits of Legitimacy,* Ch. 9; and Poulantzas, *State, Power, Socialism,* pp. 232–239.

45. Samuel H. Barnes, *Representation in Italy* (Chicago: University of Chicago Press, 1977), pp. 157–159.

46. Bologna, "The Tribe of Moles," p. 38.

47. Maria Antonietta Macciocchi, *Letters from Inside the Italian Communist Party to Louis Althusser* (London: New Left Books, 1973), pp. 94, 135-146, 205, 209–291. These themes are also explored in Lucio Magri and Filippo Maone, "L'organizzazzione comunista: strutture e metodi di direzione" [Communist organization: Structures and leadership methods], *Il Manifesto,* September 1969.

48. An elaborate personal account of this is contained in Marcello Argilli, *Un anno in sezione: vita di base del PCI* [One year in the section: life at the base of the PCI] (Milano: Feltrinelli, 1970).

49. See Magri and Maone, "L'organizzazzione comunista," pp. 29–32.

50. For a brief historical account of this phenomenon, see Serge Hughes, *The Fall and Rise of Modern Italy* (New York: Macmillan, 1967), Chs. 1 and 4. See also Gwyn Williams, *Proletarian Order* (London: Pluto Press, 1975), Ch. 1.

51. This is analyzed more fully in my article "The Historic Compromise: The Communist Party and Working-Class Politics in Italy," *Radical America*, Vol. 10, no. 6 (November-December 1976), pp. 28–42. A discussion of elite convergence as a possible response to societal crisis and polarization is contained in Giuseppe DiPalma, *Surviving Without Governing, Italian Parties in Parliament* (Berkeley: University of California Press, 1977), conclusion. See also Luigi Graziano, "On Political Compromise: Italy after the 1979 Elections," *Government and Opposition,* Spring 1980, pp. 190–193.

52. The last (and only) attempt to establish a frontist government based upon DC-PCI collaboration fell through in 1947 with the onset of the cold war, signaling thirty years of intense mutual hostility. Significantly, the economic crisis of the middle and late 1970s has produced not polarization but rather moderation and consensus at the elite level.

53. For example, Wolfgang Müller and Christel Neüssus, "The Illusion of State Socialism and the Contradiction Between Wage Labor and Capital," *Telos,* no. 25 (Fall 1975), pp. 13–90.

54. The PCF is commonly viewed as more centralist and statist than the PCI or PCE—and this is true, especially where internal party structure is concerned. Still, these generalizations remain applicable insofar as they concern the role of the state in Eurocommunist political strategy. Where the PCI is willing, for example, to encourage local and private initiative in various areas of the economy, it does not necessarily look upon this initiative as a catalyst in socialist transformation.

55. The combining of these three functions already occurs with the transition from competitive to monopoly capitalism; structural reformism would merely extend them further. This functional distinction is made by Ernest Mandel in *Late Capitalism* (London: Verso, 1978), pp. 486–487.

56. Here it is conceivable that the state might gradually displace the bourgeoisie in the accumulation process. If so, Gouldner's observation seems appropriate: Capitalism can quite clearly survive beyond the bourgeoisie, in the sense that state entrepreneurs and financiers would replace private entrepreneurs and financiers in the reproduction of capital. See *Two Marxisms,* p. 212.

57. It should be emphasized that, with the emergence of a structural reformist government, the state would have no single relationship to the market. Following Habermas's categories, at least three broad functions can be identified—"market-constituting," "market-replacing," and "market-complementing" activities. See *Legitimation Crisis,* pp. 55–57.

58. Sani, "Italy: The Changing Role of the PCI," pp. 59–63.

59. Such a statist mobilization of the technocratic middle strata is precisely

what the PCI leadership has in mind when it speaks of institutional "renewal." A dismantling of the DC patronage network would be likely to pave the way to a public sector composed of younger, more "cosmopolitan" employees oriented toward rationalization of the economy.

60. For an interesting study of the PCI's early postwar mobilization — and how it gave way to disillusionment — from the viewpoint of the participants, see Belden Paulson, *The Searchers* (Chicago: Quadrangle Books, 1966).

61. The 1975 local and regional elections, in which the PCI gained 35.7 percent of the vote, represent the high point of postwar growth.

62. This predicament was underscored by Mayor Zangheri of Bologna, himself one of the architects of the PCI's local strategy: "We Communists conquered or reconquered most of the big cities, a large number of regions, and many of the provinces. However, the character of the society in which we live has not changed. The laws are not different; nor are the relations between the state and the municipalities. The Italian state is still a highly centralized one which makes highly centralized decisions." From an interview in Joggi et al., *Red Bologna,* p. 190.

63. For an analysis of the PCI's clientelism, see Luigi Graziano, *Clientelismo e sistema politico: il caso dell' Italia* [Clientelism and the political system: The case of Italy] (Milan: Franco Angeli, 1980). Also, Peter Lange, "The PCI at the Local Level: A Study of Strategic Performance," in Blackmer and Tarrow, *Communism in France and Italy,* pp. 176–211; Jaggi et al., *Red Bologna;* Degli Esposti, *Bologna PCI;* Robert H. Evans, *Coexistence: Communism and its Practice in Bologna* (Notre Dame, Ind.: University of Notre Dame Press, 1961); and Paulson, *Searchers.*

64. The PCE constitutes a partial exception to this tendency, as we have seen. This is so for several reasons: the PCE's smaller size and relative lack of institutionalization; the strength of the anarchist and syndicalist traditions in Spain; the role of regional movements for national autonomy; and the continuing importance of broad antifascist politics. In addition, the PCE has less attachment to the middle strata at present than either the PCF or PCI.

65. Berlinguer, in an interview published in *L'Unita* (June 19, 1977) entitled "Un anno doppo," remarked, "The extemists do nothing but shout and provoke, with the result that they have no influence whatsoever in changing the course of things to the benefit of the working people. At most, they create confusion, desperation, and frustration."

66. A survey by the Italian polling agency DOXA in 1977 revealed the following preferences of young leftist voters: ultra-left groups, 11.7 percent; Radical party, 10.7 percent; PCI, 57.2 percent; and PSI, 20.4 percent. Cited in Sani, "Italy: The Changing Role of the PCI," p. 80.

67. See Maurizio Marcelloni, "Urban Movements and Political Struggles in Italy," *International Journal of Urban and Regional Research,* June 1979. Here it is necessary to emphasize that the label "radical left" has encompassed a wide variety of groups, with different structures, political strategies, and modes of relating to the popular movements. And of course there have been significant divisions *within* the radical left around the problem of democratization. For

example, many of the earlier new left organizations—Potere Operaio, Lotta Continua, Il Manifesto—stressed the goals of workers' control and self-management but were internally hierarchical even if not strictly Leninist. Later groups, including elements of the feminist movement and youth tendencies like the Metropolitan Indians, were oriented more toward internal democratic process but often retreated to forms of new left spontaneism. Other formations within the radical left—notably Avanguardia Operaio and the many "Marxist-Leninist" sects—were more traditionally Leninist in both organization and strategy. The insurrectionary group Autonomia Operaio, which emerged in 1977, contained an uneasy mixture of grassroots and Leninist elements.

68. For example, in 1977 the PCI Central Committee held a number of sessions on the problem of youth and students, some proceedings of which are reprinted in *I comunisti e la questione giovanile* (Roma: Editori Riuniti, 1977).

69. In a special issue devoted to PCI politics, the radical left periodical *Rosso* (June 1976) devoted considerable analysis to this containment of local movements—especially in the article "PCI e forze politiche," pp. 39–52. See also Marcelloni, "Urban Movements and Political Struggles," pp. 259–260.

70. The PCI's repression of the left in Bologna was one of the events that led to the decision by radical left groups to hold a conference on political repression, which convened in Bologna in September 1977 and attracted tens of thousands of supporters from several Western European countries.

71. A young militant who resigned from the PCI in 1977 wrote to the secretary of the Bolognese federation as follows:

> I feel violently angry at the stupidity shown by the party. . . . I understood that our opposition to the student movement was absurd, dictated by a policy of conciliation toward the Christian Democrats which would inevitably lead us to accept repression. One can't hide behind the trite analysis that calls the students "fascists," paid provocateurs, because this movement . . . expresses real anger, real social disintegration and a lucid awareness of the function of control over the working class assigned by capitalism to the Communist Party. We are supposed to represent "social democratic" order, good for the shopkeepers and bosses big and small, while *they* represent subversion, extremism, the wicked wolf in fairy tales.

Published in *Dear Comrades: Readers' Letters to Lotta Continua* (London: Pluto Press, 1980), pp. 9–10.

72. Aldo Tortorella, "Interpretare ed elevare le diverse esigenze ad aspirazione generale," in *Almanacco PCI '79*, p. 42.

73. At Fiat and elsewhere, terrorist methods were introduced into the class struggle and were accepted by enough workers to precipitate a real crisis of authority—not only within management-labor relations but within the unions and PCI as well. Between 1975 and 1979, three Fiat executives were murdered, seventeen were wounded, and numerous fires were set in the plants. Management responded by firing sixty-one workers in October 1979 for their presumed association with terrorist groups, setting off a series of protests and demonstrations.

74. See, for example, Enrico Berlinguer, "Report to the 15th National Congress of the PCI," reprinted in *Italian Communists,* no. 1 (January-June 1979), p. 35.

75. In April 1979, the police arrested more than twenty well-known leftists in northern Italy, charging them with "antistate" crimes in assisting the Red Brigades and "masterminding" the Moro abduction. Although evidence against those arrested was flimsy, most were still being detained many months later. The *legge reale* enables authorities to detain people without bail — and virtually incommunicado — for as long as four years. It was a PCI-oriented prosecutor in Padua who issued the arrest warrants. And the PCI has stood firmly behind these crackdowns, which included periodic bans on public demonstrations.

76. Suzanne Cowan, "Terrorism and the Italian Left, in Boggs and Plotke, *Politics of Eurocommunism,* pp. 182–187. Cowan wrote:

> ... the various actions planned and carried out by terrorist organizations ... have had an effect diametrically opposite to the one envisioned by the Red Brigades. Specifically, their outcome has been not to expose the true face of bourgeois power, but to more successfully mask it and strengthen it by unifying a broad spectrum of popular sympathy and consensus around the ruling party, and to provide the government with a handy pretext for carrying out further repression against the left. [pp. 182–183]

77. These Gramscian concepts, along with the whole mystique of Gramsci's Marxism, have been misappropriated by Eurocommunist theorists, beginning with Togliatti.

78. This critique shares some of the assumptions of Althusser's attack on the PCF's turn from Leninism at the Twenty-second Congress, except that Althusser himself repeated the fallacy of the alternative dictatorship of the proletariat versus pluralist democracy. See "The Historic Significance of the 22nd Congress," in Balibar, *Dictatorship of the Proletariat,* pp. 204–207. Mandels' critique in *From Stalinism to Eurocommunism* (pp. 164–177) is more attuned to this problem, but his analysis is flawed by a mechanistic view of power.

79. Nicos Poulantzas, "Dual Power and the State," *New Left Review,* no. 109 (May-June 1978), pp. 82–84.

Chapter Five

1. Frank Parkin, *Class Inequality and Political Order* (New York: Holt, Rinehart, and Winston, 1971), p. 121.

2. I first presented this argument, in somewhat rudimentary form, several years ago in my article "Italian Communism in the Seventies," *Socialist Review,* no. 34 (July-August 1977), pp. 105–118.

3. See, for example, Togliatti, *La via italiana al socialismo,* pp. 192–193, 213–214.

4. Tortorella, "Interpretare ed elevare le diverse esigenze ad aspirazione generale," pp. 37–38. See also Berlinguer, *La grande avanzata comunista,* pp. 96–97.

5. Weber's exchange with Nicos Poulantzas, "The State and the Transition to Socialism," *Socialist Review,* no. 38 (March-April 1978), p. 30.

6. Mandel, *From Stalinism to Eurocommunism,* pp. 33-34.

7. Fernando Claudin, "Democracy and Dictatorship in Lenin and Kautsky," *New Left Review,* no. 106 (November-December 1979), p. 65. See also Mandel, *From Stalinism to Eurocommunism,* p. 34, and Kautsky, "Karl Kautsky and Eurocommunism," passim.

8. "Social Reform or Revolution," in Howard, *Selected Political Writings of Rosa Luxemburg,* pp. 52-134. Peter Gay analyzed this problem in the context of Bernstein's thought in *The Dilemma of Democratic Socialism,* Chs. 7 and 12.

9. Adam Przeworski, "Social Democracy as a Historical Phenomenon," *New Left Review,* no. 122 (July-August 1980), pp. 51-53; Parkin, *Class Inequality and Political Order,* pp. 123-127; and Mattick, *Marx and Keynes.* Of course neither the social democrats nor the Eurocommunists have chosen to justify these policies in explicitly Keynesian terms.

10. Sweden represents probably the most advanced example of this. See Gosta Esping-Anderson, Rodger Friedland, and Erik Olin Wright, "Modes of Class Struggle and the Capitalist State," *Kapitalistate,* nos. 4-5 (Summer 1976), especially pp. 210-212.

11. See Lucio Magri, "Italy, Social Democracy, and Revolution in the West," *Socialist Revolution,* no. 36 (November-December 1977), pp. 109-112.

12. Giovanni Arrighi, "Towards a Theory of Capitalist Crisis," *New Left Review,* no. 111 (September-October 1978), pp. 17-18. In Arrighi's view, the most advanced sectors of the bourgeoisie see the state as a vehicle for establishing their hegemony over other sectors, notably the traditional sectors. This in turn generates new contradictions within the capitalist system as a whole.

13. Bahro, *Alternative in Eastern Europe,* pp. 274-275.

14. Both Bernsteinian social democracy and Eurocommunism celebrate the idea of self-governing local administration, but they are interestingly vague about its *structural* components—indicating simply the need to transfer more power to the regions and localities. But although Eurocommunism has paid some lip service to conciliar democracy, the social democrats—at least until quite recently—placed little value on it. As Gay observed, Bernstein rigidly adhered to a liberal, representative concept of democracy that owed more to John Stuart Mill than to Marx or Rousseau: "Democracy is representative, not direct, parliamentary, not plebiscitarian. Its bureaucracy is permanent and professional." *Dilemma of Democratic Socialism,* p. 246.

15. Of course the mere existence of local forms does not guarantee the conditions of democratization. They too are vulnerable to degenerative tendencies, including parochialism and bureaucratization, especially where they are not united within a larger movement. See Hodgson, *Socialism and Parliamentary Democracy,* pp. 72-78.

16. Although Eurocommunist references to "councils" and "community power" are not uncommon, no attempt has been made to specify the role of local structures (their functions, their relationship to parliament, parties, and so on) within a theory of socialist democracy. In Italy, the PCI has encouraged the

development of factory and neighborhood councils only where such forms could be strictly subordinated to the party hierarchy—in which instances, of course, they would quickly lose their participatory character and evolve into something more akin to "transmission belts."

17. For example, see Parkin, *Class Inequality and Political Order,* Ch. 4.

18. The argument that modern Communist parties in the developed countries are bearers of a "mythology of revolution" is developed by John Kautsky in *Communism and the Politics of Development* (New York: John Wiley and Sons, 1968), pp. 208–210.

19. In recognizing this convergence, PCI leaders have taken the initiative in pushing for a Western Europe–wide unity of Communist and other leftist parties. See the interview with Berlinguer in *La Repubblica,* June 7, 1980. The present absence of such unity—not to mention the antagonism between Communists and Socialists, as in France—does not necessarily negate this process of convergence. Of course differences still exist, for example, around the issue of nationalization, but these are more often questions of emphasis. A deeper source of conflict stems from historical tensions and from conditions of electoral competition.

20. On this general point, see Gouldner, *Two Marxisms,* pp. 345–351.

21. Michels, *Political Parties,* passim. See also Roth, *Social Democrats in Imperial Germany.*

22. Perhaps the most striking parallel between Austro-Marxism and Eurocommunism is the claim of staking out a "middle ground" between Leninism and right-wing social democracy. But in the first instance this pretense collapsed after World War I and the Bolshevik Revolution, when the Austro-Marxist "center" wound up politically absorbed by the Bernstein-Kautsky synthesis. See Raimund Loew, "The Politics of Austro-Marxism," *New Left Review,* no. 118 (November-December 1979), p. 50.

23. This argument is developed by Lucio Colletti in Paolo Mieli, ed., *Il socialismo diviso* [Divided socialism] (Bari: Laterza, 1978), pp. 112–114.

24. Gurley, "Capitalist and Maoist Economic Development," pp. 17–19.

25. It is precisely the emergence of these popular struggles in many of the advanced capitalist countries since the 1960s that has precipitated the contemporary "crisis of Marxism." See Elmar Altvater and Otto Kallscheuer, "Socialist Politics and the Crisis of Marxism," in *Socialist Register* (London: Merlin Press, 1979).

26. See Magri, "Italian Communism in the Sixties."

Epilogue

1. In this connection, the PCI held its first conference on Gramsci in Rome in 1958—in part the outgrowth of the theoretical ferment linked to the debates around structural reformism at the Eighth PCI Congress in 1956. Togliatti's contribution to the conference was entitled, fittingly, "Gramsci's Leninsim." It is contained in Palmiro Togliatti, *Gramsci* (Roma: Editori Riuniti, 1967), pp. 135–182.

2. Maxy Beml, "Marketing Eurocommunism," *Telos,* no. 37 (Fall 1978), pp. 120–126.

3. Pietro Ingrao, "La svolta di 1956 e la via italiana al socialismo," *Rinascita,* January 21, 1977. Ingrao's *Masse e Potere* is also sprinkled with references to Gramsci.

4. Paolo Bufalini, "Le origine della nostra politica," *L'Unita,* April 24, 1977. This article was one of many published in a special issue of *L'Unita* commemorating the fortieth anniversary of Gramsci's death.

5. Ibid. The key role of Gramsci's influence on current PCI development is also emphasized by leading PCI figure Giorgio Napolitano, who sees in the "struggle for hegemony" an imperative for socialists to manage the economy more effectively than capitalists. See *Intervista sul PCI* [Interview on the PCI], p. 46. One of the most comprehensive efforts to establish the Gramscian basis of PCI strategy since the late 1950s is Luciano Gruppi's *Socialismo e democrazia* [Socialism and democracy] (Milano: Edizioni del Calendario, 1969).

6. Carrillo, *Eurocommunism and the State,* p. 44.

7. Ibid., p. 102.

8. Claudin, *Eurocommunism and Socialism,* p. 85.

9. Franco Ferrarroti, "The Italian Party and Eurocommunism," in Morton Kaplan, ed., *The Many Faces of Communism* (New York: Free Press, 1978), p. 62.

10. Max Gordon, "The Theoretical Outlook of the Italian Communists," *Socialist Revolution,* no. 33 (May-June 1978), p. 31.

11. Antonio Gramsci, "Syndicalism and the Councils," in Quintin Hoare, ed., *Antonio Gramsci: Selections from Political Writings, 1910–1920* (New York: International Publishers, 1977), p. 109.

12. "Revolutionaries and the Elections," in Hoare, *Political Writings, 1910–1920,* p. 127.

13. Ibid., pp. 128–129.

14. "Electoralism," in Hoare, *Political Writings, 1910–1920,* p. 105.

15. "Syndicalism and the Councils," in ibid., p. 110. For an elaboration of these themes, see Carl Boggs, *Gramsci's Marxism* (London: Pluto Press, 1976), pp. 86–89.

16. "The Party and the Revolution," in ibid., pp. 142–143.

17. Ibid., p. 149.

18. "La conquista dello stato" [The conquest of the state], *L'Ordine Nuovo,* July 12, 1919, in Mario Spinella, ed., *Antonio Gramsci: scritti politici* [Political writings] (Roma: Editori Riuniti, 1967), p. 221.

19. "First: Renew the Party," in Hoare, *Political Writings, 1910–1920,* p. 160.

20. "Two Revolutions," in ibid., pp. 306–307. The Sorelian syndicalist influence upon Gramsci's early thought is evident here not only in the emphasis on extraparliamentary politics, but in the productivist bias toward strictly workplace activity.

21. "Sindacato e consigli" [Union and councils], *L'Ordine Nuovo,* October 11, 1919, in Spinella, *Antonio Gramsci: scritti politici,* p. 248.

22. "The Communists and the Elections," in Quintin Hoare, ed., *Antonio Gramsci: Selections from Prison Writings, 1921–1926* (New York: International Publishers, 1978), p. 33.

23. "The Elections and Freedom," in Hoare, *Gramsci: Prison Writings,* pp. 36–37.

24. "One Year," in ibid., p. 82.

25. "Our Trade Union Strategy," in ibid., pp. 167–168. Gramsci opposed the Bordiga-inspired strategy not only in the sphere of trade-union politics but also in other areas where it also lacked a sensitivity to popular, "spontaneous" forms of struggle.

26. "The Programme of L'Ordine Nuovo," in ibid., p. 235.

27. "The Italian Crisis," in ibid., pp. 264–266. Gramsci's analysis of fascism here was not so far-fetched as it might initially appear. In fact, the analysis was essentially correct—except of course that the crisis and mobilization cycle that Gramsci expected did not occur for another fifteen years or so, when in the context of World War II Mussolini's rule crumbled and gave way to popular resistance movements that transformed the PCI from an isolated sect into a mass party.

28. "Lyons' Theses," in ibid., pp. 340–341 and 360–361. In his analysis of social democracy, Gramsci cautioned that one should not allow the reality of fascism to obscure the fact that social-democratic currents represent not the "right wing of the proletariat" but the "left wing of the bourgeoisie."

29. Ibid., p. 357.

30. Ibid., p. 370.

31. See, for example, "The State and Civil Society," in Hoare and Nowell-Smith, *Prison Notebooks,* pp. 248–249.

32. "The Modern Prince," in Hoare and Nowell-Smith, *Prison Notebooks,* p. 160.

33. Such references can be found throughout the *Prison Notebooks.* See for example, "Notes on Italian History," p. 57, and "State and Civil Society," p. 235. The origins of such an approach can already be detected in the Lyon's theses and in some of Gramsci's earlier writings.

34. "State and Civil Society," in ibid., p. 235.

35. "Americanism and Fordism."

36. For a more comprehensive evaluation of the differences between Gramsci and Lenin, see my *Gramsci's Marxism,* Ch. 5, and Paul Piccone, "Beyond Lenin and Togliatti: Gramsci's Marxism," *Theory and Society,* Vol. 4, no. 1 (Winter 1976).

37. Gramsci died in April 1937. The available evidence, based upon reports from his brother and other visitors, indicates that Gramsci never supported Popular Front tactics. See Lucio Colletti, "Gramsci and Revolution," *New Left Review,* no. 65 (January-February 1971), pp. 91–92.

38. Charles F. Delzell, *Mussolini's Enemies: The Anti-Fascist Resistance* (Princeton, N.J.: Princeton University Press, 1961), pp. 127, 207.

39. This point is developed by Herbert Marcuse in his *Soviet Marxism,* pp. 39–41.

40. Such theoretical statements are repeated throughout Togliatti's writings, especially in the period 1958–1964. A good sampling is contained in Togliatti's *La*

via italiana al socialismo — for example, pp. 179–182, 192–196, and the sections "9 Domande sullo stalinismo" [9 questions on Stalinism], "Per un governo democratico delle classi lavoratrici" [For a democratic government of the working class], and "Per una nuova maggioranza" [For a new majority].

41. Probably Togliatti's most ambitious effort to build a connection between Gramsci and his own theory of structural reforms is his "Nel quarantesimo anniversario del partito comunista italiano" [On the twentieth anniversary of the Italian Communist party], in *Il partito* [The party] (Roma: Editori Riuniti, 1964).

42. See Mario Telo, "L'interpretazione togliattiana di Gramsci: il problema della continuita della tradizione comunista italiana" [The Togliattian interpretation of Gramsci], in Il Manifesto, *Da Togliatti alla nuova sinistra* [From Togliatti to the new left] (Roma: Alfani Editore, 1975). Telo stressed the theme of a fundamental break between Gramsci and Togliatti. See also Lucio Magri, "Italian Communism in the Sixties," p. 39. The impact of frontism on recent PCI development is analyzed by Marcello Flores in "Togliatti e i fronti popolari" [Togliatti and the Popular Fronts], in Il Manifesto, *Da Togliatti alla nuova sinistra,* pp. 63–82.

43. Foremost among such themes is the Hegelian tradition, which has exerted a compelling influence on the development of Italian Marxism since the time of Antonio Labriola. See Paul Piccone, "Labriola and the Roots of Eurocommunism," *Berkeley Journal of Sociology,* Vol. 22 (1977-1978), pp. 3–38.

44. As Pontusson noted, the Eurocommunist "need for consensus serves as a pretext to avoid the problem of coercion, and this is in part related to the way in which they [Eurocommunists] perceive the transition to socialism." He added: "The class analysis of the Latin European Communist Parties and their gradualist orientation serve to justify the evasion of the problem of coercion. For them, it is only the monopolist bourgeoisie that has an objective interest in preventing . . . democratization. . . ." See Jonas Pontusson, "Gramsci and Eurocommunism: A Comparative Analysis of Conceptions of Class Rule and Socialist Transition," *Berkeley Journal of Sociology,* Vol. 25 (1980), p. 223.

45. See Franco Rodano, *Sulla politica dei comunisti* [On the politics of the Communists] (Torino: Boringheri, 1975), pp. 106–108.

46. Weber, "Eurocommunism, Socialism, and Democracy," p. 13.

47. On the primacy of this (structural reformist) definition of the "political" in Togliatti's strategic thinking, see Claudio Pavone, "Togliatti, la 'neutralita' dello stato e delle istituzioni" [Togliatti, the 'neutrality' of the state and of institutions], in Il Manifesto, *Da Togliatti alla nuova sinistra,* pp. 138–139. The point here is not that the PCI has completely ignored the "social" or that it has failed to establish any kind of extraparliamentary presence in Italian society, but that it has subordinated this presence to instrumentalized electoral goals and thus has abandoned any real *transformative* commitment at the base.

48. It is worth mentioning here that Gramsci's own theoretical outlook suffered from a certain ambiguity and in some areas even a one-sidedness, especially in his approach to the state, where the influence of Lenin ran deep. In particular, Gramsci remained convinced that — given a favorable balance of political

forces—a direct frontal assault on the bourgeois state in its totality was a strategic necessity. Once swept away, the old political order would be replaced by a qualitatively new proletarian-socialist state the outlines of which were never specified. The problem involves not so much the obvious conceptual ambiguity of the vision of a future state, however, as lack of specificity concerning the transitional *process*. Hence Gramsci, like Lenin, never really confronted a vital question: What are the structural components of an *evolving* democratic socialism? Absent is the distinction between "participatory" and "administrative" forms of the bourgeois state—that is, between those structures and traditions that can be retained or enlarged and those that must be overturned—as well as an effort to spell out the role of local councils (including their relationship to parliament, trade unions, the party system, and a reconstituted state).

49. For a discussion of ideological hegemony in this context, see Pontusson, "Gramsci and Eurocommunism," pp. 191-197.

50. Nicola Badaloni, "Gramsci and the Problem of Revolution," in Chantal Mouffe, ed., *Gramsci and Marxist Theory* (London: Routledge and Kegan Paul, 1979), p. 103.

51. For a discussion of this problem from a slightly different angle, see Mandel, *From Stalinism to Eurocommunism,* pp. 164-177.

Index

Abortion, 73
Afghanistan, 37
Agnelli, Giovanni, 67
Agricultural production, 50–51, 54, 55–56. *See also* Italy, agriculture
Alfa Sud (company) (Italy), 56
Alienated labor, 20
Alienated politics, 89
Amendola, Giorgio, 29, 64, 81, 106
Armed Proletarian Nuclei (Italy), 99
Artisan production, 55, 59
Austerity, 83. *See also* "Politics of austerity"
Austria, 25
Austro-Marxism, 5, 115
Autogestion, 21, 41, 111
Autonomia Operaia, 80, 99–100

Baader-Meinhof group, 98
Bad Godesburg Program (1959) (Germany), 104
Balance-of-payments deficits, 51, 53, 58, 59, 117
Barca, Luciano, 59
Bebel, August, 5, 7
Belgium, 25
Berlinguer, Enrico, 24, 28, 29, 30, 32, 37, 61, 90, 106, 120, 121, 133, 135
Bernstein, Eduard, 5, 6, 7–8, 10, 11, 12, 15, 16, 18, 104, 105,

106, 107, 110, 113, 115, 121, 134, 137
Biennio Rosso, 123
Blanquism, 5
Bologna, Sergio, 88
Bologna (Italy), 36, 60, 97, 98
Bolshevik Revolution, 3, 14, 126
Bolsheviks, 8, 10, 11, 123
Bordiga, Amadeo, 5, 126
Bourgeois democracy, 4, 7, 9, 11, 12–13, 25, 27, 33, 39, 40, 58, 63, 85–86, 103, 104, 112, 125, 133, 136, 137
Bourgeois hegemony, 48, 49, 50, 51, 52, 73, 92, 111, 115
Bourgeoisie, 50, 52, 73, 76, 78, 117
  "new," 79, 80
Bourgeois institutions, 8, 13, 17, 18, 84, 106, 110, 125, 129
Bourgeois state, 2, 4, 5, 8, 9, 11, 26, 31, 38, 46, 48, 51, 64, 72, 74, 101, 110, 128
Braverman, Harry, 55
Brigatisti, 100
Bufalini, Paolo, 122
Bureaucracy, 3, 11, 43, 47, 48, 51, 66, 101. *See also* Eurocommunism, and bureaucratization
Bureaucratic centralism, 3, 4, 17, 20, 30, 32, 36, 38, 45, 53, 58, 75, 92, 94, 130

Franco, Francisco, 27, 31, 52
Francoism, 40, 52
French Communist Party (PCF), 18
  alliance strategy, 35, 71
  and capitalism, 85. *See also*
    Eurocommunism, and
    capitalism
  and centralism, 36, 85, 94
  and dictatorship of the
    proletariat, 30
  electoral successes, 24, 25, 52, 87
  and Italian and Spanish
    declaration (1977), 37
  and Italian Communist Party, 38
  and Italian joint declaration
    (1975), 37
  and Leninism, 30, 31, 36, 77,
    102, 105
  and liberal democracy, 23, 25, 84
  middle strata, 77, 78, 80
  and Socialist alliance, 20
  and socialist transformation, 84
  and Soviet Union, 26, 31, 37
  structural reformism, 89, 116
  and "third road," 24, 33
  Twenty-second Congress (1976),
    19, 31
  and working class base, 31, 78
  See also Eurocommunism; May
    Events

Gaullism, 26, 40, 52
General Confederation of Labor
  (CGT) (France), 81
Genoa (Italy), 95
German-Dutch radical left, 10
German Social Democratic party
  (SPD), 5, 7, 8, 10, 11, 12–13,
  103, 104, 112, 114
Germany, 4, 6, 12, 17, 116. *See also*
  Weimar Republic; West
  Germany
Giolitti, Giovanni, 90
Gordon, Max, 123
Görter, Hermann, 10

Gramsci, Antonio, 4, 29, 39, 49,
  55, 77, 111, 115, 119–131,
  133–134, 135, 136–137
Great Britain, 4, 6
Greece, 25
Grundrisse (Marx), 44
Gruppi, Luciano, 34

Habermas, Jürgen, 48
Hamill, Pete, 1, 2
Hegemony. *See* Bourgeois
  hegemony; Ideological
  hegemony; Proletarian
  hegemony
"Hegemony in pluralism," 39
Hitler, Adolf, 31, 131
"Hot autumn" (1969) (Italy), 26,
  79
Hungarian uprising (1956), 25, 116

Iceland, 25
Ideological hegemony, 4, 17, 39, 45,
  74, 101, 111, 120, 121, 129,
  134, 135, 136
Il Manifesto group (Italy), 26
Imperialism, 9, 13
Income distribution, 61, 69, 104
Industrialization, 21, 44–45, 50, 51,
  109
  "Fiat" model, 54, 60
  "Prussian" model, 52
Inflation, 51, 61, 62, 108, 117
Ingrao, Pietro, 34, 39, 58, 62, 106,
  121
Institutional cohesiveness, 20
"Integrated culture," 112
International division of labor, 20,
  58
International Monetary Fund, 51
Italian Communist Party (PCI), 2,
  18
  and "agro-industrial production,"
    62, 68
  alliance strategy, 35, 59, 71